"In my opinion, the great value of this very timely book is the author's ability to analyze and explain in detail the role data and information, critical success factors, leadership, and strategy have played in the COVID-19 pandemic. Moreover, the author has done this in a very careful and honest way. I also appreciate the clear and direct writing style that makes the book's themes and conclusions easily understood by all readers from scientists, medical professionals, and policy makers to the public."

—*From the foreword by Dr. John R. Talburt, Acxiom Chair of Information Quality at the University of Arkansas at Little Rock and Lead Consultant for Data Quality Management and Data Governance with Noetic Partners*

"This book bridges the fields of health care and data to clarify how to use data to manage pandemics. Written while COVID-19 was raging, it identifies both effective practices and misfires, and is grounded in clear, research-based explanations of pandemics and data strategy. Rupa Mahanti includes a cogent summary of use cases for data analytics specific to COVID-19 that will be useful in future pandemics. She also explicates crucial instances of effective visualization of data to aid the public's understanding during a pandemic. The author has written an essential book for students and professionals in both health care and data. While serving the needs of academics and experts, the book is accessible for the general reader."

—*Eileen Forrester, CEO of Forrester Leadership Group, Author of CMMI for Services, Guidelines for Superior Service*

"For those of us that care about the quality of data and the ethical use of data, the COVID-19 pandemic has raised as many questions as it has answered. In contrast to our capability to respond to the 1918 influenza, when the medical profession was in its infancy and data collection about health conditions was limited, in 2020, we were rich in information and tools to combat a global pandemic. We had a better understanding of how diseases emerge and spread. And we had an incredible apparatus for collecting the data we needed to understand what was happening. Yet human factors still got in the way of the response and millions died. Rupa Mahanti explores the connections between data and the human response to the spread of disease in her new book *How Data Can Manage Global Health Pandemics: Analyzing and Understanding COVID-19*. She recognizes the value of data and the kind of insight it can bring, while at the same time recognizing that using data to solve problems requires not just technology, but also leadership and courage. This is a book for people who want to better understand the role of data and people in solving human problems."

—*Laura Sebastian-Coleman, author of Meeting the Challenges of Data Quality Management*

"It is great to see this book tackling the current pandemic from the data-driven perspective. As the world becomes ever more interconnected, we increase the likely spread of future pandemics, but we also improve our ability to understand, track, prevent, and mitigate their impacts. This book starts out by setting a basic foundational understanding of pandemics like COVID-19 in both the real world and the data we have available to model and understand all aspects of the pandemic. Not stopping there, it then covers the critical discussions that we all need to understand in order to better leverage data, analytics, and machine learning to improve our ability to prevent future pandemics, learn as much as we can about them, and use all available resources to create a safer world for us all to live in."

—*Don Jenkins, Mirah Chief Operating Officer and Data Science Evangelist*

"Dr. W. Edwards Deming once said, 'In God we trust, all others bring data.' Good decisions are always data driven, and the author does a great job of reminding us of the advantages we have for managing global pandemics with special reference to the worldwide COVID-19 pandemic as a result of the wide availability of digital data."

—Christianna Hayes, COO VEREO/iMpact Utah

"This book embarks on an ambitious journey of showing how data and analytics can help understand and better manage pandemics in the digital age. The lessons learned not just from the current pandemic but from the analytical processes, applied to enable effective decision-making at every step in a dynamic and ever evolving global ecosystem, enables decision-makers with tools for the future. Dr. Mahanti expertly guides and enlightens the reader using the COVID-19 pandemic along with historical precedence to provide meaningful guidance in how data and analytics might better serve as a formidable defense in bringing future pandemics under control."

—Clint D'Souza, CEO & Director, CDZM Consulting

"This work is a welcome deep-dive into the potential for digital data to transform not only the ways we work and live but also how we address worldwide disease propagation."

"The book carefully traces the long, long history of pandemics and their origins. And in parallel shows us how new (digital) knowledge could better arm us going forward, if only we had the will and the open-mindedness."

"The author is a 'data person,' so her perspective is especially hopeful in these confusing and troublesome times. She shows clearly what has been achieved and what remains."

"I commend this work to you as a compelling example of the application of much of what we already know to an important and continuing worldwide health situation."

—Dr. Stan Rifkin, Master Systems Inc.

"COVID-19 has strained our society in unexpected and disruptive ways. The management and analytics of data are no exception. Rupa Mahanti does a masterful job of presenting use cases and the relevant insights gained from COVID-19 data. The lessons in this book will be valuable far past COVID-19 as they are applicable for any infectious outbreak."

—Dr. David P. Marco, President, EWSolutions & Best-Selling Data Management Author

"This book's achievements are twofold. First, it offers an excellent introduction to the disciplines of data management and analytics and their importance in the modern world. It then overlays this understanding with a detailed analysis of the critical role that data has played in that most contemporary of challenges, the COVID-19 pandemic. Employing a wealth of evidence, Mahanti examines a fascinating array of use cases including Taiwan's success in handling the crisis using advanced analytics, the role of data played in the development of vaccines, and the direct impact of mis-information on the welfare of thousands of citizens worldwide. A highly recommended read."

—Guy Bradshaw, Consulting Director, Comma Group

"Rupa Mahanti has got the right eye to connect Data and Pandemic and has shared some unimaginable insights in the book. Data world is shifting toward solving business and customer problems, and this book explores the potential of data in addressing global health pandemic problems. Great book!"

—Ravit Jain, Founder and Host of "The Ravit Show", Data Community Evangelist

How Data Can Manage Global Health Pandemics

Analyzing and Understanding COVID-19

Rupa Mahanti, Ph.D.

A PRODUCTIVITY PRESS BOOK

First published 2022
by Routledge
605 Third Avenue, New York, NY 10158

and by Routledge
2 Park Square, Milton Park, Abingdon, Oxon, OX14 4RN

Library of Congress Cataloging-in-Publication Data
A catalog record for this book has been requested

ISBN: 978-1-032-22030-7 (hbk)
ISBN: 978-1-032-22024-6 (pbk)
ISBN: 978-1-003-27091-1 (ebk)

DOI: 10.4324/9781003270911

Typeset in Garamond
by Apex CoVantage, LLC

To Mom and Papa, for their unwavering support, dedication, love, and encouragement.

To my teachers and mentors, for their guidance and patience.

To all the (living and fallen) global frontline heroes, who continue to battle COVID-19.

Contents

Figures

Tables

Tables

Foreword

A Data and Analytics Perspective on Global Pandemics: COVID-19 as an Example

As a reader, you will understand this is a book for our time! In the summer of 2019, who would have believed that the world would be thrown into the chaos and crisis of the COVID-19 pandemic—a crisis that still affects us, as of this writing, nearly two years later. While there have been other global pandemics in the past, the COVID-19 is the first to occur in the new digital age, a time when organizations, private and public, large and small, are striving to extract the maximum value from their data and information resources. This book stands at the confluence of these two streams and gives all of us some very important insights into this historic interaction. Every problem presents an opportunity to learn, and this pandemic is no exception.

It is clear to anyone who has watched the news that data are the face of the COVID-19 pandemic. Every broadcast and press update are accompanied by charts and graphs. From the counts of new infections to vaccination rates, hospitalizations, ventilator occupancy, and, sadly, to number of deaths, all types of statistics are used to convey the ever-changing contours of the pandemic to the public. However, the high-level statistics consumed by the public are only summaries of the much large data sets collected by the U.S. Center for Disease Control and Prevention (CDC), the National Institutes for Health (NIH), the U.N. World Health Organization (WHO), and many other organizations. These organizations share and aggregate these data sets into even larger data sets to drive much deeper analyses in an attempt to model the trajectory of the pandemic and to inform public policy.

In addition to the descriptive demographic data of the pandemic, even larger amounts of scientific and medical data are collected, such as medical data from the many clinical trials conducted to understand the efficacy treatments and vaccines and to identify possible adverse side effects. In addition, vast amounts of data are constantly being collected from sequencing the DNA of the virus. This type of genomic data helps scientists develop more effective drugs and treatments for the virus. Genomic data also help researchers track and monitor emerging variants of the virus, some of which may be more virulent than the original or evolve the ability to evade current treatments.

In all, there has never been this enormous amount and variety of data available to address a global pandemic. So how do the data and pandemic intersect? In my opinion, the great value of this very timely book is the author's ability to analyze and explain in detail the role data and information, critical success factors, leadership, and strategy have played in the COVID-19 pandemic. Moreover, the author has done this in a very careful and honest way. I also appreciate the clear and direct writing style that makes the book's themes and conclusions easily understood by all readers from scientists, medical professionals, and policy makers to the public.

This book covers many aspects specific to the pandemic, such as pandemic terminology, the role of leadership, human element strategies, and communication in managing pandemics. At the same time, it is a case study on the way in which so much of what we experience is directly related to data and information. In this case, our experience in dealing with the pandemic—for example, the discussions on the challenges around gathering and interpreting data in a pandemic crisis, how to overcome these challenges, and the roles played by data literacy and data visualization. In addition, it covers how data and analytics help in the other industry sectors during the pandemic and the overall lessons learned from the COVID-19 experience.

I believe the author was able to effectively convey this information to the reader because of her extensive data and information background. She has expertise in several data management sub-disciplines and is the author of several books on data governance and data quality.

Data governance is a relatively new information management practice. While data governance involves some information technology, it is largely about people and changing the culture of an organization. It is about getting people in an organization to think about data and information in a new way, not as a commodity, but as a unique resource and an asset capable of creating value for the organization and value for the people who use the information products produced by the organization.

Data governance has emerged over the past few years as a framework for defining the roles and responsibilities each employee of an organization has with respect to the data and information the employee uses. The author's experience in helping organizations understand data issues and helping them fix their data has clearly informed the depth, breadth, and quality of her analyses given in this book. The same experience and background have also given her the ability to communicate these analyses to the reader in a clear and understandable manner. Given my own background, I also appreciate the inclusion of Chapter 5, introducing the readers to the principles of data quality and best practices in managing data quality.

While the COVID-19 pandemic will eventually end, this book will continue to have value as a resource for public policy makers and medical and technology professionals alike who will no doubt face similar crises in the future. Because of its extensive citation of published materials and objective analysis, I believe it will also become a valued academic resource from both a medical and epidemiological research perspective, as well as, for data scientists. It also provides readers with some basic background information science concepts such as varieties of data, data governance practices, data quality, data management, data strategy, and data analytics. I will not be surprised to see it being used as a textbook in the growing number of data and information science programs, especially at the graduate level.

John R. Talburt
Acxiom Chair of Information Quality at the
University of Arkansas at Little Rock and Lead Consultant for
Data Quality Management and Data Governance with Noetic Partners.

Preface

As I write this, the COVID-19 pandemic continues to play havoc across the world. The COVID-19 pandemic started at the end of year 2019. Since then, it has affected all continents across the world, with Antarctica being the last continent to be directly impacted. Per the WHO COVID-19 dashboard, as of August 7, 2021, more than 201 million cases have been identified, and more than 4.27 million deaths have been recorded worldwide. In addition to the large number of deaths, the COVID-19 pandemic has transformed the lives of people across the globe, and has had and continues to have a global health, social, cultural, political, and economic impact.

Pandemics have been a part of human history from ancient times through today. Pandemics are always characterized by fear, uncertainty, suddenness, panic, different degrees of stigma, and deaths, and have a devastating multisectoral impact (social, political, cultural, health, and economic).

Historically, pandemics have forced humans to break with the past and imagine their world anew. This one is no different. It is a portal, a gateway between one world and the next.

—Arundhati Roy, 2020

Pandemics that occurred in the non-digital age were characterized by limited availability/collection of related data due to the absence of digital technologies. For example, in the non-digital age, the Spanish flu pandemic shook the world a little more than century ago in 1918–1919 and resembled COVID-19 in its lethality and widespread reach. However, information collection and organization were so poor that we will never know how many millions actually died from Spanish flu (Tworek, 2020).

In contrast, the timing of the COVID-19 pandemic intersects with the digital age, characterized by sophisticated technologies which enable collection and storage of massive amounts of data. We are literally drowning in an ocean of data. We are currently living in a digital world and armed with sophisticated technology that can be used to leverage data and derive insights that can help in combating pandemic of a scale similar to COVID-19, in ways that were not possible in previous centuries. This is because the variety and amount of data available today and the technologies to leverage data to derive insights were not there in the previous centuries. Also, the COVID-19 pandemic has resulted in the acceleration in the pace of digitization more than any other recent event.

The biggest development of 2020 was the **COVID-19 pandemic**, which accelerated the pace of digital transformation around the world, in personal and professional life.

—Madanmohan Rao, 2021

Data and analytics have a critical role to play in managing a pandemic. Data have been and are being actively used to fight the COVID-19 pandemic, and will be used beyond it to recover from the pandemic. It is important to be able to understand the nature of the contagion, and measures that help manage and prevent spread of the disease. It is also important to understand the wider impact to the economy and businesses such as changes in consumer behavior, supply chain impact, resourcing issues, and risks. Data sit at the heart of this exercise.

Given the adverse impacts of pandemics in general and the COVID-19 pandemic in particular, it is imperative that students, professionals, and the general public understand what a pandemic is, the origin of pandemics, the related terms (such as epidemic, outbreak, super spreader, and patient zero), the trajectory of a new disease, the butterfly effect of contagious diseases, digital contact tracing, epidemiological parameters, factors that determine the pandemic potential of a disease, how to prepare for a pandemic and strategies to combat a pandemic in the digital age, the role of data, including external data, data strategy, data sharing, data privacy, data literacy, big data, analytics and data visualization in preventing and combating a pandemic, pandemic myths, critical success factors in managing a pandemic, and lessons learnt from pandemics. This book discusses these with special reference to COVID-19 in detail.

Target Audience

- On a broad level, the target audience is the scientific community, policy makers, and professionals across the domains of health, management, risk, strategy, and data. The book is specifically beneficial for university students, academicians, professors, researchers, and industry professionals. Even the general public will find this book useful and interesting.
- Courses where health, pandemics, strategies, and data analytics are a part of the course curriculum. Some courses include bachelor's and master's degrees in information technology, computer science, data analytics, epidemiology, biomedical informatics, and management.

The book does not assume any prior or specialist knowledge in pandemics, strategies, data, data analytics, or data visualization. While this book talks about data, the use cases of analytics, and data visualization from a pandemic perspective, it does not speak about the technical details of how to do analytics or data visualization. This book is technology agnostic and contains a large number of illustrations and examples from COVID-19, making it easy for the readers to understand and relate to the concepts discussed in this book.

The book is divided into ten chapters.

Chapter 1, "Pandemic—An Introduction," introduces the audience to the concept of pandemic, the characteristics of a pandemic, the origin of pandemics, and notable pandemics in history of mankind. The last section of the chapter briefly discusses the role of technology, data, and data analytics in managing pandemics.

Chapter 2, "Data—Management, Strategy, Quality, Governance, and Analytics," discusses in brief some key concepts around data such as definition of data, varieties of data, traditional data versus big data, organization of data, data management, data strategy, data quality, key data quality dimensions, data governance, data analytics, and the role, data quality and data governance play in data analytics.

Chapter 3, "Trajectory and Stages of a New Disease," discusses the trajectory of new diseases, some terminologies associated with pandemics, the butterfly effect of contagious disease, and the different stages that a disease passes through before it achieves pandemic proportions, stages of disease pandemic spread, the concept of contact tracing, data using in digital contact tracing and the apps used for the same, the different epidemiological parameters, and the role of data and analytics in measuring these parameters to help manage a pandemic. The role data and analytics play in flattening the curve is also discussed in this chapter.

Chapter 4, "COVID-19—A Pandemic in the Digital Age," discusses COVID-19, its features, the predictions in relation to COVID-19 pandemic, coronaviruses, the family of viruses that SARS-CoV-2 (that causes COVID-19) belongs to, and the spread and impacts of COVID-19 from a data perspective.

Chapter 5, "Data and Pandemic in the Digital World," discusses how data can help in managing a pandemic, the concept of traditional data and big data, the use of external data and data sharing in the pandemic, the big data sources that can assist in pandemic prevention and management, challenges around traditional data and big data (such as data quality, data protection and privacy, data collection, misinformation, credibility of sources, data definition, and metadata) in managing a pandemic with special emphasis on the COVID-19 pandemic.

Chapter 6, "Data Analytics and Pandemics," discusses data analytics and data analytics use cases in a pandemic, data visualization, and their role in a pandemic with special reference to COVID-19.

Chapter 7, "Disease and Pandemic Potential," discusses some of the pathogens (paramyxoviruses, Nipah, influenza, and coronavirus), their pandemic potential, and the factors determining the pandemic potential of a disease.

There are a number of elements that play a crucial role in controlling a disease outbreak and pandemic, such as government and leadership, capacity to test, trace, and treat, pandemic preparedness and strategies, communication, technology and quality data, education and training, and collaboration, coordination, and global solidarity. Chapter 8, "Pandemic and Critical Success Factors," discusses each of these elements. How data and technology intersect with these factors has also been discussed.

Chapter 9, "Pandemic Preparedness and Strategies," discusses the strategies for preparing for and combating a pandemic. The role of data strategies in managing a pandemic, and the key data strategy lessons learnt during the COVID-19 pandemic have also been discussed in this chapter.

Chapter 10, "Pandemic—Lessons Learned and Future Ahead," discusses the mistakes made in handling the COVID-19 pandemic (for example, misinformation, delay in release of crucial information, and more), and lessons learnt from past pandemics as well as the COVID-19 pandemic.

Rupa Mahanti

Roy, A. (April 4, 2020) Arundhati Roy: 'The pandemic is a portal'. The Financial Times

Rao, M. (April 1, 2021) 'The pandemic has been a great teacher' – 25 quotes from India's COVID-19 struggle. *Yourstory*, Last accessed on September 10, 2021, from https://yourstory.com/2021/04/quotes-storybites-covid19-pandemic-teacher/amp

Tworek, Heidi. (10 December, 2020) The Promise and Peril of Anti-pandemic Technology. Stream Available at: www.brookings.edu/techstream/the-promise-and-peril-of-anti-pandemic-technology/

Acknowledgments

I am very grateful to Taylor and Francis Group for giving me an opportunity to publish this book. I am grateful to Guy Loft, Senior Editor, Taylor and Francis Group, for initially reviewing the book proposal and forwarding it to his colleague Kristine Rynne Mednansky, Senior Editor, Business Improvement—Healthcare Management, Taylor and Francis Group, for further consideration. I am particularly thankful to Kristine (Kris) for her continued cooperation and support for this project. She was patient and flexible in accommodating my requests. Thanks to the Taylor and Francis team for helping me to make this book a reality. I am also thankful to Marsha Hecht, Project Editor, Ganesh Pawan Kumar Agoor, Project Manager and his team who made the process and the experience smooth and enjoyable.

I am thankful to the reviewers for their time and constructive feedback that helped improve the quality of this book. Many thanks to Dr. John R. Talburt, Laura Sebastian-Coleman, Dr. Stan Rifkin, Eileen Forrester, Christianna Hayes, Clint D'Souza, Dr. Victor Squires, and George Firican for their feedback and helpful suggestions that helped make this a better book.

I had a few questions on book publishing and I am extremely thankful to Dr. Karl Wiegers and Dr. Victor Squires for answering them.

I have been writing research articles in various domains for many years. My book writing journey began in 2017, when I approached Paul O'Mara, Managing Editor at ASQ Quality Press, with a draft of the first chapter of my first book—*Data Quality*. I had very little idea about book proposals then, and I am very thankful to Paul for his consideration, encouragement, and continued support throughout that project. The successful publication of *Data Quality* gave me impetus to write six more books after that, with this book being the seventh book. I owe a big thanks to Paul, who helped me get started on my book writing journey.

I am also thankful to a lot of my colleagues and friends, who have been an active part of conversations related to data and data management. Special mentions are Allan Wu, Anurag Behera, and Clint D'Souza.

I am grateful to my teachers at Sacred Heart Convent, DAV JVM, and Birla Institute of Technology, where I received education that created opportunities that have led me to where I am today. Thanks to all my English teachers and special thanks to Miss Amarjeet Singh, because of whose efforts I have acquired good reading and writing skills. My years in PhD research have played a key role in my career and personal development, and I owe a special thanks to my PhD guides—Dr. Vandana Bhattacherjee and Late Dr. S. K. Mukherjee—and my teacher and mentor Dr. P. K. Mahanti who supported me during and beyond that period.

Last, but not the least, many thanks to my parents for their unwavering support, encouragement, and optimism. They have been my rock throughout my life, even when they are not near me and hence share credit for every goal I achieve. They have been my inspiration and my determination to finish this book.

About the Author

Rupa Mahanti is a business and information management consultant with extensive and diversified consulting experience in different solution environments, industry sectors, and geographies (the United States, the United Kingdom, India, and Australia). She has expertise in different information management disciplines, business process improvement, regulatory reporting, and more. Her research interests include quality management, information management, software engineering, empirical study, environmental management, compliance, simulation and modeling, and more. With a work experience that spans industry, academics, and research, Rupa has guided a doctoral dissertation, published a large number of research articles, and is the author of the books—*Data Quality, Data Governance and Compliance, Data Governance and Data Management, Data Governance Success, Data Humour*, and *Thoughts*. She is also a reviewer for several international journals.

Chapter 1

Pandemic—An Introduction

"It's been said that there are decades where nothing happens; and then there are weeks when decades happen."

—**Vladimir Ilyich Lenin**

Introduction

I am writing this book as the world continues to be overwhelmed by coronavirus—the COVID-19 pandemic, a respiratory disease which supposedly originated in the city of Wuhan in China in the end of 2019 (Zhu et al., 2020). In a few months, since its emergence, COVID-19 took the shape of a pandemic, and it has spread to every continent. The disease continues to spread like wild fire, and its longevity and cure remain unknown and uncertain. While from a prevention perspective, a number of vaccines have been manufactured and tested; a certain percentage of the people who have been administered vaccines since early 2021 have still contracted the disease. COVID-19 is the greatest challenge that countries have faced since World War II.

Pandemics have been a part of human history from ancient times through today. However, not all have the misfortune to experience a pandemic in their lifetime. While those who hear about a pandemic but are not directly impacted by it, might not remember the scale and impact, pandemics are generally characterized by fear, uncertainty, suddenness, panic, different degrees of stigma, and deaths, and have a devastating impact. Responding to a pandemic requires rigorous public health measures. The stricter the measures, the greater is the disruption of normal life, and more adverse is the economic impact. In addition, pandemics also have an impact on demography, social customs, culture, and religion.

In contrast to the 1918 Spanish flu pandemic which occurred in a non-digital age, the timing of the COVID-19 pandemic intersects with the digital age or information age which is characterized by the collection and availability of large amounts of data and sophisticated technologies that enable digital transformation, and an economy based on information technology. Data and technology are being used to combat this digital age pandemic in ways that were not possible in the pre-digital/non-digital age, when limited data were collected and digital technology was absent.

DOI: 10.4324/9781003270911-1

In this chapter, we discuss what a pandemic is, the characteristics of a pandemic, the origin of pandemics, and notable pandemics in the history of mankind, and briefly discuss the role of technology, data, and data analytics in managing pandemics.

What Is a Pandemic?

The term pandemic originated in the mid-17th century from the Greek roots, from pan "all" + dēmos "people" or pandēmos, that is, all the people [Lexico]. The first known use of the word pandemic, in 1666, referred to "a *Pandemick,* or *Endemick,* or rather a *Vernacular* Disease (*a disease always reigning in a Country*)" (Harvey, 1666).

It can be used as an adjective (in terms of the high magnitude of spread) as well as a noun (in connection with the disease).

Pandemic — Definitions

There is no universally accepted and standard definition of the term. For example, there have been arguments along the lines that level of explosive transmissibility is sufficient to declare a pandemic versus insistence by some that the severity of infection should also be considered when assigning pandemic status to a disease (Cohen, 2009; Enserink, 2009; Swine flu, 2009; Altman, 2009; Morens et al., 2009a).

In some ways, declaring a pandemic is more art than science. "Pandemics mean different things to different people," National Institute of Allergy and Infectious Diseases Director Dr. Anthony Fauci said in February 2020. "It really is borderline semantics, to be honest with you" (Ducharme, 2020).

Merriam-Webster's Dictionary defines the term as follows:

Pandemic (adjective)—definition:

—occurring over a wide geographic area and affecting an exceptionally high proportion of the population [Merriam-Webster Dictionary].

Pandemic (noun)—definition:

—an outbreak of a disease that occurs over a wide geographic area and affects an exceptionally high proportion of the population [Merriam-Webster Dictionary].

Collins Dictionary defines the term pandemic as follows:

A pandemic is an occurrence of a disease that affects many people over a very wide area [Collins Dictionary].

World Health Organization (WHO) defines pandemic as (WHO, 2010):

"the worldwide spread of a new disease."

Anthony Fauci, Director of the National Institute of Allergy and Infectious Diseases, told USA TODAY (Shannon, 2020):

A pandemic is a global outbreak of a serious new illness that requires "sustained transmission throughout the world."

Dana Grennan, MD, in her article "What is a Pandemic?" defines pandemic as (Grennan, 2019): "a health condition that has spread globally."

Madhav et al. (2017) define pandemic as:

"large-scale outbreaks of infectious disease that can greatly increase morbidity and mortality over a wide geographic area and cause significant economic, social, and political disruption (Jamison et al., 2017)."

All the aforementioned definitions have one characteristic in common—the large-scale spread of the disease.

Characteristics of Pandemics

While there is no single accepted definition of the term "pandemic," characteristics of pandemics have been derived by studying diseases commonly said to be pandemic and identifying key features that apply to all or almost all of them (Morens et al., 2009a). These are as follows and summarized in Figure 1.1.

Large Geographic Spread

Almost all definitions of the term "pandemic" refer to diseases that have a large geographic spread. Some examples of diseases that evolved into a pandemic and had a large geographic spread are the 14th-century plague (the Black Death), cholera, influenza, and human immunodeficiency virus (HIV)/AIDS. In a review of the history of pandemic influenza, pandemics were categorized as transregional (greater than or equal to two adjacent geographic regions of the world), interregional (greater than or equal to two nonadjacent geographic regions), and global (Taubenberger and Morens, 2009; Morens et al., 2009a).

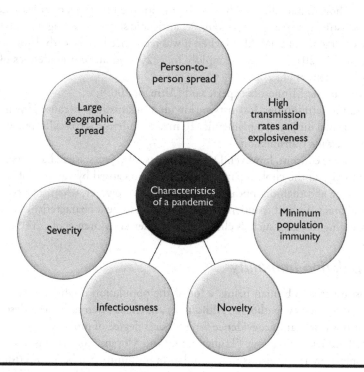

Figure 1.1   Characteristics of a pandemic.

Source: Adapted from Morens et al. (2009a)

Person-to-Person Spread

In addition to extensive geographic spread, most uses of the term pandemic imply spread of the disease from person to person via transmission that can be traced from one place to another place, as has been done historically for centuries (for example, the Black Death) (Morens et al., 2009a).

High Transmission Rates and Explosiveness

Diseases with slow rates of transmission or low rates of symptomatic (that is symptoms are manifest) are rarely classified as pandemics, even when they spread widely across multiple geographic regions. For example, West Nile virus infection spread from the Middle East to both Russia and the Western hemisphere in 1999; however, this disease spread has not generally been called a pandemic, most probably because transmission rates have been moderate and symptomatic cases have been relatively few. Infamous pandemics have tended to exhibit not only high transmission rates but also "explosive" spread—that is, multiple cases appearing within a short period of time. This epidemiologic feature characterizes both common-source acquisition and extremely contagious diseases of short incubation periods—for example, the 14th-century plague, cholera in 1831–1832, and flu on many occasions (Morens et al., 2009a).

Novelty

The term pandemic has been used most commonly to describe diseases that are new (that is associated with a new pathogen) and affecting human beings for the first time, or at least associated with novel variants of existing pathogens—for example, antigenic shifts occurring in influenza viruses as they mutate, the emergence of HIV/AIDS when it was recognized in the early 1980s, and COVID-19, which originated in 2019 and spread rapidly in 2020, and ancient epidemics of diseases (for example, plague) (Morens et al., 2009a).

As Dr. Osterholm, the Minnesota expert, said (Altman, 2009),

"you can't use the terminology for just worldwide transmission, because if you did that, you would say every seasonal flu year is a pandemic. To me, a pandemic is basically a new or novel agent emerging with worldwide transmission."

Novelty is a relative concept, however. During the past 200 years, there have been seven cholera pandemics. Seemingly, all the cholera pandemics have been caused by variants of the same organism. Pandemics come and then disappear for long periods. However, when they come back again, they are still pandemics. Indeed, pandemicity can be said to be a characteristic feature of certain repeatedly re-emerging diseases, such as cholera and influenza (Moren et al., 2009).

Minimal Population Immunity

When a new disease attacks human being, a lot of the population might not have the immunity power to fight against the new pathogen. Although pandemics often have been described in partly immune populations (for example, evidence for a modest degree of protection in persons >60 years of age in the 1918 influenza pandemic (Taubenberger and Morens, 2009)), it is obvious that in limiting microbial infection and transmission, population immunity can be a powerful antipandemic force. However, immunity is a relative concept that does not necessarily imply full protection from infection (Krause et al., 1997). For example, pandemic diseases such as cholera and influenza are associated with new subtypes or drifted strains, and immunity may not be able to fully protect the victim from these new subtypes or strains (Morens et al., 2009b).

Infectiousness

Some diseases have a large geographical spread and may be rising in global occurrence but are not infectious. The term pandemic has less commonly been used to describe such disease situations.

A disease or condition is not usually considered a pandemic simply because it is widespread or kills or affects a large number people; it must also be infectious. For example, diseases such as cancer, heart diseases, obesity, or risk behaviors, such as cigarette smoking or alcoholism, affect a large population worldwide, but they are not considered a pandemic because these diseases or risk behaviors are not infectious (Dumar, 2009; Kvicala, 2003; Shafey et al., 2003).

Such uses of the term generally show up less in scientific discussions, but they generally show up more in public health communication and education. The intent is to emphasize the importance of the health problem by using the term pandemic in an informal rather than scientific sense (Morens et al., 2009a).

A lot of infectious diseases regarded as pandemic by public health officials are transmittable from person to person. A common example is influenza. Other diseases have several means of transmission. These include occasionally contagious diseases that are more commonly transmitted by different methods, such as plague (by fleas) and cholera (by water) (Morens et al., 2009a).

Severity

The classic definition of a pandemic does not talk about disease severity; that is, there is no strict definition as to how serious the illness should be (Shope, 1958). However, organizations and researchers have included disease severity in the definition to increase public awareness and garner financial support for pandemic preparedness, and the term pandemic has been applied to severe or fatal diseases (for example, the Black Death, HIV/AIDS, and SARS that have caused a large number of deaths) much more commonly than it has been applied to mild diseases (Morens et al., 2009a).

However, diseases of low or moderate severity, for example, AHC in 1981, and cyclical international reappearances of diseases, for example scabies (an infestation, not an infection), also have been called pandemic when they exhibit explosive behavior as in case of AHC, or widespread and recurrent behavior as in case of scabies (Morens et al., 2009a).

Origin of Pandemic

In the history of mankind, the "zoonotic" transmission of pathogens from animals to humans has been behind the origin of most new pandemics (Murphy, 1998; Woolhouse and Gowtage-Sequeria, 2005). Zoonosis or zoonotic disease is a disease that can be transmitted from animals, birds, or insects to humans or, more specifically, a disease that normally exists in animals but that can infect humans. They are frequently novel diseases or have increased virulence in populations that lack immunity. Some examples of zoonoses are plague, anthrax, rabies, bird flu, malaria, dengue fever, swine flu, West Nile fever, HIV/AIDS, SARS, and COVID-19.

The course that an animal pathogen takes into the human population varies. Some do not make the animal, bird, or insect sick, but are disease carriers, and will infect human beings. Such organisms are called vectors or intermediate hosts and they act as intermediate species for transmission to human. The SARS outbreak originated from bats of the species known as *Rhinolophus*, and its emergence in humans is thought to have been assisted through intermediate hosts in the wet markets of southern China (Webster, 2004; Wang and Eaton, 2007). While bats may indeed be the initial reservoir for SARS, human infections by these viruses are acquired mainly from intermediate animal hosts that frequently encounter humans (for example, domestic pigs, and wild animals sold for food) (Wolfe et al., 2007).

Zoonoses enter into human populations from both domesticated animals (such as farmed swine, pigs, or poultry) and wildlife (such as bats, civets, or chimpanzees). A number of historically important zoonoses were introduced through amplified human–animal contact resulting from domestication, and possibly high-risk zoonoses (including avian influenzas) continue to arise from livestock production systems (Van Boeckel et al., 2012; Wolfe et al., 2007) including the hunting and consumption of wild species such as bushmeat, wild animal trade and other contact with wildlife (Pike et al., 2010; Wolfe et al., 2007).

Zoonosis can be caused by a range of pathogens such as virus, bacteria, fungus, parasites. Figure 1.2 shows the classes of zoonoses and corresponding zoonotic diseases.

Zoonoses can be transmitted in various ways such as, but not limited to, through the air (droplets and/or aerosols), by eating contaminated meat or produce or animal derivatives, through close contact with an infected animal or bird, by touching an area, surface, or object contaminated by the touch of an infected animal, drinking or coming in contact with water that has been contaminated with feces from an infected animal, or through bites, scratches, or

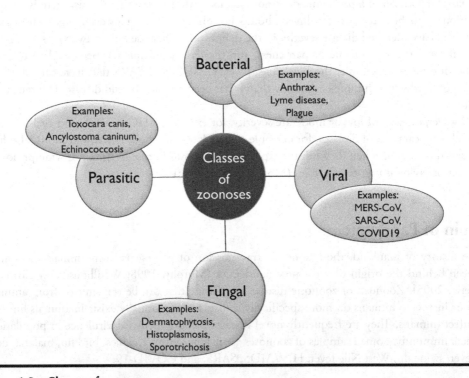

Figure 1.2 Classes of zoonoses.

contact with saliva. It is important to understand the mode of transmission to stop or contain the spread of the disease.

Zoonoses may appear all of a sudden and be quite infectious, as illustrated by HIV which ignited the AIDS pandemic, and the coronaviruses responsible for the SARS and COVID-19 pandemic.

Zoonotic pathogen's ability to infect humans depends on their ability to survive within and spread between human hosts. For an animal pathogen to become a thriving human pathogen (Pike et al., 2010):

- It must develop into a pathogen capable of infecting humans.
- It must be able to sustain long-term human-to-human transmission without the need for reestablishment from the original animal host which typically serves as the reservoir for the pathogen.

The disease emergence model provides a theory for how pathogens arise from animals and demonstrates the scale of animal pathogen infectivity in the human population (Pike et al., 2010). This process can be categorized into five progressive stages (Wolfe et al., 2007; Pike et al., 2010; WHO 2009) as follows (see Figure 1.3):

Stage 1: Stage 1 involves animal pathogens that are not present in humans under natural conditions, such as most malarial plasmodia.

Stage 2: When a pathogen evolves such that it can be transmitted to a human under natural conditions but cannot support sustained human-to-human transmission, it has entered Stage 2. An example of such a pathogen is West Nile viruses.

Most animal pathogens are not transmitted to human beings; that is, they do not even pass from Stage 1 to Stage 2, and hence are harmless to humans.

Stage 3: Transition from Stage 2 and into Stage 3 is defined by secondary transmission between humans as in human beings can get infected from another human being who has contracted

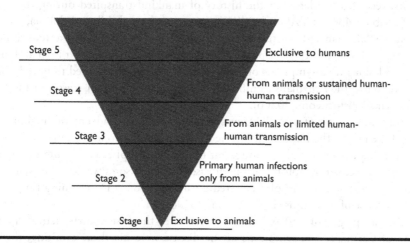

Figure 1.3   Zoonotic disease emergence model outlining the 5 stages of pathogen emergence from animals to humans.

Source: Adapted from Pike et al. (2010), Wolfe et al. (2007)

the disease and show symptoms or are asymptotic. Stage 3 includes pathogens that go through only a few cycles of secondary transmission between humans. Examples of these pathogens are Ebola, Marburg, and human monkeypox viruses.

Although some Stage 2 and 3 pathogens, such as Marburg agents, are contagious, they claim few victims at present and is therefore low impact. However, if they made the transition to Stage 4 or 5, their worldwide impact effect would be overwhelming.

Stage 4: Stage 4 includes diseases that exist in animals and that have a natural cycle of infecting humans by primary transmission from the animal host, but which go through prolonged series of secondary human-to-human transmission with no participation of animal hosts. Influenza A, *Vibrio cholerae*, and dengue virus are some examples of such diseases.

Stage 5: Stage 5 represents diseases that are exclusive to humans, with pathogens confined to human beings only. Agents accountable for some of history's most worrisome diseases belong to this stage. These include pathogens such as smallpox, human immunodeficiency virus (HIV) that causes AIDS, and tuberculosis (Wolfe et al., 2007; Pike et al., 2010).

Most zoonotic pathogens are not well adapted to human beings and progress to stage 2 and/or stage 3, appear intermittently through spillover events, and may lead to localized outbreaks, called stuttering chains (Pike et al., 2010; Wolfe et al., 2005). These episodes of "viral chatter" make available, opportunities for viruses to become better adapted to spreading within a human population, thus increasing the pandemic risk. Pathogens that are past stage 3 are source of extreme apprehension, because they are suitably adapted to humans to cause long transmission chains between humans (either directly or indirectly through vectors), and their geographic spread is not constrained by the habitat range of an animal reservoir (Morens et al., 2009a).

Notable Pandemics in History

There have been several devastating pandemics in the history of mankind:

■ The first recorded pandemic in the history of mankind transpired during the Peloponnesian War about 430 B.C. After the disease traversed through Libya, Ethiopia, and Egypt, it crossed the Athenian walls as the Spartans laid siege. The disease had a devastating impact and as much as two-thirds of the population died. Fever, thirst, bloody throat and tongue, red skin, and lesions were symptoms of the disease. The disease, assumed to have been typhoid fever, weakened the Athenians significantly and was an important reason in their defeat by the Spartans (History.com, 2020b).

■ The Antonine plague of 165 A.D. was probably an initial advent of smallpox that first infected the Huns. The Huns then infected the Germans, who in turn infected the Romans. The returning troops spread it throughout the Roman empire. Fever, sore throat, and diarrhea were immediate symptoms of the disease. Pus-filled sores was another symptom if the patient survived longer. This plague lasted until about 180 A.D., claiming Emperor Marcus Aurelius as one of its victims (History.com, 2020b).

■ The Cyprian plague of 250 A.D. was named after the first known victim, the Christian bishop of Carthage. The symptoms of the disease were diarrhea, vomiting, throat ulcers, fever, and gangrenous hands and feet. Possibly originating in Ethiopia, it traversed through Northern Africa, into Rome, then onto Egypt and northward. There were recurrent disease outbreaks over the following three centuries. In 444 A.D., it hit Britain (History.com, 2020b).

■ The Plague of Justinian of 541 A.D. was ascribed to the bubonic plague. The plague killed 25–50 million people in one year [Ancient History Encyclopedia].

■ The Black plague killed millions of people from 1347 to 1351, including those who died in Middle Eastern lands, China, and India, in addition to Europe. This pandemic was caused by a bacterium, called Yersinia pestis, rather than a virus. Epidemiologists think that the Black Death started in Asia. Rodents carrying bacteria-infected fleas spread this disease [Medical News Today].

■ In the decades and centuries following the Black Death, doctors got greater confidence, mortality dropped, and governments began to take a more vigorous role in managing the plague. People became habituated to plague as it became a consistent feature of life in many places. London suffered seventeen outbreaks between 1500 and 1665. France suffered from plague for nearly three hundred years from 1500 to 1720. In Egypt, it emerged every eight to nine years (McMillen, 2016; [New World Encyclopedia]).

While there was no scientific understanding of contagion, they knew that it had something to do with proximity. This propelled forward-thinking officials in Venetian-controlled port city of Ragusa decided to keep newly arrived sailors in seclusion until they could prove they did not have the disease. Initially, sailors were kept on their ships for 30 days, which came to be known in Venetian law as a trentino. With the passage of time, the Venetians increased the forced seclusion to 40 days or a quarantino, which is the origin of the word "quarantine" and the start of its practice in the Western world (History.com, 2020a).

■ The Russian flu of 1889 is regarded as the first major flu pandemic. It possibly had its origins in Siberia and Kazakhstan. The disease then spread to Moscow, and then made its way into Finland, and then Poland. From Poland, it spread throughout the rest of Europe. By next year, it had spread into North America and Africa. By the end of 1890, the disease had killed around 360,000 people (History.com, 2020b).

■ The Spanish flu pandemic of 1918 resulted in the death of over 50 million people in one year, including 675,000 Americans (Centers for Disease Control and Prevention, 2019).

■ The smallpox pandemic of the 20th century claimed between 300 and 500 million human lives. In 1979, Edward Jenner substantiated that cowpox provided protection against smallpox infection. In 1959, the World Health Organization (WHO) launched a huge campaign to globally eradicate smallpox. In 1980, smallpox was declared eradicated—the only human disease that has been eradicated to date (Voigt et al., 2016).

■ The ongoing tuberculosis pandemic continues to claim more than 1.5 million human lives annually. Even with the availability of effective treatment, multi-drug resistance has countered efforts to reverse the progression of the pandemic [TB Alliance].

■ Originating in Hong Kong and traversing throughout China and then into the United States, the Asian flu of 1957 became widespread in England where, over a period six months, there were 14,000 deaths. A second wave followed in early 1958, causing around 1.1 million people to die worldwide, with 116,000 deaths in the United States alone (History.com, 2020b).

■ Over the previous two centuries, cholera has touched pandemic proportions seven times. The cholera pandemic of 1961–1975 is considered as the seventh one by experts. Cholera is a bacterial infection of the small intestine caused by certain strains of V. cholerae. It can be fatal within hours. The seventh cholera pandemic was caused by a strain of V. cholerae known as El Tor, which was first identified by scientists in 1905. The disease outbreak appears to have started in Sulawesi, which is an island in Indonesia. From there, it spread to Bangladesh, India, and the Soviet Union, including Ukraine and Azerbaijan. By 1973, the disease had also reached Japan, Italy, and the South Pacific. Latin America had not experienced cholera for 100 years. However, in the 1990s, though the pandemic had officially ended, the same strain reached Latin America. There were a minimum 400,000 infected individuals and 4,000 deaths [Medical News Today].

■ 1981 to present: HIV—Since the early 1980s, HIV has resulted in deaths of around 32 million people. At the close of 2018, there were roughly 37.9 million infected people [Medical News Today].

■ In 2002, severe acute respiratory syndrome (SARS) became the first pandemic of the 21st century and was caused due to a coronavirus, known as SARS-CoV. It originated in China. The virus originated in bats, but it moved into civets before infecting humans. SARS infected an estimate of 8,000 people in 29 countries across the world. It had a mortality rate of approximately 10% [Medical News Today].

■ According to the Centers for Disease Control and Prevention (CDC), between April 2009 and April 2010, the swine flu pandemic affected an estimated 60.8 million people. The swine flu pandemic resulted in 274,304 hospitalizations and 12,469 deaths. It had a mortality rate of around 0.02% [Medical News Today].

■ The most recent pandemic is the COVID-19 pandemic which originated in 2019 and spread rapidly in 2020. The disease was caused due to a coronavirus, known as SARS-CoV-2. As of August 2021, the global COVID-19 cases has topped 197.7 million, with more than 4.21 million deaths, according to the Johns Hopkins University (Business Standard, 2021).

Table 1.1 summarizes the major pandemics in the history of mankind.

Table 1.1 Major Pandemics in the History of Mankind

Name	Time Period	Type/Pre-Human Host	Death Toll
Plague at Athens	430–426 BCE	Believed to be typhoid	100,000
Antonine plague	165–180	Believed to be either small pox or measles	5M
Plague of Justinian	541–542	Yersinia Petis Bacteria/ Rats, flea	30M–50M
Black Death	1347–1351	Yersinia Petis Bacteria/ Rats, flea	200M
Russian Flu	1889–1890	Believed to be H2N2 (avian origin)	360,000
Spanish Flu	1918–1919	H1N1 virus /Pigs	50M
Smallpox	1520–1980	Variola major virus	300M–500M
Tuberculosis	1720–till date	Mycobacterium tuberculosis	
Asian Flu	1957–1958	H2N2 virus	1.1M
Cholera	1817–1990	*V. cholerae* Bacteria	1M+

Name	Time Period	Type/Pre-Human Host	Death Toll
HIV/AIDS	1981–Present	Virus/Chimpanzees	25–35M
SARS	2002–2003	Coronavirus/ Bats, Civets	770
Swine Flu	2009–2010	H1N1 virus /Pigs	200,000
COVID-19	2019–till date	Bats	Approximately 4.7 million deaths as of September 21, 2021

Note: Many of the death toll numbers listed in this table are best estimates.

Source: Adapted from LePan (2020), History.com (2020b), Barberis et al. (2017)

Pandemics, COVID-19, Technology, Data, and Analytics in the 21st Century

In the previous section, we listed the notable pandemics in the history of mankind, which shows that pandemics have been there since ancient ages. What is usually new or different:

- Is a new pathogen or new strain of an old pathogen causing the pandemic?
- How is the pandemic managed?

How a pandemic is managed and contained depends on the leadership decisions, infrastructure, and technology available during the occurrence of the pandemic.

Managing a pandemic (like managing data) is as much about people, leadership, strategy, process, and culture, as it is about the nature of the pathogen itself.

A health pandemic is a complex crisis, influenced by a range of factors and having a range of adverse consequences. Hence, it needs much more than human experience and approaches based on conviction, perceptiveness, and acumen to be able to assess all these factors and consequences and combat it. Data replace intuition with objectivity, and powerful tools like analytics that leverage data to provide useful insights are needed in addition to human element and strategy, to fight such a crisis.

We are currently living in a digital world and armed with sophisticated technology that can be used to leverage data and derive insights that can help in combating pandemic of a scale similar to COVID-19, in ways that was not possible in previous centuries. This is because the variety and amount of data available today as well as the technologies available to leverage data to derive insights were not there in the previous centuries. From the 1800s to modern times, the time for new technologies to diffuse has shrunk from around 100 years to within a decade for multiple technologies (Comin and Hobijn, 2004; World Bank, 2008), thereby ushering in a new environment where access to technologies, information, and data has become increasingly common across the globe (Sheng et al., 2020).

Until the advent of computers, limited facts were documented and stored in paper files, given the expense, scarcity of resources, and effort to store and maintain them. While electronic storage and processing of data started at the end of the 19th century, owing to the cost and limitations of storage, the amount of data that could be stored was relatively less. The advancement of technology enabled increasing volumes of data to be captured, processed, and stored for operational, analysis, and reporting purposes (Mahanti, 2021). However, the storage of data was more centralized and sharing of data was somewhat restricted.

Post advent of internet in the mid-1990s, there was further progress of information technologies and this era was characterized by declining cost of disk hardware and availability of cloud storage. As the internet became worldwide, social media, mobile apps, and websites steadily grew to become platforms for sharing data. Electronic generation, capture, processing, and storage of large volumes of data via a large variety of channels became common. The advancement in technologies enabled sourcing and processing massive amounts of data from heterogeneous sources using various software tools and technologies (for example, data warehousing tools, big data technologies, data analytics, and reporting tools) (Mahanti, 2021).

Data and analytics have been at the heart of every COVID-19 pandemic research effort. In fact, they will form the base for any pandemic research effort. This is because pandemics are characterized by global spread of disease as well as lot of unknowns which require researchers to analyze massive amounts of data from different sources—which cannot be accomplished manually.

COVID-19 pandemic requires us to use new sources of data in thoughtful and creative ways to help understand the cause–effect relationship as well as the relative risk. Fortuitously, technology and data companies are continuously innovating new methods to aggregate and present data that can help us make more informed, data-rich decisions in difficult times brought about by the COVID-19 pandemic [Cruickshank and O'Mara].

Real-time data have been a principal focus throughout the COVID-19 pandemic. The Center for Systems Science and Engineering (CSSE) at Johns Hopkins University released a web-based dashboard tracking real-time data on confirmed COVID-19 cases, fatalities, and recoveries for all impacted countries. This was first publicly shared on January 22, 2020, which was a few months before the US had implemented quarantine and social distancing measures (Kent, 2020).

The dashboard signified the pivotal role data and technology would play in the coming months, as leaders across world worked on strategies to combat the pandemic. Big data analytics tools have featured principally in the industry's response to coronavirus infections, and these technologies will possibly continue to be an essential part of healthcare going forward (Kent, 2020).

While healthcare industry sector is the worst hit during a pandemic, a pandemic takes a toll over other industry sectors too. This is because human resources form a part of every industry sector and pandemics target human beings which in turn has a multisectoral impact. Data and analytics not only play a role in combating diseases and the healthcare industry, but also play a role in other industry sectors. For example, pandemic is characterized by change in consumer spending patterns, and the retail industry can use data and analytics to study these patterns and devise strategies to meet consumer needs. However, data need to be of good quality else results will be of no use. The different data challenges, ways to overcome those challenges, and the role of data and analytics in managing a pandemic will be discussed in the subsequent chapters.

However, while technology, data, and the insights that can be drawn from data are powerful enablers, they are not the drivers; human beings are the drivers. Data, even inferences, alone are impotent in most crises. There have to be minds ready to look at the data, capable of understanding the data, be open to new possibilities, a bias toward action, and creation and execution of appropriate strategies driven by effective leadership. The saying "you can bring a horse to water" applies here—where water can be thought of as data, and human being the horse. You can bring water to the horse, but it is the horse's choice to drink it or not drink it. Similarly, data and inferences might be available for people to use. It is their choice to use them to make informed decisions or to ignore them and do nothing.

Concluding Thoughts

Humankind has always been vulnerable to disease outbreaks. Diseases have been constant companions of all living beings. With larger cities, increased interconnectivity and extensive travel, global trade routes, and increased contact with different populations of people, animals, and ecosystems, the likelihood of diseases growing into pandemics becomes greater.

While it is not possible to stop a new disease from emerging and infecting mankind, it is definitely possible to a certain extent to learn lessons from past pandemics and plan better for a new disease, by investing in better healthcare infrastructures. Also, once a new disease has been discovered, it is important to understand the characteristics of the disease, to devise strategies to stop it from evolving into a pandemic as well as strategies to deal with it once it takes shape of a pandemic.

We are currently living in a digital world, armed with sophisticated technology that can be used to leverage data and derive insights that can help in combating pandemic of a scale similar to COVID-19, in ways that was not possible in previous centuries. Data and analytics can play a crucial role in reporting, managing, and combating a pandemic, and the technological achievements (for example, big data analytics tools) will continue to feature in the industry sectors, beyond the pandemic.

References

Altman, L. K. (June 8, 2009) Is This a Pandemic? Define 'Pandemic'. *New York Times*, 1998 Available at: www.nytimes.com/2009/06/09/health/09docs.html. Accessed 24 August 2009.

[Ancient History Encyclopedia], Justinian's Plague (541–542 CE). Updated 26 December 2014.

Barberis, I., Bragazzi, N. L., Galluzzo, L., and Martini, M. (March 2017) The History of Tuberculosis: From the First Historical Records to the Isolation of Koch's Bacillus. *Journal of Preventive Medicine and Hygiene*, 58(1), pp. E9–E12 Available at: www.ncbi.nlm.nih.gov/pmc/articles/PMC5432783/. Accessed 4 November 2020.

Business Standard (2021) Global Covid-19 Caseload Tops 197.7 Million: Johns Hopkins University, *Business Standard*, August 1 2021 Available at: www.business-standard.com/article/current-affairs/global-covid-19-caseload-tops-197-7-million-johns-hopkins-university-121080100087_1.html.

Centers for Disease Control and Prevention (2019) 1918 Pandemic (H1N1 Virus). Updated 20 March 2019.

Cohen, J. (June 12, 2009) Here Comes Swine Flu Phase 6, Severity Available at: http://blogs.sciencemag.org/scienceinsider/2009/06/swine-flu-who-r.html. Accessed 24 August 2009.

[Collins Dictionary], Definition—Pandemic Available at: www.collinsdictionary.com/dictionary/english/pandemic. Accessed 1 June 2020.

Comin, D., and Hobijn, B. (2004) Cross-Country Technology Adoption: Making the Theories Face the Facts. *Journal of Monetary Economics*, 51, pp. 39–83.

[Cruickshank and O'Mara] Cruickshank, C., and O'Mara, M. Data-Driven Operational Strategies in the Pandemic Era. *AreaDevelopment Online, COVID-19 Response* Available at: www.areadevelopment.com/covid-19-response/Q3-2020/data-driven-operational-strategies-in-the-pandemic-era.shtml. Accessed 1 May 2021.

Ducharme, J. (March 11, 2020) World Health Organization Declares COVID-19 a 'Pandemic.' Here's What That Means. *Time.com* Available at: https://time.com/5791661/who-coronavirus-pandemic-declaration/. Accessed 4 November 2020.

Dumar, M. (2009) *Swine Flu: What You Need to Know*. Wildside Press LLC, p. 7. ISBN 978–1434458322.

Enserink, M. (June 9, 2009) Swine Flu: WHO "Really Very Close" to Using the P Word. *Sciencemag Blog*. Available at: http://blogs.sciencemag.org/scienceinsider/2009/06/here-comes-phas.html. Accessed 24 August 2009.

Grennan, D. (March 5, 2019) What Is a Pandemic? *JAMA Patient Page* Available at: https://jamanetwork.com/journals/jama/fullarticle/2726986. Accessed 4 November 2020.

Harvey, G. (1666) *On the Original, Contagion, and Frequency of Consumptions*. Harvey, Morbus Anglicus. London Nathaniel Brook, pp. 2–14.

History.com (27 March, 2020a) How 5 of History's Worst Pandemics Finally Ended Available at: www.his tory.com/news/pandemics-end-plague-cholera-black-death-smallpox.

History.com (April 1, 2020b) Pandemics That Changed History Available at: www.history.com/topics/ middle-ages/pandemics-timeline.

Jamison, D. T., Gelband, H., Horton, S., et al., editors. (November 27, 2017) *Disease Control Priorities: Improving Health and Reducing Poverty*. 3rd ed. Washington, DC: The International Bank for Reconstruction and Development/The World Bank.

Kent, J. (December 24, 2020) Intersection of Big Data Analytics, COVID-19 Top Focus of 2020, *Health IT Analytics*, Available at: https://healthitanalytics.com/news/intersection-of-big-data-analytics-cov id-19-top-focus-of-2020. Accessed 24 August 2021.

Krause, R. M., Dimmock, N. J., and Morens, D. M. (1997) Summary of Antibody Workshop: The Role of Humoral Immunity in the Treatment and Prevention of Emerging and Extant Infectious Diseases. *The Journal of Infectious Diseases*, 176, pp. 549–559.

Kvicala, J. (February 20, 2003) Americans Experiencing "Pandemic of Obesity," Says Director of Centers for Disease Control and Prevention in Atlanta, *Terry College of Business Press Releases* Available at: www. terry.uga.edu/news/releases/2003/gerberding.html. Accessed 24 August 2009.

LePan, N. (March 15, 2020) A Visual History of Pandemics. *World Economic Forum*, Available at: www.wefo rum.org/agenda/2020/03/a-visual-history-of-pandemics. Accessed 4 November 2020.

[Lexico], Powered by Oxford, Definition—Pandemic Available at: www.lexico.com/definition/pandemic. Accessed 1 June 2020.

Madhav, N., Oppenheim, B., Gallivan, M. et al. (November 27, 2017) Pandemics: Risks, Impacts, and Mitigation. In: Jamison DT, Gelband H, Horton S et al., editors. *Disease Control Priorities: Improving Health and Reducing Poverty*. 3rd ed. Washington, DC: The International Bank for Reconstruction and Development/The World Bank. Chapter 17 Available at: www.ncbi.nlm.nih.gov/books/ NBK525302/ doi:10.1596/978-1-4648-0527-1_ch17.

Mahanti, R. (2021) *Data Governance and Data Management: Contextualizing Data Governance Drivers, Technologies, and Tools*. Springer, Book. doi:10.1007/978-981-16-3583-0; Print ISBN—978-981-16-3582-3.

McMillen, C. W. (2016) *Pandemics: A Very Short Introduction*. Oxford: Oxford University Press.

[Medical News Today], Comparing COVID-19 with Previous Pandemics Available at: www.medicalnewsto day.com/articles/comparing-covid-19-with-previous-pandemics#20092010:-H1N1-swine-flu.

[Merriam-Webster Dictionary], Definition—Pandemic Available at: www.merriam-webster.com/dictionary/ pandemic. Accessed 1 June 2020.

Morens, D. M., Folkers, G. K., and Fauci, A. S. (October 1, 2009a) What Is a Pandemic? *The Journal of Infectious Diseases*, 200(7), pp. 1018–1021. https://doi.org/10.1086/644537 Available at: https://academic. oup.com/jid/article/200/7/1018/903237. Accessed 11 November 2020.

Morens, D. M., Taubenberger, J. K., and Fauci, A. S. (2009b) The Persistent Legacy of the 1918 Influenza Virus. *The New England Journal of Medicine*, 361, pp. 109–113.

Murphy, F. A. (1998) Emerging Zoonoses. *Emerging Infectious Diseases*, 4(3), pp. 429–435.

[New World Encyclopedia] Black Death. Updated 3 September 2019.

Pike, B. L., Saylors, K. E., Fair, J. N., Lebreton, M., Tamoufe, U. et al. (2010) The Origin and Prevention of Pandemics. *Clinical Infectious Diseases*, 50(12), pp. 1636–1640.

Shafey, O., Dolwick, S., and Guindon, G. E. (2003) *Tobacco Control Country Profiles 2003*. Atlanta: Atlanta American Cancer Society.

Shannon, J. (March 2020) Coronavirus Has Been Declared a Pandemic: What Does That Mean, and What Took So Long? *USA Today* Available at: www.usatoday.com/story/news/nation/2020/03/11/coronavi rus-pandemic-world-health-organization/5011903002/. Accessed 4 November 2020.

Sheng, J., Amankwah-Amoah, J., Khan, Z., and Wang, X. (November 2, 2020) COVID-19 Pandemic in the New Era of Big Data Analytics: Methodological Innovations and Future Research Directions. *British Journal of Management*, https://doi.org/10.1111/1467-8551.12441.

Shope, R. E. (1958) Influenza: History, Epidemiology, and Speculation the R E. Dyer Lecture. *Public Health Reports*, 73, pp. 165–178.

Swine Flu (June 6, 2009) Swine Flu: Let's Scrap the Pandemic Alert System Effect Measure. *Scienceblogs*. Available at: http://scienceblogs.com/effectmeasure/2009/06/swine_flu_lets_scrap_the_pande.php. Accessed 24 August 2009.

Taubenberger, J. K., and Morens, D. M. (2009) Pandemic Influenza: Including a Risk Assessment of H5N1. *Revue Scientifique et Technique*, 28, pp. 187–202.

TB Alliance. The Pandemic.

Van Boeckel, T. P., Thanapongtharm, W., Robinson, T., Biradar, C. M., Xiao, X. et al. (2012) Improving Risk Models for Avian Influenza: The Role of Intensive Poultry Farming and Flooded Land During the 2004 Thailand Epidemic. *PLOS ONE*, 7(11), p. e49528.

Voigt, E. A., Kennedy, R. B., and Poland, G. A. (2016) Defending Against Smallpox: A Focus on Vaccines. *Expert Review of Vaccines*, 15(9), pp. 1197–1211. doi:10.1080/14760584.2016.1175305.

Wang, L. F., and Eaton, B. T. (2007) Bats, Civets and the Emergence of SARS. *Current Topics in Microbiology and Immunology*, 315, pp. 325–344.

Webster, R. G. (2004) Wet Markets-a Continuing Source of Severe Acute Respiratory Syndrome and Influenza? *Lancet*, 363(9404), pp. 234–236.

WHO (2009) Pandemic Influenza Preparedness and Response: A WHO Guidance Document Available at: www.ncbi.nlm.nih.gov/books/NBK143061/. Accessed 4 November 2020.

WHO (2010) What Is a Pandemic Available at: www.who.int/csr/disease/swineflu/frequently_asked_questions/pandemic/en/. Accessed 11 November 2020.

Wolfe, N. D., Daszak, P., Kilpatrick, A. M., and Burke, D. S. (2005) Bushmeat Hunting, Deforestation, and Prediction of Zoonotic Disease. *Emerging Infectious Diseases*, 11(12), pp. 1822–1827.

Wolfe, N. D., Dunavan, C. P., and Diamond, J. (2007) Origins of Major Human Infectious Diseases. *Nature*, 447(7142), pp. 279–283.

Woolhouse, M. E. J., and Gowtage-Sequeria, S. (2005) Host Range and Emerging and Reemerging Pathogens. *Emerging Infectious Diseases*, 11(12), pp. 1842–1847.

World Bank (2008) *Global Economic Prospects: Technology Diffusion in the Developing World*. Washington, DC: World Bank.

Zhu, H., Wei, L. and Niu, P. (2020) The Novel Coronavirus Outbreak in Wuhan, China. *Global Health Research and Policy* 5, 6 https://doi.org/10.1186/s41256-020-00135-6

Chapter 2

Data—Management, Strategy, Quality, Governance, and Analytics

> *"Data is the key link in a chain of components that define the helix at the heart of every organisation; it is a continuous spiral of events repeating over the passage of time."*
>
> **—Pete Smith, Jason Edge, Steve Parry and Dave Wilkinson,**
> **Crossing the Data Delta**

We are currently living in the digital age with data being the key differentiator. Data promises to be for the 21st century what steam power was for the 18th, electricity for the 19th, and hydrocarbons for the 20th century (Mojsilovic, 2014).

The volume of data being created, generated, captured, processed, and stored within organizations' IT infrastructures is growing exponentially. Evolution of IT and internet way of things have attributed to widespread sharing of data and data having a universal presence.

This growing trend to capture data in different forms and feeds to achieve new functions is called datafication, and is being driven by new opportunities, methods, and tools to deal with volumes in the order of peta—and exabytes rather than giga—and terabytes (Natarajan et al., 2017). The sheer volume of data that exists in the new economy is enabled by advancements in low-cost technology to collect, store, transport, and analyze it.

The pervasiveness of data has changed the way we conduct business, transact, undertake research, and communicate. Data have played a crucial role in the management of the COVID-19 pandemic too.

In fact, data have become more important due to the COVID-19 pandemic. In the words of Chief Performance Officer Greg Useem—"People are seeing more clearly how important data is in solving problems" (Jaiani and Audet, 2020).

In this chapter, we discuss in brief some key concepts around data such as definition of data, varieties of data, traditional data versus big data, organization of data, data management, data strategy, data quality, key data quality dimensions, data governance, data analytics, and the role data quality and data governance play in data analytics.

DOI: 10.4324/9781003270911-2

Delving into the Definition of Data

The Cambridge Dictionary defines data as "information, especially facts or numbers, collected to be examined and considered, and used to help decision-making." From an IT perspective, the Cambridge Dictionary defines data as "information in an electronic form that can be stored and used by a computer."

The International Organization for Standardization (ISO) defines data as "re-interpretable representation of information in a formalized manner suitable for communication, interpretation, or processing" [ISO 11179]. A singular datum provides "a fixed starting point of a scale or operation." Data are representation of facts related to entities, where an entity can be a concept, object, event, phenomena, party, or location. It stands for things other than itself (Chisholm, 2010). Data can even represent other data, that is, data about data or metadata (Sebastian-Coleman, 2013).

In order for data to be understood, one needs to understand the context of data. This includes the context of creation of data, characteristics of the entities that the data are supposed to represent, the context of usage of data, and the conventions of representation they employ to convey meaning. These conventions of representation translate features of entities into numbers, identifiers, codes, or other symbols based on decisions made by people. To understand the meaning of a piece of data, one must understand not only what the data are supposed to represent, but also the conventions of representation they employ to convey meaning (Sebastian-Coleman, 2013). These conventions can be thought of as data about data or metadata.

Data represent selective features of entities. Since there are usually more than one way to represent entities and their respective features, different people often make different choices when representing entities and their corresponding features. This results in different representations of the same entities and data taking on different forms, types, and sizes.

Varieties of Data

With respect to data, variety refers to the assortment of data types and data sources and can be grouped into three types:

- Structured data,
- Unstructured data, and
- Semi-structured data.

Traditional data are structured data that can be stored in tables in relational databases. Largely, traditional data sources fall in the structured data domain ([NTNU]; Mahanti, 2021c).

Structured Data

Structured data are data that have clearly defined data types, and are structured by predefined data models and schema. Structured data can be stored in relational database tables in rows and columns. Structured data are predictable, and are easier to search. Structured Query Language commonly known as SQL is used to search structured data stored in relational database tables. Data stored in relational databases are the most common examples of structured data.

Unstructured Data

Unstructured data are data that have no identifiable structure and are not structured via pre-defined data models or schema, and hence are not stored in relational database tables. Unstructured data are usually stored in non-relational databases such as NoSQL databases. Unstructured data are complex and are difficult to search and process. Examples of unstructured data are text (documents, social media data, and so on), audio, images, and video streams.

Unstructured data can be human generated (such as word documents, social media data like texts posted on LinkedIn, Facebook, and presentations) and/or machine generated (such as sensor data and satellite data).

Semi-Structured Data

Semi-structured data lie between structured and non-structured data. Semi-structured data are data that may be erratic or incomplete, have a structure that may change rapidly or unpredictably, and organizational structures that makes it easier to analyze. It does not have the same level of structure and predictability as structured data, but generally has some structure such as tags to separate data elements and help to identify the data for later retrieval. However, semi-structured data do not conform to a fixed schema. Web logs, XML files, and JSON files are examples of semi-structured data.

Big Data versus Traditional Data

While traditional data or data are structured data, big data constitutes structured data, unstructured data, as well as semi-structured data.

The term big data is often thought as large volumes of data, as implied by the term itself and also because of the fact that the term was used to refer to the volumes of data requiring new, large-scale systems/software to process the data in a reasonable time frame as the volume had increased to the point that it could no longer be processed on traditional system platforms (Talburt and Zhou, 2015). In short, big data is high-volume, high-velocity, and/or high-variety information assets that demand cost-effective, innovative forms of information processing that enable enhanced insight, decision-making, and process automation [Gartner Information Technology Glossary].

The differences between big data and data or traditional data are along the lines of volume, velocity, and variety. These aspects are popularly known as the three V's of big data (Mahanti, 2021c).

Volume

If the volume of the data is very large—in the order of petabytes (1 million gigabytes) or exabytes (1 billion gigabytes) so that it cannot be stored in one location or an ordinary database, or needs specialized tools and technologies to organize or analyze the data, then the data in question is big data. On the other hand, traditional data have comprehensible proportions and can be captured or processed by traditional data processing software.

Velocity

If data are generated at exceptionally high rates or changes rapidly, such that traditional software cannot capture, store, or organize it, then such data falls under the realm of big data.

While traditional data has batch velocity, big data has real-time velocity. For example, before the advent of smart metering, meter data were captured once per month and stored as a record in relational databases. However, with the advent of smart metering, meter data are read at a much greater frequency, once every 30 minutes and qualify as big data.

Variety

Variety refers to the assortment of data types and data sources. Big data is multi-structured and has a wide variety of formats, data structure types, and semantics, sourced from a wide variety of data sources. Big data can be structured, semi-structured, and unstructured. Traditional data are structured data that can be stored in relational databases. Most traditional data sources are in the structured realm [NTNU].

Organization of Data

Organizations have a large number of systems that store data—database systems and file systems, which in turn have large number of tables and files, respectively (Mahanti, 2021c).

Data in organizations are usually stored in a standard structure in *tables* of columns and rows in a multitude of *database systems*. Each horizontal row in a table is called a *record*.

Data are also stored in *file systems*; that is, data are stored in *data files* that are organized in folders, and the folders are organized under a hierarchy of directories and subdirectories.

The most granular level of data is the *data element* which is the most basic unit of data and the smallest named unit in the database or data file that has meaning for the user and can be defined for processing. The data element represents an attribute or collection of attributes of a real-world entity (Mahanti, 2019).

A *data set* is a set of records (both rows and columns) extracted from data files or database tables, for a specific purpose (Mahanti, 2021a).

Databases are a collection of related tables. There are different types of databases. Relational databases are the most popular database for storing structured data. *NOSQL databases* are primarily used to store data that are not structured and big data, though they can store structured data too.

The database structure is attained by appropriately organizing the data with the aid of a database model. A *database model* determines the logical organization of a database and the manner in which the data can be stored, structured, linked, and manipulated [Wikipedia].

In addition, to tables and databases, data are stored in a variety of other digital means such as excel files, XML (Extensible Markup Language) files, JSON files, fixed width text files, delimited text files (for example, CSV (Comma Separated Value) files and TSV (Tab Separated Value) files).

A *data warehouse* also known as an *enterprise data warehouse* (EDW) is a database repository that sources, integrates, and consolidates data from multiple heterogeneous sources (Inmon, 2005). It is a trusted source for integrated enterprise data. *Data marts* are fundamentally, specialized, sometimes local databases or custom-built data warehouse offshoots that store data related to individual business units (e.g., sales, human resources, and marketing) or specific subject areas (e.g., product, customer, employee, asset, and event) or for addressing concerns of a particular business problem (e.g., increasing operational efficiency) (Mahanti, 2019).

Data warehouses and data marts store structured data (that is, data that complies to specific format and are created using a predefined schema). However, organizations also have a great deal of unstructured data and semi-structured data. While data warehouses store only structured data in tables in the databases, *data lakes* can store any data (that is, structured data, unstructured data, and/or semi-structured data), including data types not supported by a data warehouse, in their raw and native format in a scalable manner (Mahanti, 2021c).

Data Management

Data management is the process of capturing, processing, storing, organizing, securing, and maintaining the data that is created, generated, and/or collected by an organization.

Data management encompasses all disciplines associated with managing data as an asset. The concept of data management arose in the 1980s as technology moved from sequential processing to random access storage (Hoare, 1985). However, data management has evolved over a period of time and at present is a complex cross functional enterprise-wide program and discipline, having several intertwined sub-disciplines such as but not limited to data security management, data quality, data architecture, master data management, reference data management, and data governance. Data governance is the adhesive tying together all these different data management sub-disciplines (Mahanti, 2021c).

Data can be used to make informed decisions. However, absence of proper data management can result in data residing in silos, outdated data, inconsistent data, and other data quality issues. Analysis of such data leads to incorrect inferences and bad decisions, thus defeating the purpose of using data.

A well-designed data governance program is a very important component of effective data management strategies. A solid focus on data quality is also very important. This is because both data governance and data quality are key to having accurate, consistent, and current data. Good data are at the core of any type of analytics. Technology is an enabler, but if the input data is of questionable quality, the output results will be of questionable quality too. Charles Babbage's famous quote—"garbage in, garbage out" applies here. The next sections focus on data strategy, data quality, data governance, and data analytics.

Data Strategy

"Not having a data strategy is analogous to allowing each person within each department of your organization to develop their own chart of accounts and use their own numbering scheme."

—Sid Adelman, Data Warehousing Expert (Adelman et al., 2005)

Before we delve into data strategy, let's try to understand what a strategy is. The Oxford English Dictionary defines strategy as

a plan of action designed to achieve a long-term or overall aim.

Liddell and Scott (1999) define strategy as

a high-level plan to achieve one or more goals under conditions of uncertainty.

M. Daniell (2006) defines strategy as

the art and science of informed action to achieve a specific vision, an overarching objective or a higher purpose for a business enterprise.

However, there is no single or universally accepted definition of "strategy." More widely accepted business definitions of strategy, emphasize what an organization can do differently to outperform its peers (Coleman, 2021).

Like strategy, the term "data strategy" does not have a universally accepted definition too. Lotame defines data strategy as

> a vision for how a company will collect, store, manage, share, and use data.

The MIT CISR Data Board defines data strategy as (Lotame, 2019):

> a central, integrated concept that articulates how data will enable and inspire business strategy.

Ramesh Dontha (2016) defines data strategy as

> a strategy that lays out a comprehensive vision across the enterprise and sets a foundation for the company to employ data-related or data-dependent capability.

While having a data strategy can open doors to the power that data can bring and can also help in leveraging it to gain a competitive advantage, only one in ten organizations have an enterprise data strategy, given the difficulty in getting a buy-in from the executive level or because of a lack of realization of the benefits that an effective strategy can bring to the organization (Eckerson, 2011; Mahanti, 2021b).

An organization's data strategy sets the foundation for everything that an organization does in relation to data. An effective and robust data strategy needs to be aligned with overarching corporate and business goals and also recognize the importance of the broader data ecosystem, outside business boundaries (Coleman, 2021).

A data strategy should lay out a comprehensive plan to mature in analytic capabilities and transition from making decisions based on hindsight (that is using descriptive analytics) to making decisions with foresight (that is using predictive analytics) (Analytics8, 2021).

A data strategy should be specific and actionable. An organization's data strategy should evolve as its corporate and business objectives evolve. Also, an organization should also be able to adjust its data strategy as circumstances change.

For example, with the COVID-19 pandemic, consumer behaviors, company operations, and supply chain behaviors have changed. As a result of these changes, the underlying data have also changed and will continue to change through the duration of the pandemic as well as beyond the pandemic. Organizations need to adapt their data strategies to align with changes and at the same need to be in tandem with the organizations' wider business strategies.

Data quality, data architecture, data governance, data security and data privacy, and analytics have been important elements of a data strategy but have become more so to combat the COVID-19 pandemic crisis.

The role of data strategies in managing a pandemic, and the key data strategy lessons learnt during the COVID-19 pandemic will be discussed in Chapter 9 of this book.

Data Quality

"Businesses will live or die by their data quality competence."

—Gartner Group

Data quality is the capability of data to satisfy the stated business, system, and technical requirements of an enterprise. Data quality is an insight or an evaluation of data's fitness to serve their purpose in a given context (Mahanti, 2019).

From a data management function perspective, data quality or data quality management (DQM) is management of combination of right people, processes, and technologies to achieve high-quality data to achieve desired business outcomes (Mahanti, 2019; [Knowledgent]; Mahanti, 2021c). In short, DQM can be defined as the "quality-oriented management of data as an asset" (Weber et al., 2009, p. 4:4).

The ultimate goal of DQM is not to improve data quality for the sole sake of having high-quality data, but to realize the desired business outcomes that bank on high-quality data [Knowledgent].

The degree of data quality excellence that should be attained and sustained is driven by the criticality of the data, the business need, the purposes for which the data are used, and the cost and time to achieve the defined degree of data quality (Mahanti, 2019).

Data Quality Dimensions

Data quality can be defined as follows:

> Data quality is the capability of data to satisfy the stated business, system, and technical requirements of an enterprise,

and

> Data quality is an insight or an evaluation of data's fitness to serve their purpose in a given context.

Both these definitions are holistic but abstract. Hence, it is a challenge to measure data quality using the aforementioned two definitions (Mahanti, 2019).

Data quality as a property of data is a multidimensional concept. It has many attributes or dimensions called data quality dimensions that can be used to measure the quality of data. Each data quality dimension captures a specific measurable characteristic of data quality (Mahanti, 2019, 2021c).

There is no universal agreement on the number, categorization, and definition of data quality dimensions, with several researchers, practitioners, authors, and organizations having approached and/or approaching data quality dimensions and/or their categorization differently (Mahanti, 2019, 2021c).

Some of the key data quality dimensions are as follows:

- **Completeness**—Completeness relates to whether data values are present or not, or the extent to which data values are present or absent. Completeness is vital because missing data can have a significant effect on the conclusions drawn from the data, and decisions those conclusions drive (Mahanti, 2021c).
- **Accuracy**—Data accuracy relates to the extent to which data correctly describes the real-world object, entity, situation, phenomena, or event, and their characteristics. It is a measure of the correctness of the content of the data (which requires an authoritative source of reference to be identified and available for validation) (Mahanti, 2021c).

- **Consistency**—Consistency relates to the extent to which the data values are matching for all instances of an application. The data across the enterprise should be in sync with each other. The format and presentation of data should be consistent across the whole data set relating to the data entity (Mahanti, 2019, 2021c). If the data values are inconsistent, then at least one of the values is not accurate.
- **Timeliness**—Timeliness refers to whether the data are available in a timely manner. It is driven by the fact that it is possible to have data that are current, but that do not serve any purpose, because they are delayed for a particular usage (Batini et al., 2009; Mahanti, 2019).
- **Currency**—Currency refers to the degree to which the data are sufficiently up-to-date for the specific context and usage.
- **Data Coverage**—Data coverage refers to the extent of the availability and comprehensiveness of the data in comparison to the total data universe or the population of interest (McGilvray, 2008). More the data coverage, the greater is the ability of the data to suit multiple applications, business processes, and functions (Mahanti, 2021c).
- **Relevance**—Relevance refers to the degree to which the data content as well as its coverage is relevant for the purpose for which it is to used, and the extent to which it meets the existing and prospective future needs (Mahanti, 2019).
- **Data Security**—Data security refers to the extent to which access to data is secured so as to prevent illicit access and the extent to which data are protected from unauthorized modifications, deletes, insertions, and corruption throughout the data life cycle. More sensitive the data, greater are implications from compromise of the data. Hence, greater security measures and control need to be integrated and enforced to ensure that sensitive data is secure (Mahanti, 2021c).
- **Reliability**—Reliability refers to the extent data are complete, relevant, accurate, free of duplicates, consistent, and traceable to a trustworthy source (Mahanti, 2021c).
- **Credibility**—Credibility refers to the extent to which the good faith of a provider of data or source of data can be counted upon to ensure that the data actually represents what it is supposed to represent, and that there is no intent to misrepresent what the data are supposed to represent (Chisholm, 2014).
- **Trustworthiness**—Trustworthiness refers to the extent to which the data are sourced from data sources that are dependable. Several dynamics such as ability to trace data back to authoritative sources, number of data issues reported, number of requests to use the data, and availability of data quality statistics have a bearing on trustworthiness (Mahanti, 2021c).
- **Reputation**—Reputation refers to the extent the data are trusted and highly regarded in terms of their source and content. Reputation of data is built over time, and both data and data sources can build reputation (Wang and Strong, 1996).

A single data quality dimension by itself is rarely able to provide a holistic picture of the quality of data. Also, there is no single combination of data quality dimensions that can be applied in all situations. Depending upon context, situation, the data itself, business or research problem, usage of data, and the industry sector, diverse permutations and combination of data quality dimensions would be needed to be applied (Mahanti, 2019). Data quality challenges with respect to these data quality dimensions from a pandemic perspective have been discussed in Chapter 5. For a detailed study of data quality dimensions and their assessment, refer to the book—*Data Quality: Dimensions, Measurement, Strategy, Management and Governance.*

Data Quality Management

Data quality management is not just the technical quality management of data throughout its life cycle. While technology does play a crucial role in managing data quality, data quality management also includes defining the data quality requirements correctly and ensuring that processes and standards to capture, transform, and store data are adequate. While business is aware of the context of usage of data, the purpose the data serve, and business rules that need to be applied, the IT team understand how the data are stored technically, the data structures, the data models and the data linkages, and the technical rules used to implement the business rules. Hence, both business and IT teams need to work together for defining data quality thresholds for respective data quality dimensions relevant to the context of usage of the data, measuring and assessing data quality dimensions, performing root cause analysis to analyze the gaps, defining the layout, proposing possible solution options for data quality improvement, agreeing on the optimal solution option, and implementing the action plan for improvement (Mahanti, 2019). These activities help ensure that data are either fit for use or have to be fixed for use (Mahanti, 2021c).

Data quality management includes establishing data quality policies and processes, and other activities such as data quality assessment, data cleansing, data quality process improvement, data validation, data monitoring, data quality awareness, and education of stakeholders. Data governance helps bringing together cross-functional team consisting of various stakeholders as well as provides support for facilitation of these activities (Mahanti, 2021c).

Data quality management consists of a mix of reactive approach to fix data issues that can surface at any point of the data life cycle and proactive approach to prevent data quality issues from occurring in the first place by improving processes to capture high-quality data and sustain data quality (Mahanti, 2021c).

Data Governance

"If you value your data, you care about the governance around it."

—Graeme Thompson

Data governance is the exercise and enforcement of policies, processes, guidelines, rules, standards, metrics, controls, decision rights, roles, responsibilities, and accountabilities to manage data as a strategic enterprise asset (Mahanti, 2021c).

Data governance is one of the "pillars" of data management (Advisiondigital, 2016). However, it is often viewed as "nice to have." If an organization collects, stores, and uses data, then it needs to have data governance in place. This is because data are an important asset and an effective data governance program is crucial in managing this asset. With the importance of data increasing exponentially, and compliance and analytics calling for better quality data and improved data protection, data governance is no longer optional, but is a "must have" (Mahanti, 2021c).

Not all data need to be governed with the same rigor. Critical data that are sensitive data, data that need to be of high quality, and data that are widely shared need to be governed rigorously, while public data that does not contained sensitive information can be governed with lesser rigor (Mahanti, 2021c).

Data governance provides guidelines, standards, and rules regarding data quality and data quality management. Without data governance, it is extremely difficult to achieve and sustain data quality throughout the enterprise. This is because a lack of data governance is characterized by the absence of a governing framework which is rigorous in its definition, enforcement of data standards and policies, clear accountabilities, and responsibilities around data.

Since data governance is cross-functional, it involves stakeholders from different business units. Each stakeholder needs to have clearly defined roles and responsibilities concerning the data. Active collaboration is needed to have a consensus regarding data decisions and a common understanding associated with different aspects of data (for example, data security and data quality). For these reasons, the implementation of data governance needs an operating model and organization structure. While the data governance operating model and organization structure are different for different organizations, common groups/bodies involved in data governance at different levels are executive steering committee, data governance council, data stewardship council, data governance office (DGO), and information technology partners as shown in Figure 2.1. Some of the common stakeholders are data producers, data consumers, data owners, data stewards, and data custodians as shown in Figure 2.1 (Mahanti, 2021a).

Data Analytics

"Information is the oil of the 21st century, and analytics is the combustion engine."

—Peter Sondergaard

Data and analytics have been used to combat COVID-19, a pandemic of the digital age in ways that was not possible in case of non-digital age pandemics. Data analytics or analytics is often referred to as fact-based decision-making (Harris, 2015), with data being the common denominator of all analytics (see Figure 2.2), be it:

■ descriptive analytics,
■ diagnostic analytics,
■ predictive analytics, or
■ prescriptive analytics.

Descriptive Analytics

Descriptive analytics is the simplest class of analytics reporting on data that helps answer what has happened in the past and what is happening in the present using traditional business intelligence, data mining, and visualization. Traditional data and big data (if stored) can be used for descriptive analytics (Mahanti, 2021c).

Diagnostic Analytics

Diagnostic analytics uses historical data to help answer, why something happened, using drill-down, data discovery, data mining, and correlation techniques.

Predictive Analytics

Predictive analytics uses data to help answer what is likely to happen in future, using statistical and machine learning algorithms that are probabilistic in nature.

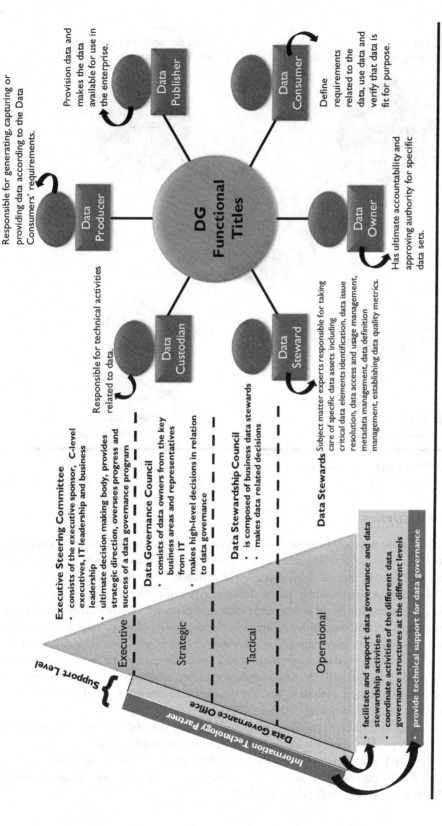

Figure 2.1   People aspect of data governance.

Source: Mahanti (2021a, 2021c)

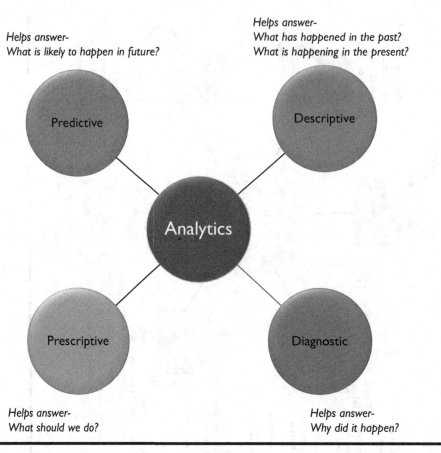

Figure 2.2 Different types of analytics.
Source: Mahanti (2021c)

Prescriptive Analytics

Prescriptive analytics is the next step from predictive analytics. Prescriptive analytics uses data to predict what is going to occur next and provide guidance on how to react to the prediction using optimization and simulation algorithms. In short, it helps answer—"what should we do (Mahanti, 2021c)."

Figure 2.3 shows value and maturity of the different types of analytics. Prescriptive analytics which provides future direction has the maximum value and maturity, followed by predictive analytics, diagnostic analytics, and descriptive analytics in the decreasing order of value and maturity.

Both data quality and data governance have a key role to play in analytics. Raw data from different sources in big data environments are complex and not in an appropriate format for analytics purposes. They need to be assessed, cleansed, stitched together, and converted to an appropriate format suitable for sophisticated analysis so that the data are adequate quality. This process of data preparation is known as data wrangling (Mahanti, 2021c).

Governance needs to document policies, processes, roles, accountabilities, and responsibilities around data preparation. Also, there should be ability of tracing the results back to the data sources, with adequate metadata to show context and representation, as well as the business rules used for transformation. Effective governance is needed to help trace the data lineage and the establishment of trust in the data analytics results (Mahanti, 2021c).

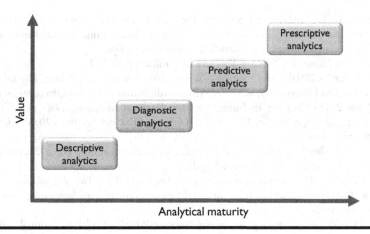

Figure 2.3   Analytical value versus maturity.
Source: Adapted from Shah and Jiles (2020)

Concluding Thoughts

Data play a dominant role in every aspect of our life. Technological advancements and low-cost storage have enabled the capture, processing, and storage of huge amounts of data through a large number of channels. Data management is no longer a simple discipline like it was in the early days of computing, when limited data were captured, stored, and processed. In the present digital age, which is characterized by data explosion and universal presence of data, data management is a multifaceted discipline comprising several closely interacting sub-disciplines or functions such as, but not limited to data quality, data governance, and data analytics.

The world has been reshaped by the COVID-19 pandemic which spread across the globe in 2020. Leverage of data by analytics empowered by advances in computing has enabled the visualization of the spread of COVID-19, almost in real time, as well as the effect the virus is having on economies across the world. However, massive data sets sit at the heart of this exercise.

Data have been and are being actively used to fight the pandemic and will be used beyond it to recover from the pandemic. The data challenges and role of data, data strategy, data governance, and data analytics use cases in the pandemic will be discussed in the subsequent chapters.

References

Adelman, S., Moss, L., and Abai, M. (2005) *Data Strategy*. Addison-Wesley.

Advisiondigital. (November 22, 2016) Why Do You Need Data Governance? *WorleyParson Group*, Last accessed on November 9, 2018, from http://digital.advisian.com/curious/why-do-you-need-data-governance/.

Analytics8. (April 9, 2021) 7 Elements of a Data Strategy, Last accessed on May 3, 2021, from www.analytics8.com/blog/7-elements-of-a-data-strategy/.

Batini, C., Cappiello, C. et al. (2009) Methodologies for Data Quality Assessment and Improvement, *ACM Computing Surveys*, Vol.41, No.3, 1–52, doi:10.1145/1541880.1541883.

Chisholm, M. (2010) *Definitions in Data Management: A Guide to Fundamental Semantic Metadata*, Design Media, Print.

Chisholm, M. (May 6, 2014) Data Credibility: A New Dimension of Data Quality? Found, Last accessed on August 08, 2017, from www.information-management.com/news/data-credibility-a-new-dimension-of-data-quality.

Coleman, S. (February 12, 2021) Data Strategy: How an Ecosystem Approach Can Help Shape Your Vision, *Open Data Institute*, Last accessed on May 3, 2021, from https://theodi.org/article/data-strategy-how-an-ecosystem-approach-can-help-shape-your-vision/.

Daniell, M. (2006) *The Elements of Strategy*, Palgrave Macmillan pp. 1–110.

Dontha, R. (December 16, 2016) Data Strategy—What, Why, When, Who, Where, *Digital Transformation Pro*, Last accessed on December 3, 2018, from https://digitaltransformationpro.com/data-strategy-5ws/

Eckerson, W. (June, 2011) Creating an Enterprise Data Strategy: Managing Data as a Corporate Asset, http://docs.media.bitpipe.com/io_10x/io_100166/item_417254/Creating%20an%20Enterprise%20Data%20Strategy_final.pdf.

[Gartner Information Technology Glossary], Big Data, Last accessed on June 20, 2021, from www.gartner.com/en/information-technology/glossary/big-data.

Harris, J. (August 20, 2015) Data Governance and Analytics, *The Data Roundtable, SAS Blog*, Last accessed on October 14, 2018, from https://blogs.sas.com/content/datamanagement/2015/08/20/data-governance-analytics/.

Hoare, C. A. R. (1985) *Communicating Sequential Processes*, Prentice Hall International, ISBN 978-0-13-153271-7.

Inmon, W. H. (2005) *Building the Data Warehouse*, 4th ed., Wiley, ISBN: 978-0-7645-9944-6.

[ISO 11179] www.iso.org/obp/ui/#iso:std:iso-iec:11179:-4:ed-2:v1:en.

Jaiani, V., and Audet, R. (2020) 8 Data Leaders on Leveraging Data During and After COVID-19, *GCN, Data Leaders Roundtable*, September 17, https://gcn.com/articles/2020/09/17/data-leaders-roundtable.aspx.

[Knowledgent] Building a Successful Data Quality Management Program, *Knowledgent Group Inc.*, Last accessed on January 2, 2017, from https://knowledgent.com/whitepaper/building-successful-data-quality-management-program/.

Liddell, H. G., and Scott, R. (1999) *A Greek-English Lexicon*, Perseus.

Lotame (May 28, 2019), How to Build a Data Strategy, Last accessed on December 3, 2019, from www.lotame.com/how-to-build-a-data-strategy/.

Mahanti, R. (2019) *Data Quality: Dimensions, Measurement, Strategy, Management, and Governance*, Quality Press, ASQ, ISBN: 9780873899772.

Mahanti, R. (2021a) *Data Governance and Compliance: Evolving to our Current High Stakes Environment*, Springer, Number 978-981-33-6877-4.

Mahanti, R. (2021b) *Data Governance Success: Growing and Sustaining Data Governance*, Springer.

Mahanti, R. (2021c) *Data Governance and Data Management: Contextualizing Data Governance Drivers, Technologies, and Tools*, Springer, Book, doi:10.1007/978-981-16-3583-0, Print ISBN—978-981-16-3582-3.

McGilvray, D. (2008) *Executing Data Quality Projects*, 1st ed., Paperback, ISBN: 9780123743695, Imprint: Morgan Kaufmann.

Mojsilovic, A. (December 5, 2014) The Age of Data and Opportunities, *IBM Big Data and Analytics Hub*, Last accessed on July 29, 2017, from www.ibmbigdatahub.com/blog/age-data—and—opportunities.

Natarajan, P., Frenzel, J. C., and Smaltz, D. H. (2017) *Demystifying Big Data and Machine Learning for Healthcare*, 1st ed., CRC Press. https://doi.org/10.1201/9781315389325.

[NTNU], Introduction to Big Data, Opphavsrett: Forfatter og Stiftelsen TISIP, Learning Material, www.ntnu.no/iie/fag/big/lessons/lesson2.pdf.

Sebastian-Coleman, L. (2013) *Measuring Data Quality for Ongoing Improvement*, Morgan Kaufmann, Print ISBN-13: 978-0-12-397033-6.

Shah, H., and Jiles, L. (September 1, 2020) A Data-Driven Approach to the Pandemic, *SF Magazine*, Last accessed on November 14, 2020, from https://sfmagazine.com/post-entry/september-2020-a-data-driven-approach-to-the-pandemic.

Talburt, J. R., and Zhou, Y. (2015) *Entity Information Life Cycle for Big Data: Master Data Management and Information Integration*, 1st ed., Morgan Kaufmann Publishers Inc., San Francisco, CA.

Wang, R. Y., and Strong, D. M. (1996) Beyond Accuracy: What Data Quality Means to Data Consumers, *Journal of Management Information Systems*, Vol.12, No.4, 5–33.

Weber, K., Otto, B., and Osterle, H. (2009) One Size Does Not Fit All—A Contingency Approach to Data Governance, *ACM Journal of Data and Information Quality*, Vol.1, No.1, Article 4.

[Wikipedia] Data Model. https://en.wikipedia.org/wiki/Database_model#:~:text=A%20database%20model%20is%20a,uses%20a%20table%2Dbased%20format.

Chapter 3

Trajectory and Stages of a New Disease

"The reasons for this unusual severity of human disease have remained unclear."

—Malik Peiris

Introduction

In the first chapter, we discussed what a pandemic is, the characteristics of a pandemic, the origin of pandemics, and notable pandemics in the history of mankind.

However, in addition to pandemic, there are a number of other terms associated with diseases such as epidemic, outbreak, and endemic. These terms are related and are often used interchangeably though they are not same. However, it is important to realize the difference between these terms to better comprehend public health news and appropriate public health responses. These terms will be discussed in this chapter. In addition to these, there are many other terms such as index case, primary case, secondary case, patient zero, and super spreaders associated with cases or patients in epidemics and pandemics, which will also be discussed in this chapter.

A disease does not achieve pandemic status from its inception itself. The trajectory of new diseases and the role that data analytics plays in this trajectory, the butterfly effect of contagious disease, role of digital contact tracing in breaking the infection chain, the different stages that a disease passes through before it achieves pandemic proportions, the different epidemiological parameters, the role of data and models to compute these parameters, stages of disease pandemic spread, the datasets needed at each stage, and role of data and analytics in flatting the curve are also discussed in this chapter.

DOI: 10.4324/9781003270911-3

New Disease Trajectory—From Darkness to Light

There are known knowns; there are things we know that we know. There are known unknowns; that is to say there are things that, we now know we don't know. But there are also unknown unknowns—there are things we do not know we don't know.

—Donald Rumsfeld, while serving as U.S. Secretary of Defense, February 12, 2002

From my perspective, there are three distinct chapters in the way a new disease becomes known (see Figure 3.1).

Dark: Unknown Unknowns—In the initial stage, the disease itself is unknown and hence the cure, prevention, symptoms, or its causes are also unknown. A person who contracts the disease is usually diagnosed by trying to find similarities with known diseases.

Grey: Known Unknowns—This is the phase when the significant number of people show the same symptoms, but cure for existing diseases do not work and the impacts may be severe (critically ill and/or deaths). That's when it becomes established as a new disease and becomes known. However, the prevention, cure, causes, and how the disease transmits etc. are still unknown. As research is conducted, we proceed to uncover some of these.

Data and analytics can specifically help in this phase to make sense of the disease and to understand different aspects such as disease transmission, high-risk patients, risk factors, origin, diagnostics, disease severity, potential therapies, and vaccines. For example, in case of the COVID-19 pandemic, two graduates from the Data Science Institute at Columbia University launched a startup named EVQLV that produces algorithms which have the capability to computationally generate, screen, and optimize a large number (in the order of hundreds of millions) of therapeutic antibodies (Kent, 2020).

Using this technology, they aimed to determine treatments that would possibly help individuals infected by the virus that causes the COVID-19 disease. The machine learning algorithms are able to swiftly screen for therapeutic antibodies with a high likelihood of success (Kent, 2020).

Light: Known Knowns—This is the phase when almost all that is there to know about the disease is known. Light does not necessarily mean all is well. There might still be some known unknowns, but it has been acknowledged that, those cannot be resolved in a definitive time frame. For example, while there is a vaccine to prevent polio, there is no cure for polio.

Not all diseases are created equal, that is not all diseases are equally infectious or impact a large population or spread globally or have the same degree of adverse impact (some may be mild while some may cause fatalities). Also, an impact of a disease changes with time; the impact might be mild, over a period

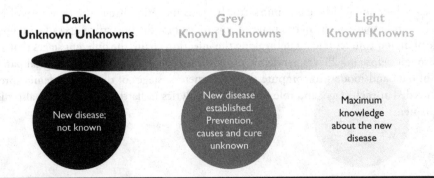

| **Dark** | **Grey** | **Light** |
| Unknown Unknowns | Known Unknowns | Known Knowns |

New disease; not known

New disease established. Prevention, causes and cure unknown

Maximum knowledge about the new disease

Figure 3.1   Trajectory of a new disease.

of time, when a prevention or cure is invented (for example polio) or the disease may disappear, if the cause itself ceases to exist, for example, a virus might down mutate and eventually disappear.

Contagious Disease and Butterfly Effect

When a contagious pathogen surfaces, the highly contagious disease can have a butterfly effect, with COVID-19 being a live example of the "butterfly effect" as shown in Figure 3.2.

The "butterfly effect," which became extensively known after a lecture delivered by MIT mathematician Edward Lorenz entitled "Predictability: Does the Flap of a Butterfly's Wings in Brazil Set Off a Tornado in Texas?" at a meeting of the American Association for the Advancement of Science in 1972, indicates that tiny changes might result in unpredictable effects.

The term butterfly effect has its roots in the "Chaos Theory," which defines the term as the sensitive dependence on initial conditions in which a trivial change in one state of a deterministic nonlinear system can result in significant differences in a later state (Boeing, 2016; [Wikipedia]). It refers to the way the fluttering of a butterfly's wing, which is in itself an insignificant occurrence, can have a major impact on weather which is a complex system. When butterflies sit on flowers for sucking nectar, pollens stick to their wings. The fluttering of the butterfly wings is an action, which in itself represents an insignificant change in the initial state of the system; however, this action has a ripple effect as it triggers a sequence of events: pollens sticking to the wings and in the atmosphere start moving through the air, which causes a gazelle to sneeze, which in turn triggers a stampede of gazelles, which raises a cloud of dust, which partially blocks the sun, which results in alteration in the atmospheric temperature (Walker and Talend, 2011), which in due course of time changes the path of a hurricane on the other side of the world. It implies that small things can have non-linear impacts on a complex system and a big phenomenon comprises a long chain of successive small events (Mahanti, 2019). It can be thought of as "ripple effect" or "domino effect" or "chain reaction," with a cumulative result, when one incident sets off a distant change.

There are various factors that determine pandemic potential and each of these and a combination of these factors can have a domino effect. The various factors that determine pandemic potential will be discussed in Chapter 7—Disease and Pandemic Potential.

From a perspective of a contagious disease, the butterfly effect alludes to the large scale of impact and spread across different geographies to the extent of it developing into a pandemic. As illustrated in Figure 3.2 with reference to the COVID-19 pandemic, in the beginning, there was just one infected patient (patient zero), and from him/or her the disease spread to more individuals who in turn passed it on to more number of people across a wider geographical area and the chain reaction continued, to the extent that it evolved into a full blown pandemic.

Contact Tracing and Disease Transmission

Contact tracing is the process of identifying individuals with close contact with infected patients and can be considered as one of the main weapons to tackle the spread of a contagious disease. In the context of public health and infection control, it is the key measure to find and isolate contacts with an infectious person to try and limit onward spread and hence, limit the generation of secondary cases (The Royal Society, 2020).

The intent is to efficiently detect people who have been in close contact with infected individuals, so they can be properly advised without delay on the next steps to follow. Contact tracing

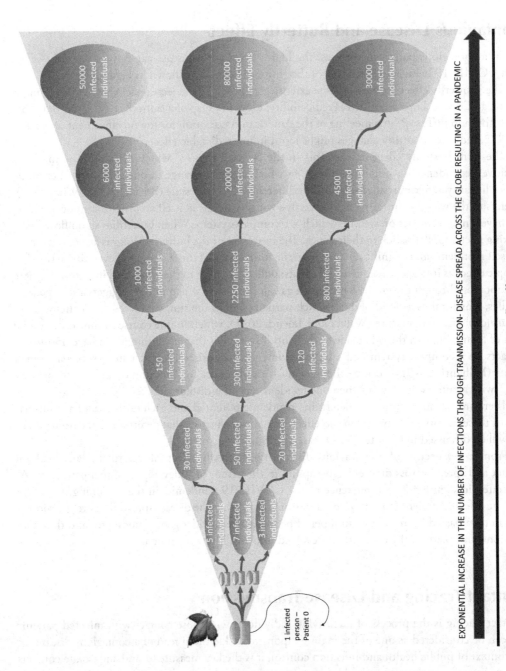

EXPONENTIAL INCREASE IN THE NUMBER OF INFECTIONS THROUGH TRANMISSION- DISEASE SPREAD ACROSS THE GLOBE RESULTING IN A PANDEMIC

Figure 3.2 COVID-19 pandemic—illustration of the butterfly effect.

enables potentially infected individuals to be easily detected and self-isolated even before showing symptoms. Therefore, the infection chain and disease transmission are interrupted as early as possible, thereby mitigating the butterfly effect of a disease.

Contact tracing has been exercised extremely successfully in the control of sexually transmitted infections for many decades across the globe. In an international context, contact tracing has been utilized successfully in a number of countries/regions, including South Korea, Taiwan, Singapore, China, Japan, and Hong Kong (The Royal Society, 2020).

Digital contact tracing is a method of contact tracing relying on tracking systems, most often based on mobile devices, to determine contact between an infected patient and a user. The concept came to prominence during the COVID-19 pandemic, where it was deployed on a wide scale for the first time through multiple government and private COVID-19 mobile apps (Ferretti et al., 2020; Choudhury, 2020; Barbaschow, 2020). The goal of digital contact tracing is to detect new potential sources of infection as soon as possible so that the COVID-19 spread can be mitigated without delay. Two types of mobile apps can be found so far (Martin et al., 2020):

- Contact tracing apps
- Location sharing apps

A *contact tracing app* is based on the digital contact tracing relying on proximity wireless technology such as BLE. Bluetooth, specifically its Low Energy (BLE) power-conserving variant, has emerged as the most promising short-range wireless network technology to implement the contact tracing service. When two app users are in close proximity, the smartphones send their identity in terms of ephemeral IDs or pseudonyms to each other. Each smartphone records all its encounters that transpired within a specific period of time, say, the last 14 days. If a user affirms a COVID-19 infection, then all their encountered users that were assessed at risk are alerted of the status quo through a central server, operating as an information dispatching office, and are requested to remain in self-isolation (Martin et al., 2020).

A *location sharing app* depends on the smartphone positioning information, i.e., via GPS tracking or cell tower mapping. For such an app, the user needs to accept that their smartphone sends at regular intervals of time, for example, every 5 minutes, its location to a central server, which can map every single user for an indefinite period of time. If a user announces a COVID-19 infection, then all the users that were within a close range to the infected user during the last, say, 14 days are cautioned of the state of affairs. As with contact tracing apps, all the concerned users are requested to self-isolate (Martin et al., 2020).

Location sharing apps seem to be far less privacy preserving for the users than contact tracing apps as the location sharing apps must agree to share continuously their location with a central server. In the case of contact tracing apps, only the—sometimes anonymized—information related to the encounters is shared (Martin et al., 2020).

Epidemic, Pandemic, Outbreak, and Endemic

Besides pandemic, there are a number of other terms associated with diseases as follows:

- Epidemic,
- Outbreak, and
- Endemic

The term epidemic is approximated 2500 years old and is derived from the Greek words *epi* [on] plus *demos* [people]. The term epidemic was first used by Homer. It took its medical meaning when Hippocrates used it as the title of one of his famous treatises. During that period, the term epidemic was used to refer to a group of clinical syndromes, such as coughs or diarrheas, occurring and spreading during a specific period at a specific geographic location. However, the form and meaning of the term have changed over a period of time (Martin and Martin-Granel, 2006).

Successive epidemics of plague in the Middle Ages gave shape to the definition of an epidemic as the spread of a single, well-defined disease (Martin and Martin-Granel, 2006). An epidemic is a disease that affects an enormous number of people within a community, population, or region. An epidemic is often localized to a region, but the number of those infected in that specific region is pointedly higher than normal. However, the term epidemic is not just used with infectious diseases but with non-diseases (such as gun violence and opioids) and any scenario that leads to a detrimental rise of health risks within a society (for example, the rise in obesity globally (often described as an "obesity epidemic")) [Physiopedia]. It is sometimes used colloquially to describe behavior (*There's an epidemic of tantrums among preschoolers!*) or behavioral phenomena (such as "epidemic hysteria"). Hence, the edges of these definitions are a bit blurry and cause confusion (Brabaw, 2020; Torrey, 2020).

A pandemic is a worldwide outbreak of a disease. It is an epidemic that spreads across a wider geographic range, for example, a number of countries and continents. Hence, a disease is first classified as an epidemic and when it spreads across a wider geographic range and affects a significant population then it gets classified as a pandemic. For example, when COVID-19 was limited to Wuhan and the Hubei province in China, it was an epidemic. However, the worldwide spread of COVID-19 resulted in it being reclassified as a pandemic.

When an epidemic crosses over into pandemic, the biggest difference is that more régimes are involved in attempting to prevent or slow the progression of the disease and, potentially, treat the people who have it. Also, the strategies to treat the disease might change. For example, according to the CDC, the U.S. Food and Drug Administration (FDA) may initiate the issue of "emergency use authorizations" (EUAs) during a pandemic, which allows doctors to use medications outside of the FDA-approved use to diagnose, treat, or prevent serious or life-threatening diseases or conditions caused by biological and other agents when "no adequate, approved, and available alternatives" exist. In 2009, during the swine flu pandemic, the FDA issued EUAs for two antiviral drugs to attempt to prevent the flu in young children and to treat patients who've had symptoms for more than two days (which Tamiflu is not prescribed for) (FDA, 2007; Brabaw, 2020).

Endemic is derived from Greek word "en" meaning in and "demos" meaning people. An endemic is something that belongs to a particular group of people or a particular country. Endemics are a perpetual presence in a specific location but at low frequency. Each country may have a disease that is very specific to that country or to a region within that country. For example, the disease, malaria is endemic to parts of Africa. The disease dengue is endemic in certain parts of the world (Intermountain Healthcare, 2020). It can be associated with non-disease too like presence and use of illicit drugs in some neighborhoods.

An outbreak is "a sudden rise in the incidence of a disease" and is typically restricted to a localized area or an exclusive group of people. However, outbreak may be treated no less aggressively than a pandemic if it has the potential to expand beyond its borders or spread to a significant population (Torrey, 2020).

Should an outbreak become more severe (affects a significant population), and less localized, it may be characterized as an epidemic. If it extends still further and impacts a significant portion of the population, the disease may be categorized as a pandemic [Merriam-Webster]. Pandemic

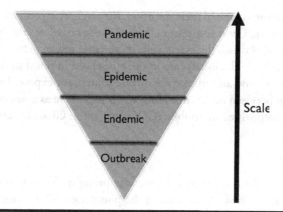

Figure 3.3 Scale of impact of pandemic, epidemic, endemic, and outbreak.

is an outbreak that touches most of the world. In short, pandemic can be thought of as a global epidemic, or a global outbreak.

The inverted pyramid can be used to describe the scale of impact of outbreak, endemic, epidemic and pandemic as shown in Figure 3.3.

The distinction between the terms "pandemic," "epidemic," "outbreak," and "endemic" is regularly blurred, even by medical experts or epidemiologists. While the terms may imply that there is an explicit threshold or limit by which a disease event is acknowledged as an outbreak, epidemic, or pandemic, the distinction is frequently blurred. Also, the definition of each term is fluid and changes as some diseases become more prevalent or lethal with time, over a period of time, while in case of some diseases the opposite is true. For example, with HIV/AIDS, a disease spread across much of the planet, the term *pandemic* has been increasingly replaced by *epidemic* given the widespread distribution of effective treatment and decreasing rates in some previously hyper-prevalent regions.

Index Case, Primary Case, Secondary Case, Patient Zero, and Super Spreaders

There have been many terms such as index case, primary case, secondary case, patient zero, and super spreaders associated with cases or patients in epidemics and pandemics, and it is important to understand the meaning and significance of these terms.

Index Case

In a medical context, the *index case* is the first documented disease case (that is the first documented patient) in an epidemic within a population, or the earliest documented case of a disease included in an epidemiological study [NIH; WordNet Search 3.0].

In genetics, the index case is the case of the original patient (propositus or proband) that kindles investigation of other family members to discover a likely genetic factor (Farlex, 2012).

The term has also been used in non-medical context, for example to identify the first computer or user to be infected with malware on a network, which then infected other systems.

With respect to the "first case noticed," since at least the 1930s, health investigators involved in contact-tracing work have used the axiom "index case" to mark the first person in a household or community whose symptoms grabbed their attention. Researchers investigating tuberculosis in Tennessee during the time of the Great Depression defined "index case" as "that person through whom attention was drawn to the household." Crucially, these same researchers were quick to emphasize that this person might not be "the initial case in the household in point of time" (McKay, 2010).

The index case may or may not indicate the disease source, the expected spread, or which reservoir holds the disease in between outbreaks. However, it may serve as a wakeup call of an emerging outbreak and alert the authorities and public (CDC.gov, 1994; Giesecke, 2014).

Primary Case

In contrast to index case which is the first disease case brought to the attention of the epidemiologist, the *primary case* is the first disease case in the population. The index case is not always the primary case as the first disease case may not have been the first to get noticed.

Secondary Case

Secondary case is an individual who become infected with a disease that has been introduced into a population, from contact with the primary case.

Patient Zero

As per Dictionary.com, the expression *patient zero* comes from epidemiology, or "the study of the spread of disease" [Dictionary.com].

Dictionary.com defines patient zero as follows:

> *Patient zero* is a popular medical term referring to the first person infected in an epidemic.
> *Patient zero* can also be a metaphor for initial actions that have major downstream consequences.

Origin, Confusion, and Stigma Around the Term—"Patient Zero"

"Patient zero" is a striking phrase which got accidently coined in association with the AIDS epidemic in the 1980s. It shares a linguistic connection to 20th-century military terms such as "zero hour" (when an action begins) and "ground zero" (the point below where a bomb detonates), and hence it also communicates a feeling of excitement (McKay, 2010). In relation to the SARS pandemic, the WHO in due course assessed that roughly 4,000 of the world's total SARS cases (that is about half of the total number of SARS cases) during that outbreak could be traced back to the Patient Zero's stay at the Metropole Hotel. News reports around the world named the hotel as a SARS hotspot and a ground zero for the SARS pandemic (Huddleston Jr., 2020). Meliandou, Guinea is named as ground zero for the Ebola epidemic (Beukes, 2014).

The Origin and Evolution of the Phrase—Patient Zero

In the 1980s, researchers toiled to find out why gay men in Los Angeles (LA) were dying of a mysterious disease, later known as HIV/AIDS. Behavioral scientist Dr. William Darrow at the Centers for Disease Control and Prevention (CDC) interviewed some of the infected men and found that many of the men who had been infected with the disease had slept with the same Canadian flight attendant, Gaëtan Dugas. In publishing his research and results in 1984, Darrow branded Dugas, an out-of-town subject, *Patient O* (letter *O*) for "outside of California," and concluded Dugas was at the center of the HIV/AIDS outbreak in LA.

A researcher, apparently, misunderstood *Patient O* for *Patient Zero* (0). The term itself became popular when designation *patient zero* (for Gaëtan Dugas) was adopted by the *San Francisco Chronicler* journalist and author Randy Shilts, based on what was communicated to him by the researcher. Randy Shilts's work on the AIDS epidemic and designation *patient zero* (for Gaëtan Dugas) was subsequently broadcasted through his influential book *And the Band Played On* on AIDS in 1987 ([Dictionary.com]; McKay, 2010).

It was later found that Gaëtan Dugas was not, —the *patient zero*—who started the AIDS outbreak in LA. It had started in New York City in the 1970s. But the term *patient zero* stuck, and took the place of the synonymous *index patient* (or *index case*), recorded in the early 1900s in many medical contexts [Dictionary.com].

Patient zero quickly entered the popular lexicon. By the *1990s*, it was already being used to label imaginary scenarios, for example, the first person infected in a zombie apocalypse, taken more commonly to denote the beginning of a fast-spreading epidemic [Dictionary.com].

There is a lot of confusion around the term "Patient zero." As per Dr. Richard McKay, it is often used interchangeably for three different scenarios: first case noticed, first case here, and first case ever. He states that, while there are legitimate reasons for discussing each of these situations, better terminology exists for doing so (McKay, 2010).

Using the word, "cases" instead of "patients" makes it possible to be more specific. By doing so, individuals who may be infected and infectious are included. However, they do not attain the official "patient" status by seeking treatment (McKay, 2010).

Significance of Patient Zero

Patient zero carries the disease in its most basic form. From a medical and public health perspective, in a disease outbreak or epidemic, it is extremely important to find "patient zero." This is because knowing that person's history can help researchers determine how, when, and where exactly the disease started and provide some inkling as to the source of the disease, its transmission course, the possible risk events and activities that can lead to contracting the disease, and pave a way to devise preventive strategies to stop the spread and start working toward a cure too. Patient zero helps to find distinguishable elements that might have led to ill health in the community.

Once a "patient zero" is uncovered the next steps involves to find out how the person got infected in the first place, when exactly did he start feeling sick, what activities did he carry out before that, how were those activities carried, and what places did he visit, to find out the root cause.

Challenges in Locating Patient Zero

However, finding patient zero is not easy, as he or she could have already infected a number of people undetected. Hence, locating patient zero requires considerable back tracing and rigorous detective work. With the passage of time, tracing back to the patient zero becomes even more difficult. Also, the first person infected might have had mild symptoms or be asymptotic (that is, presents no symptoms of the disease) or could have even passed away undetected. Since a new disease is not known, the symptoms could be likened to an existing disease which could lead to delays in recognizing the outbreak. Lack of adequate and timely testing could also be a blocker in locating the first person to be infected. The key to locating the first person infected is ruled by the fact as in how quickly is the disease outbreak recognized and having effective and timely testing unless the person is an asymptotic carrier and survivor.

In some cases, the person labeled as "patient zero" may simply be the person with a positive test result whose likely date of infection is the earliest on record (McKay, 2010).

Examples of Patient Zero or Index Case in the History of Pandemics

■ The most famous patient zero was "Typhoid Mary." Her real name was Mary Mallon and was an index case of a typhoid outbreak which plagued New York in the early 1900s. While she herself was apparently a healthy carrier, she infected 47 people while being employed as a cook. In due course she was secluded, so as to stop her from spreading the disease to others (PBS, 1938; Brockell, 2020).

■ A 44-year-old schoolteacher named Mabalo Lokela, was the first recorded victim of the Ebola virus. Mabalo Lokela died on September 8, 1976, 14 days after symptom onset (Yong, 2017).

■ Liu Jianlun, a 64-year-old Guangdong doctor, spread SARS internationally by infecting other super-spreaders during a stay in the Hong Kong Metropole Hotel in 2003 (Huddleston Jr, 2020; Fleck, 2003).

■ Emile Ouamouno, a one-year-old kid is believed to be patient zero in the 2014 Ebola epidemic in Guinea and West Africa (Beukes, 2014).

Super Spreaders

"I think the thing we worry about as health officials is a thing called 'super spreading' where we have certain individuals that are not just infectious but highly infectious. This happened in a health care setting in Wuhan China where one patient transmitted the virus to 14 health care workers."

—Dr. Michael Osterholm

Super spreaders have been identified as those individuals who expel a greater than the normal number of pathogens during the time they are infectious. This causes their contacts to be exposed to greater pathogen loads than would be seen in the contacts of non-super spreaders with the same period of exposure (Rothman et al., 2008).

A *super spreader* is an extraordinarily infectious organism who has been infested with a disease. In relation to a human-borne disease, a super spreader is an individual who is more likely to infect other individuals, than a normal infected individual as demonstrated in Figure 3.4. Such super spreaders are worrisome in epidemiology. As shown in Figure 3.4, the individual in the center is a super spreader who has spread infection to significantly large number of individuals.

Some infected people may not spread the disease further, but super spreaders infect a disproportionate number of others, whether as a consequence of genetics, social habits, or simply being in the wrong place at the wrong time (KHN, 2020). Some cases of super spreading conform to the Pareto Principle or the 80/20 rule (that is 20% of causes are responsible for 80% of the failures) (Galvani and May, 2005), where around 20% of infected individuals are accountable for 80% of transmissions. However, super spreading can still be said to occur when super spreaders account for a higher or lower percentage of transmissions (Lloyd-Smith et al., 2005).

For example, in case of outbreak of severe acute respiratory syndrome (SARS) in 2003, five different super spreaders were identified who helped the spread of the SARS outbreak that infected over 8,000 people, killing 774 of them (Huddleston Jr., 2020).

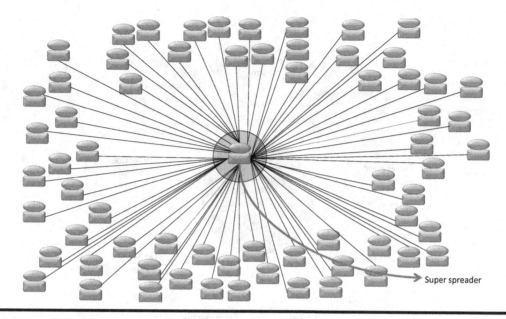

Figure 3.4 Super spreader and infected individuals.

One of those cases was linked to a Chinese respiratory doctor, Dr. Liu Jianlun a super spreader. He spread the disease to seven other people (who happened to stay on the same floor of the same hotel) during a one-night hotel stay in Hong Kong. Several of them travelled to other countries, thus resulting in community spread in the other geographic locations helping to give the disease a much larger global footprint (Huddleston Jr, 2020).

Contact tracing can help contain spread by early detection and notification of contact with the infectious person thus breaking the infection chain.

Epidemiological Parameters

Understanding the parameters that effect the course of an epidemic is crucial for health-related decision-making. These parameters are measurable factors and help in planning of strategies to mitigate and control diseases, as well as provision of care to those infected and sick (Guerra et al., 2020). These parameters are known as epidemiological parameters. While the level of disease occurrence can be described in many ways, it is primarily defined by epidemiological parameters.

Some key epidemiological parameters are as follows and summarized in Figure 3.5 (The Royal Society, 2020; [Barratt et al.]; Rothman et al., 2013):

- **The critical community size**
  The size of the susceptible population.
- **The transmission rate**
  The transmission rate β is the rate at which infectious cases cause secondary or new cases in a population, P, with S susceptible individuals. It is a rate constant and has units of inverse time.
- **Infectious mortality rate**
  The infectious mortality rate δ represents the rate at which infected people die.

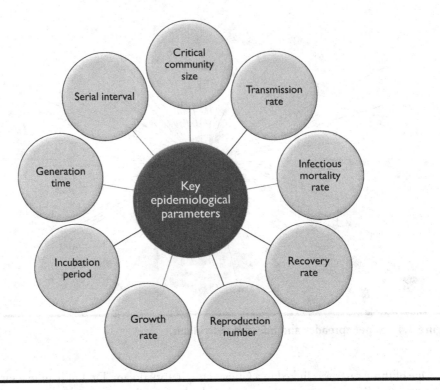

Figure 3.5 Key epidemiological parameters.

■ **The recovery rate**
The recovery rate γ is the inverse of the infection period.

■ **The reproduction number**
This number reflects the infectious potential of a disease. It is also known as reproduction ratio. As an infection is transmitted to new people, it reproduces itself.

R_0 represents the basic reproduction number, which is the number of secondary infections generated from an initial case at the beginning of an epidemic, in an entirely susceptible population [Barratt et al.]. It is an important epidemiological parameter for all infectious diseases (Anderson, 1991).

R_0 excludes new cases produced by the secondary cases [Barratt et al.].

The basic reproductive number is affected by several factors [Barratt et al.]:

– The rate of contacts in the host population,
– The probability of infection being transmitted during contact, and
– The duration of infectiousness.

In general, for an epidemic to occur in a susceptible population R_0 must be >1, so the number of cases is increasing (Rothman et al., 2013).

In numerous circumstances not all contacts will be vulnerable to infection. This is measured by the effective reproductive number (R). The *effective reproductive number* (R) is the average number of secondary cases per infectious case in a population comprised of both susceptible and non-susceptible hosts [Barratt et al.].

The effective reproduction number can be estimated by the product of the basic reproduction number and the fraction of the host population that is susceptible (x). Hence [Barratt et al.],

$$R = R_0 x$$

- If R>1, the number of cases will increase, such as at the start of an epidemic.
- If R=1, the disease is endemic, and
- If R<1, the number of cases will decrease. To successfully eliminate a disease from a population, R needs to be less than 1 [Barratt et al.].

However, *R* does not tell us, how *quickly* things are changing. This is because *R* is not a rate, and there is no time period involved. R is a ratio of cases by infection generation.

In contrast to the basic reproduction number, the momentary reproduction number, R_t, is the reproduction number at time t since the start of the epidemic. As more individuals are infected or immunized, R_t captures the number of secondary infections generated from a population consisting of both naïve/susceptible and exposed/immune individuals and therefore it both changes in value over time (The Royal Society, 2020).

■ The growth rate:

The rate of change of the epidemic and represents the number of new infections at an increasing or decreasing exponential rate. It captures how quickly the number of infections is changing on a daily basis. The growth rate, r, is dependent on the reproduction number and timescale between infections (The Royal Society, 2020).

The growth rate, r, is more easily measured than the reproduction number R.

The growth of cases of a disease is modeled using an exponential curve. It can be a positive number (the number of new infections is increasing) or a negative number (the number of new infections is decreasing) (The Royal Society, 2020). Negative values for the growth rate in infections, r, clearly reveals a contracting epidemic.

r is sometimes explained in a more comprehensible manner through use of the closely related doubling time of the epidemic (the number of days or time units which leads to a doubling in cases) (The Royal Society, 2020).

The doubling time is an intuitive number—the time taken for cases to double—and so it facilitates understanding during the early stages of this epidemic, but it has limited usefulness during the current phase where the number of new infections is stable or declining slowly. As the value of r potentially switches from positive to negative (and possibly back again during a resurgence), it passes through zero, at which point the doubling time briefly tends to infinity. For a stable decline in infections, r informs us about the halving time, the time required for the number of cases to halve and hence how rapidly or slowly the remaining cases will decline to eradication (The Royal Society, 2020).

As highlighted earlier, it is driven by a combination of R—the higher the number of cases caused by each infectious individual, the faster the epidemic will grow—and the timescale over which infections occur (The Royal Society, 2020).

A useful comparison for understanding the effects of R and the generation time of new infections is provided by HIV, which has an R_0 of around 2 in some populations, and influenza, which has an R_0 around 1.329, the most important being the reproduction number R, but the timescale from one infection to the next is days for influenza but months or years for HIV (The Royal Society, 2020).

◼ **Incubation period**

The time between infection and symptoms showing onset of the disease.

◼ **The generation time**

For an infectious disease, it is the time between infection events in an infector–infectee pair of individuals. In conjunction with estimates of R, the generation time T can provide insights into the speed of epidemic spread (The Royal Society, 2020).

It is a challenge to measure the generation time precisely, as it is difficult to determine the time of infection due to the fact it is generally overlooked.

◼ **Serial interval**

The time period between the onset of symptoms in an index (infector) case and the onset of symptoms in a secondary (infectee) case. It is the average time between symptoms of infection in the transmitter and when the person he or she infects develops symptoms. Serial interval, s, is easier to measure than the generation time as symptom onset is easier to identify than time of infection acquisition (The Royal Society, 2020).

Serial interval is often used interchangeably with the generation time, since it is easier to measure via contact tracing studies. However, ignoring the difference between the serial interval and generation time can lead to biased estimates of R (Britton and Tomba 2019).

In the case of COVID-19, serial interval has less relevance given that many infections especially in the young do not seem to generate marked and easily identifiable symptoms. Some studies suggest that between 5% and 80% of infected people do not show clear symptoms of infection (The Royal Society, 2020).

The ongoing assessment of key epidemiological parameters is strengthened by high-quality data. Estimation of key epidemiological parameters starts with data and no amount of sophisticated modeling can make up for inadequate measurement (The Royal Society, 2020). The availability of accurate real-time data is vital to the effective management of any epidemic or pandemic (The Royal Society, 2020).

For example, as per a report published by the Royal Society, UK in 2020, bad data quality and slow access to information on COVID-19 spread and impact collected by different government organizations such as Pubic Health England, Office for National Statistics (ONS) and NHS Trusts have been a major impediment to good epidemiological analysis of the state of the epidemic and predictions of future trends. Timelines are important; so are other data quality parameters such as accuracy and consistency. Data definitions should be standardized too. An authoritative body should both acquire timely and relevant data at scale in accordance with governance policies and through standard processes across government bodies, and distribute it openly through a carefully curated portal. Processes should be designed to ensure that national database is effectively fed by local public health bodies, and this national information portal feeds back to facilitate local action (The Royal Society, 2020). Effective data governance mechanisms should be there to facilitate the same.

The most edifying data on epidemic trends arise from longitudinal cohort-based studies of seroprevalence of past infection and the incidence of new infections, stratified by the appropriate variables such as home and work locations, age, gender, and ethnicity (The Royal Society, 2020).

Human mobility is a major factor in the spread of contagious diseases and mobile phone location data can be used to predict disease spread and understanding disease transmission dynamics.

Contact tracing is an important technique in epidemiological study, since it can generate information on key epidemiological parameters such as R, the generation time, T, the serial interval, s, and the incubation period. It also furnishes information on the distributional properties of these elements (The Royal Society, 2020).

Hong Kong, Singapore, and Japan did contact tracing from the initial days of COVID-19 disease spread. Thus R_0 and k values could be estimated very early in the epidemic which resulted in their being effectively able to control and prevent many transmission chains as well as super spreading events (The Royal Society, 2020).

It is important to determine the disease prevalence (the proportion of people affected within a population) and incidence (the occurrence of a disease over a specific period of time) to direct the appropriate public health response.

Simulation models are extensively used to model spread and control of many different infectious diseases. In these models, transmission rates are used to describe the flow of individuals in a population going from a susceptible state to an infected state, and it is imperative to obtain an accurate estimate of the transmission rates in order to create useful and realistic simulation models for decision support (Zadoks et al., 2001; Caley and Ramsey, 2001; Otten et al., 2003). Accurate estimation of the transmission rate is vital because it can have a key impact on model predictions and conclusions (Zadoks et al., 2001; Halasa et al., 2009). It is hard to estimate this parameter for most host-pathogen models because natural processes are stochastic, and transmission events are influenced by parameters that cannot be included in a transmission model (McCallum et al., 2001; Elkadry, 2013). Thus, large datasets are often required to reach a good estimate (Kirkeby et al., 2017).

Stages of a Disease and Pandemic Status

A disease passes through different stages before it attains pandemic status. Different organizations, researchers, and countries have defined different levels or stages that a disease has to cross before it can be declared as a pandemic.

WHO and CDC define six levels for a disease, with the sixth level being the level when disease attains pandemic status. Yigitcanlar et al., 2020; Bharat, 2020 define four stages for a disease, with the fourth stage being the pandemic stage. Each of these have been discussed in detail in the following sections. Each country also has its own policies when defining such levels; for example, China splits natural disasters, accidental disasters, and public health incidents into four levels—important (level I), significant (level II), large (level III), and general (level IV). Factors such as the extent of social harm and the scope of influence are used to determine the level (Qiong et al., 2020). Greater the extent of social harm and the scope of influence, higher the level.

According to WHO Director-General Tedros Adhanom Ghebreyesus, PhD, it was not an easy decision to categorize COVID-19 as a pandemic. The decision resulted from concern for "the alarming levels of spread and severity, and by the alarming levels of inaction" (Brabaw, 2020).

While WHO declared COVID-19 as a pandemic on March 11, 2020, it had expressed concerns over its pandemic potential much earlier. WHO Director-General Tedros Adhanom Ghebreyesus told reporters on February 24, 2020, that the number of new cases in recent days in Iran, Italy and South Korea was "deeply concerning."

However, he added:

> For the moment we are not witnessing the uncontained global spread of this virus and we are not witnessing large scale severe disease or deaths. Does this virus have pandemic potential? Absolutely, it has. Are we there yet? From our assessment, not yet.

> **(BBC, 2020)**

Disease Stages as Defined by Centers for Disease Control and Prevention

A pandemic is the highest possible level of disease, in terms of the number of people that contracted the particular disease and the extent of its spread geographically. However, before a disease reaches pandemic proportions, it has to exceed a few other levels, according to the Centers for Disease Control and Prevention (CDC) (Torrey, 2020; Brabaw, 2020) (see Figure 3.6):

Sporadic: Infrequent and irregular occurrence of a disease. Small number of people infected. For example, foodborne pathogens, such as Salmonella or E. coli, can often cause sporadic disease outbreaks (Riley, 2019; Torrey, 2020).

Cluster: Larger numbers of isolated occurrence of a disease even though the actual number or cause may be uncertain. For example, a group of cancer cases often reported after a disaster in a chemical or nuclear plant ([Farlex]; Torrey, 2020).

Endemic: A continuous presence and/or typical occurrence of a disease or infection within a geographic area (Riley, 2019; Torrey, 2020).

Hyperendemic: Persistent high levels of disease occurrence significantly well above what is seen in other populations. For example, AIDS-HIV disease is hyperendemic in parts of Africa,

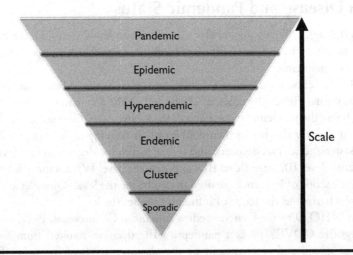

Figure 3.6 Disease stages as defined by Centers for Disease Control and Prevention.

with as many as one in five adults being infected with the disease, in these geographies (Center for Strategic & International Studies, 2019; Torrey, 2020).

Epidemic: A sudden surge in the number of cases of a disease—more than what's characteristically expected for the population in that area [Merriam-Webster]. An **outbreak** carries the same definition as an epidemic but is frequently used to describe a more limited geographic event [WHO].

Pandemic: A worldwide outbreak or an epidemic that has spread across several countries or continents, affecting a huge number of people.

Disease Stages as Defined by WHO

The WHO has identified six phases that it follows before declaring a pandemic (WHO, 2009). The phases are as follows and summarized in Table 3.1.

- Phase 1—A virus is seen in animals but has not been seen to cause infections in humans.
- Phase 2—A known animal virus has caused an infection in humans.
- Phase 3—Scattered or isolated occurrence of cases or small clusters of the disease; infections occurring in humans; likely cases of human-to-human transmission but not at a level to cause community-level outbreaks.
- Phase 4—Human-to-human transmission at a speed that causes an outbreak in communities.
- Phase 5—Disease spread between humans is now obvious in more than one country.
- Phase 6—Community-level disease outbreaks are observed in at least one additional country other than that seen in Phase 5.

Phase 1 represents the lowest risk and phase 6 is a full-blown pandemic. Phases 1–3 are related with preparedness, including capacity development and response planning activities, while Phases 4–6 undoubtedly signal the need for response and mitigation efforts (WHO, 2009).

Table 3.1 Six-Phase Pandemic-Tracking Model

Interpandemic phase New virus in animals, No human cases	Low risk of human cases	1	
	Higher risk of human cases	2	
Pandemic alert New virus causes human cases	No or very limited human-to-human transmission	③→	Organization should develop risk mitigation plans at Phase 3
	Evidence of increased human-to-human transmission	4	
	Evidence of significant human-to-human transmission	5	
Pandemic	Efficient and sustained human-to-human transmission	6	

Stages of Spread of a Pandemic as Defined by Yigitcanlar et al. (2020), Bharat (2020)

A pandemic disease can be broken into four stages as follows (Yigitcanlar et al., 2020; Bharat, 2020):

Pre-Concave

The first stage (Stage 1) of the spread of a pandemic disease, is the pre-concave stage. Only people in the region where that outbreak has occurred and those who have travelled from this region test positive for the disease. Local transmission does not occur at this stage (Bharat, 2020).

There are a small number of human infections at this stage. This stage involves the understanding of the epidemiological parameters, and the risks of transmission of the disease to different countries. The primary sources of data used in this stage are (Adiga et al., 2020):

■ line lists,
■ clinical investigations,
■ prior literature on similar diseases,
■ mobility data such as airline flows, and
■ information on travel restrictions.

Concave-Up

The concave-up stage is the second stage (Stage 2) of the spread of a pandemic disease. Local transmission occurs at this stage. The disease sources, for example, originally infected patients who possibly had travel history to other already affected countries, are known and can be located. At this stage, the disease might be contained through preventive and containment measures, but the risk of community transmission still grows, and the number of new cases show increase.

This stage encompasses modeling spread patterns at diverse spatio-temporal scales, and deriving short-term forecasts and projections. A diverse group of datasets is used for developing models, including mobility, populations, and activities. These datasets are combined with different types of time-series data and covariates such as weather data for forecasting purposes (Adiga et al., 2020).

Linear

The linear stage is the third stage (Stage 3) of the spread of a pandemic disease. At this stage, transmission rate of the disease becomes stable; that is, the number of new cases stay the same or vary with smaller difference in the linear stage.

This stage, involves the implementation of numerous interventions (which are mostly non-pharmaceutical in the case of a novel pathogen), by government agencies, once the outbreak has spread within the population. This stage also involves understanding the impact of interventions on the number of infected cases and health infrastructure necessities, while also taking into account individual attitudes and behaviors. Additional datasets on behavioral changes and hospital capacities are needed in this stage (Adiga et al., 2020).

Concave-Down

The fourth stage (Stage 4) of the spread of a pandemic disease is the concave-down stage. At this stage, the transmission rate of the disease shows a decline—in other words, the number of new cases drop.

This stage is characterized by approaches designed to control the outbreak by contact tracing, isolation, and vaccination. In this stage, data on contact tracing, associated biases, vaccine production calendars, compliance, and hesitancy are needed (Adiga et al., 2020).

Flattening the Curve

During a pandemic situation, a tall, steep, and lean curve of infected people to date as shown by the navy blue/dark color curve in Figure 3.7 is extremely undesirable. This means that a lot of individuals will contract the disease at the same time, and disease spreads to a large number of people in a short period of time. This happens when no or inadequate containment and preventive measures are undertaken to prevent disease transmission. While most individuals might not get sick enough to be hospitalized, those who do could easily overwhelm the number of beds, equipment, and healthcare staff available (Gavin, 2020; Yigitcanlar, 2020).

On the other hand, with adequate containment and prevention measures, the number of infected people can be lesser and disease spread can be slower, thus resulting in a more flattened curve as shown by the yellow/greyish curve in Figure 3.7, lowering the stress on the healthcare systems, and increasing time scale of the pandemic, so that a potential vaccine can become available at some future point in time that can help immunize the masses. This is re-enforced by Dr. Bertha Hidalgo, associate professor in the School of Public Health's Department of Epidemiology, University of Alabama at Birmingham in her statement as follows (Herfurth, 2020):

> You want to spread out the rate of infection so as to not overwhelm our health care system and infrastructure. If everyone is out and about, it's more likely that everyone will get sick at once. But if you're able to spread out how many people get sick, over time, patients can get the treatment they need because hospitals and other resources will not be exhausted.

Data, data analytics, and data visualization can play a crucial role in flattening the curve. Data from different subject areas and channels can be analyzed to drive informed decisions that lessen the number of people infected over a period of time, thus resulting in flattening of the curve. This can be done by identifying population movement and infection rates, identifying densely populated areas and infection clusters, identifying the highly vulnerable communities, and monitoring quarantined people. At the heart of all these exercises is high-quality data and analytics. These can help to answer the questions such as:

- Where is the disease likely to spread?
- How many people are getting infected on a daily basis?
- Where are the most vulnerable communities?

For example, in Belgium, anonymized mobility data was harnessed to identify the areas with greater movement and infection rates. This data was used to impose lockdown in a stepwise fashion in

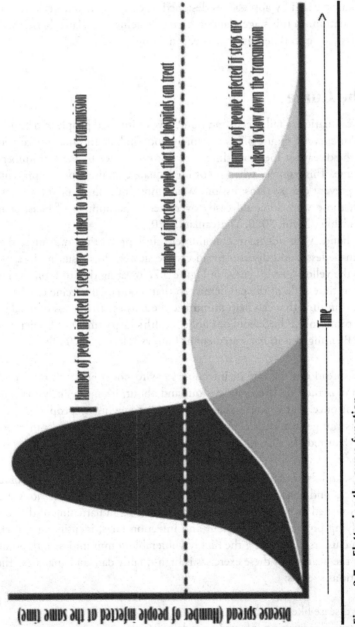

Figure 3.7 Flattening the curve function.

Source: Adapted from Yigitcanlar (2020), Gavin (2020)

these areas. Mobility was reduced by an average of 54% throughout the country (LightCastle Analytics Wing, 2020; Zaimova, 2020). Due to these prompt data-driven measures, Belgium was able to bring down its death rate down to half and had seen a recovery rate of 67% by April 13, 2020 (The Economic Times, 2020).

Identifying the most vulnerable communities can be significant for health officials to direct response efforts like health infrastructure improvements, emergency funding allocation, and preventive measures. For example, in case of COVID-19, the Location Analytics (LOCAN) team at Dalberg Research based in Kenya is analyzing risk profiles in multiple African countries. The underlying data is a combination of available primary data collection, data from national bureaus of statistics, and satellite images. The results are then fed back into epidemiological models as input for informed decision-making on the crisis response (LightCastle Analytics Wing, 2020; Zaimova, 2020).

Concluding Thoughts

The spread of a new infectious disease follows a convoluted dynamic course and the outcome can vary between mild to drastic. A large number of factors have a role to play in the spread of new infectious disease or existing infectious disease created by a new strain of pathogen, and each factor or a combination of these factors can have a domino effect. These factors include transmission modes, the rate of spread, the initial delay in recognizing the disease (which allows the disease to spread unknown and unseen), transparency and clarity of communication, variable individual susceptibility to the pathogen (e.g., by age and health conditions), number of super spreaders, variable individual behaviors (e.g., practice of good hygiene, compliance with social distancing, and the use of facemasks), different response strategies implemented by governments (e.g., travel restrictions, shutting down of effective areas, quarantining high-risk areas, level of restrictions on social gatherings, school and workplace closure policies, and criteria for testing), and potential availability of non-pharmaceutical and pharmaceutical interventions.

While transparency, clarity of communication, adequate response strategies and people's compliance with this strategies, and availability of non-pharmaceutical and pharmaceutical interventions can check spread, the converse can accelerate spread. Also, since the spread of disease at a pandemic might not be evident immediately or even gradually, but rather suddenly, after a time lag when a large number of people start showing symptoms, governments need to be prepared to respond to the changing dynamics of a pandemic. Informed decisions driven by good quality data and analytics can play a crucial role in controlling a pandemic and mitigating its effects.

References

Adiga, A., Chen, J., Marathe, M. et al. (2020) Data-Driven Modeling for Different Stages of Pandemic Response, *The Journal of the Indian Institute of Science*, 100, 901–915, https://doi.org/10.1007/s41745-020-00206-0.

Anderson, R. M. (May 1991) *Infectious Diseases of Humans: Dynamics and Control*. Oxford: Oxford University Press.

Barbaschow, A. (April 22, 2020) Australia Looks to 'Go Harder' with Use of COVID-19 Contact Tracing App. *ZDNet*. Last accessed on April 18, 2021, from https://www.zdnet.com/article/australia-looks-to-go-harder-with-use-of-covid-19-contact-tracing-app/

[Barratt et al.] Barratt, H., Kirwan, M., and Shantikumar, S. Epidemic Theory (Effective & Basic Reproduction Numbers, Epidemic Thresholds) & Techniques for Analysis of Infectious Disease Data

(Construction & Use of Epidemic Curves, Generation Numbers, Exceptional Reporting & Identification of Significant Clusters), *Health Knowledge*, Last accessed on April 18, 2021, from www.health-knowledge.org.uk/public-health-textbook/research-methods/1a-epidemiology/epidemic-theory.

BBC (February 25, 2020) Coronavirus: World Must Prepare for Pandemic, Says WHO, Last accessed on June 1, 2020, from www.bbc.com/news/world-51611422.

Beukes, S. (October 28, 2014) Finding Ebola's 'Patient Zero'. *The Guardian*, Last accessed on November 28, 2014, from www.theguardian.com/world/2014/oct/28/ebola-virus-guinea-first-victim-patient-zero.

Bharat, D. (2020) COVID-19: The Four Stages of Disease Transmission Explained, Last accessed on June 25, 2020, *netmeds.com* from www.netmeds.com/health-library/post/covid-19-the-4-stages-of-disease-transmission-explained.

Boeing, G. (2016) Visual Analysis of Nonlinear Dynamical Systems: Chaos, Fractals, Self-Similarity and the Limits of Prediction, *Systems*, 4(4), 37, doi:10.3390/systems4040037.

Brabaw, K. (March 13, 2020) Epidemic vs. Pandemic: What Exactly Is the Difference? *Health*, Last accessed on June 1, 2020, from www.health.com/condition/infectious-diseases/epidemic-vs-pandemic.

Britton, T., and Tomba, G. S. (2019) Estimation in Emerging Epidemics: Biases and Remedies. *Journal of the Royal Society Interface*, 16, 20180670, https://doi.org/10.1098/ rsif.2018.0670.

Brockell, G. (March 17, 2020) Yes, There Really Was a 'Typhoid Mary,' an Asymptomatic Carrier Who Infected Her Patrons, *The Washington Post*, Last accessed on November 4, 2020, from www.washingtonpost.com/history/2020/03/17/typhoid-mary-st-patricks-day-coronavirus/.

Caley, P., and Ramsey, D. (2001) Estimating Disease Transmission in Wildlife, with Emphasis on Leptospirosis and Bovine Tuberculosis in Possums, and Effects of Fertility Control, *Journal of Applied Ecology*, 38, 1362–1370.

CDC.gov (January 1, 1994) *Sporadic STEC O157 Infection: Secondary Household Transmission in Wales.* Centers for Disease Control and Prevention, Retrieved November 3, 2010.

Center for Strategic & International Studies (2019) The World's Largest HIV Epidemic in Crisis: HIV in South Africa, Updated April 2, 2019.

Choudhury, S. R. (March 25, 2020) Singapore Says It Will Make Its Contact Tracing Tech Freely Available to Developers. *CNBC*. Last accessed on November 4, 2020, from https://www.cnbc.com/2020/03/25/coronavirus-singapore-to-make-contact-tracing-tech-open-source.html

[Dictionary.com], Patient Zero, Last accessed on November 4, 2020, from www.dictionary.com/e/pop-culture/patient-zero/.

The Economic Times (April 13, 2020) Covid-19: The Countries That Have Flattened the Curve Are All Led by Women, https://economictimes.indiatimes.com/news/international/world-news/covid-19-the-countries-that-have-flattened-the-curve-are-all-led-by-women/pandemic-curves/slideshow/75116659.cms.

Elkadry, A. (2013) Transmission Rate in Partial Differential Equation in Epidemic Models. Ph.D. Thesis, Marshall University.

Farlex (2012) Definition of Index Case. The Free Medical Dictionary by Farlex, Farlex Partner Medical Dictionary © Farlex 2012.

[Farlex], the Free Dictionary by Farlex. Disease Cluster.

[FDA, 2007] U.S. Food and Drug Administration, July 2007, *FDA Guidance: Emergency Use Authorization of Medical Products*, Last accessed on June 1, 2020, from www.fda.gov/oc/guidance/emergencyuse.html.

Ferretti, L., Wymant, C., Kendall, M., Zhao, L., Nurtay, A., Abeler-Dörner, L., Parker, M., Bonsall, D., and Fraser, C. (March 31, 2020) Quantifying SARS-CoV-2 Transmission Suggests Epidemic Control with Digital Contact Tracing, *Science*, 368(6491), eabb6936, doi:10.1126/science.abb6936. ISSN 0036–8075.

Fleck, F. (2003) How SARS Changed the World in Less Than Six Months, *Bulletin of the World Health Organization*, 81(8), Last accessed on November 4, 2020, from https://scielosp.org/pdf/bwho/v81n8/v81n8a14.pdf.

Galvani, A. P., and May, R. M. (2005) Epidemiology: Dimensions of Superspreading, *Nature*, 438(7066), 293–295. Bibcode:2005Natur.438.293G. doi:10.1038/438293a. PMC 7095140. PMID 16292292.

Gavin, K. (2020) Flattening the Curve for COVID-19: What Does It Mean and How Can You Help? Last accessed on June 25, 2020, from https://healthblog.uofmhealth.org/wellness-prevention/flattening-curve-for-covid-19-what-does-it-mean-and-how-can-you.help.

Giesecke, J. (2014) Primary and Index Cases, *The Lancet*, 384(9959), 2024, doi:10.1016/s0140-6736 (14)62331-x. PMID 25483164.

Guerra, G. L., de Morais, O. A. F., Amaral, A. A., Maia, S. L. A., Araújo, M. Y. R., Maria, A., Ganem, dos S. F. S., Navegantes, A. W., Fernandes, de O. M. R., and Maia, P. H. (2020) Ten Epidemiological Parameters of COVID-19: Use of Rapid Literature Review to Inform Predictive Models During the Pandemic, *Frontiers in Public Health*, 8, doi:10.3389/fpubh.2020.598547, ISSN=2296–2565, Last accessed on April 25, 2021, from www.frontiersin.org/article/10.3389/fpubh.2020.598547.

Halasa, T., Nielen, M., Huirne, R., and Hogeveen, H. (2009) Stochastic Bio-Economic Model of Bovine Intramammary Infection. *Livestock Science*, 124, 295–305.

Herfurth, H. (April 28, 2020) What Exactly Does It Mean to 'Flatten the Curve'? UAB Expert Defines Coronavirus Terminology for Everyday Life, *UAB News*, Last accessed on June 2021, from www.uab.edu/news/youcanuse/item/11268-what-exactly-does-it-mean-to-flatten-the-curve-uab-expert-defines-coronavirus-terminology-for-everyday-life.

Huddleston Jr., T. (February 16, 2020) This Hotel Is Infamous as Ground Zero for a SARS 'Super Spreader' in the 2003 Outbreak—Here's What Happened, *CNBC*. Last accessed on June 1, 2020, from www.cnbc.com/2020/02/14/hong-kong-hotel-hosted-super-spreader-in-the-2003-sars-outbreak.html.

Intermountain Healthcare (April 2, 2020) What's the Difference Between a Pandemic, an Epidemic, Endemic, and an Outbreak? Last accessed on June 1, 2020, from https://intermountainhealthcare.org/blogs/topics/live-well/2020/04/whats-the-difference-between-a-pandemic-an-epidemic-endemic-and-an-outbreak/.

Kent, J. (December 24, 2020) Intersection of Big Data Analytics, COVID-19 Top Focus of 2020, *Health IT Analytics*, Last accessed on August 24, 2021, from https://healthitanalytics.com/news/intersection-of-big-data-analytics-covid-19-top-focus-of-2020.

KHN (April 13, 2020) Researchers Try to Solve Mystery of 'Super Spreaders' to Help Control Pandemic's Spread, Last accessed on November 4, 2020, from https://khn.org/morning-breakout/researchers-try-to-solve-mystery-of-super-spreaders-to-help-control-pandemics-spread/.

Kirkeby, C., Halasa, T., Gussmann, M. et al. (2017) Methods for Estimating Disease Transmission Rates: Evaluating the Precision of Poisson Regression and Two Novel Methods. *Scientific Reports*, 7, 9496, https://doi.org/10.1038/s41598-017-09209-x.

LightCastle Analytics Wing (June 7, 2020) Flattening the Curve by Harnessing Data Intelligence: Data-Driven Approaches in Fighting COVID-19, *Light Castle Partners*. www.lightcastlebd.com/insights/2020/06/flattening-the-curve-by-harnessing-data-intelligence-data-driven-approaches-in-fighting-covid-19.

Lloyd-Smith, J. O., Schreiber, S. J., Kopp, P. E., and Getz, W. M. (2005) Superspreading and the Effect of Individual Variation on Disease Emergence, *Nature*, 438(7066), 355–359. Bibcode:2005Natur.438.355L. doi:10.1038/nature04153. PMC 7094981. PMID 16292310.

Mahanti, R. (2019) *Data Quality: Dimensions, Measurement, Strategy, Management, and Governance*. Milwaukee, WI: Quality Press, ASQ.

Martin, P. M. V., and Martin-Granel, E. (June 2006) 2,500-Year Evolution of the Term Epidemic, *Emerging Infectious Diseases [Serial on the Internet]*, http://dx.doi.org/10.3201/eid1206.051263.

Martin, T., Karopoulos, G., Hernández-Ramos, J. L., Kambourakis, G., Nai Fovino, I. (2020) Demystifying COVID-19 Digital Contact Tracing: A Survey on Frameworks and Mobile Apps, *Wireless Communications and Mobile Computing*, vol. 2020, Article ID 8851429, 29 pages, 2020, https://doi.org/10.1155/2020/8851429.

McCallum, H. Barlow, N., and Hone, J. (2001) How Should Pathogen Transmission Be Modelled? *Trends in Ecology & Evolution*, 16, 295–300.

McKay, R. (April 1, 2010) Patient Zero: Why It's Such a Toxic Term, *The Conversation*, Last accessed on November 4, 2020, from https://theconversation.com/patient-zero-why-its-such-a-toxic-term-13472.

[Merriam-Webster], When Does an Outbreak Become an Epidemic?

Otten, W., Filipe, J., Bailey, D., and Gilligan, C. (2003) Quantification and Analysis of Transmission Rates for Soilborne Epidemics, *Ecology*, 84, 3232–3239.

[NIH] Diseases—Activity 1—Glossary, Page 3 of 5, Last accessed on October 11, 2017, from science.education.nih.gov.

PBS (1938) The Most Dangerous Woman in America | In Her Own Words. *PBS Nova*. 1938–11–11. Retrieved 2010–11–03, Last accessed on November 4, 2020, from www.pbs.org/wgbh/nova/typhoid/letter.html.

[Physiopedia], Endemics, Epidemics and Pandemics, Last accessed on June 1, 2020, from www.physio-pedia.com/Endemics,_Epidemics_and_Pandemics.

Qiong, J., Guo, Y., Wang, G., and Barne, S. J. (August 2020) Big Data Analytics in the Fight Against Major Public Health Incidents (Including COVID-19): A Conceptual Framework, *International Journal of Environmental Research and Public Health*, 17(17), 6161, https://doi.org/ 10.3390/ijerph17176161

Riley, L. W. (2019) Differentiating Epidemic from Endemic or Sporadic Infectious Disease Occurrence. *Microbiology Spectrum*, 7(4), doi:10.1128/microbiolspec.AME-0007-2019.

Rothman, K. J., Lash, T., and Greenland, S. (2013) *Modern Epidemiology* (3rd ed.). Lippincott Williams & Wilkins.

Rothman, K. J., Greenland, S., and Lash, T. L. (2008) *Modern Epidemiology* (3rd ed.). Philadelphia: Lippincott, Williams & Wilkins, p. 561.

The Royal Society (August 24, 2020) Reproduction Number (R) and Growth Rate (r) of the COVID-19 Epidemic in the UK: Methods of Estimation, Data Sources, Causes of Heterogeneity, and Use as a Guide in Policy Formulation, Last accessed on April 25, 2021, from https://royalsociety.org/-/media/policy/projects/set-c/set-covid-19-R-estimates.pdf.

Torrey, T. (May 5, 2020) Difference Between an Epidemic and a Pandemic, *Very Well Health*, Last accessed on November 4, 2020, from www.verywellhealth.com/difference-between-epidemic-and-pandemic-2615168#citation-2.

Walker, J., and Talend (2011) The Butterfly Effect on Data Quality, Talend White Paper, Last accessed on March 3, 2018, from www.datatechnology.co.uk/data-quality-4/.

WHO (2009) Pandemic Influenza Preparedness and Response: A WHO Guidance Document. Last accessed on November 4, 2020, from www.ncbi.nlm.nih.gov/books/NBK143061/.

[WHO] World Health Organization. Disease Outbreaks.

[Wikipedia], Butterfly Effect, Last accessed on January 2021, from https://en.wikipedia.org/wiki/Butterfly_effect.

[WordNet Search 3.0], Princeton University, Last accessed on November 3, 2010, from wordnetweb.princeton.edu.

Yigitcanlar, T., Kankanamge, N., Preston, A. et al. (2020) How Can Social Media Analytics Assist Authorities in Pandemic-Related Policy Decisions? Insights from Australian States and Territories. *Health Information Science and Systems*, 8, 37, https://doi.org/10.1007/s13755-020-00121-9.

Yong, E. (December 14, 2017) 40 Years Later, Some Survivors of the First Ebola Outbreak Are Still Immune, *The Atlantic*, Last accessed on November 4, 2020, from www.theatlantic.com/science/archive/2017/12/forty-years-later-some-survivors-of-the-first-ebola-outbreak-are-still-immune/548339/.

Zadoks, R. et al. (2001) Analysis of an Outbreak of Streptococcus Uberis Mastitis, *Journal of Dairy Science*, 84, 590–599.

Zaimova, R. (March 31, 2020) How Data Can Help Fight a Health Crisis Like the Coronavirus, *World Economic Forum*, www.weforum.org/agenda/2020/03/role-data-fight-coronavirus-epidemic/.

Chapter 4

COVID-19—A Pandemic in the Digital Age

"Historically, pandemics have forced humans to break with the past and imagine their world anew. This one is no different. It is a portal, a gateway between one world and the next."

—Arundhati Ray

Introduction

The COVID-19 pandemic, also branded as the coronavirus pandemic, is a current pandemic of coronavirus disease 2019 (COVID-19). COVID-19 is an infectious respiratory and vascular disease caused by a corona virus named severe acute respiratory syndrome coronavirus 2 (SARS-CoV-2).

COVID-19 is a perilous disease in terms of scale as well as severity, with several disease variants—Alpha, Beta, Gamma, Delta, Epsilon, Zeta, Eta, Theta, Iota, Kappa, Lambda and more. COVID-19 has presented and continues to present unprecedented challenges to not only global health, but also to work, supply chains, and the economy. It has spread all over the world. As of September 2, 2021 (more than a year and a half, since the first disease outbreak in Wuhan, China), more than 219 million cases have been confirmed globally, and more than 4.5 million deaths have been attributed to COVID-19. The International Labour Organization (ILO) in its report labels the coronavirus pandemic as "the worst global crisis since World War II."

While there were some predictions around the COVID-19 pandemic, some of which are eerie, none of these predictions propelled the world to be prepared for preventing it from evolving into pandemic proportions. These predictions have been discussed in the first section of the chapter. The next section discusses coronaviruses and the family of viruses that SARS-CoV-2 belongs to.

The timing of the COVID-19 pandemic intersects with the digital age, when we are literally drowning in an ocean of data. Data and analytics can play a key role in managing the pandemic. COVID-19 and the spread and impacts of COVID-19 in line with the data collected are discussed in the next sections.

COVID-19 Pandemic Predictions

"The influenza pandemic that gripped the world from 1918 to 1919 sickened 500 million individuals and killed almost 50 million, many of them young and otherwise healthy. . . . One hundred years later, we have not experienced anything like the pandemic that shook the world in the early 20th century. But are we being complacent? Is another pandemic lurking in our future, and are we ready for such an event?"

—Laurie Saloman (2018)

"It's just a matter of when and where it starts. The possibility that we could have a 1918-type pandemic again is actually very real."

—Michael Osterholm (Saloman, 2018)

Eerily, the COVID-19 pandemic which first hit in the end of 2019 and spread rapidly across the globe in the beginning of 2020 had been predicted by a couple of authors, a long time before its year of occurrence. Written nearly 40 years ago before the COVID-19 pandemic, thriller writer Dean Koontz's fiction novel, "The Eyes Of Darkness" published in 1981, mentions a virus called Wuhan-400, created as a bioweapon in a Chinese laboratory.

Twenty Twenty, the fourth novel written by the acclaimed author Nigel Watts, was published by Hodder and Stoughton in August 1995. What made "Twenty Twenty" extraordinary was its "prediction" of a viral pandemic, a world of virtual communication, and a planet heading toward environmental catastrophe in 2020, very similar to what we are experiencing with COVID-19 today (Mearns, 2020).

First published 12 years before the COVID-19 pandemic spread in 2020, in 2008, Sylvia Browne's book entitled "End of Days: Predictions and Prophecies about the End of the World," Ms Browne prophesied a widespread pneumonia pandemic. While the coronavirus is not absolutely pneumonia, the coronavirus can cause flu-like and pneumonia-like symptoms (Kettley, 2020).

Her book reads: "In around 2020 a severe pneumonia-like illness will spread throughout the globe, attacking the lungs and the bronchial tubes and resisting all known treatments."

"Almost more baffling than the illness itself will be the fact that it will suddenly vanish as quickly as it has arrived, attack again 10 years later, and then disappear completely (Browne, 2008)."

Director Steven Soderbergh and screenwriter Scott Z Burns's film "Contagion" released in 2011 apparently foretold the coronavirus pandemic too. The film is about a fictitious illness called MEV-1. The disease was caused by a fictional virus, which had a 72-hour incubation period and high fatality rate, according to The Sun. In the film, the disease becomes a global pandemic after a bat spread it to a pig, who spread it to an individual who didn't rinse his hands before shaking hands with another individual (Hoffower, 2020).

Notable flu and disease experts, scientists and government officials, Bill Gates, and former White House officials have been warning of a pandemic for a number of years (Hoffower, 2020).

In his 2008 book—"Global Catastrophes and Trends," scientist, Vaclav Smil, cautioned of the unavoidable threat of another influenza pandemic (Smil, 2008).

In a 2015 TED talk, Bill Gates stated that the world was "not ready for the next epidemic (Hoffower, 2020)." Three years down the line, in a discussion about epidemics hosted by the Massachusetts Medical Society and the New England Journal of Medicine in 2018, he said a pandemic could happen within the next decade (Hoffower, 2020).

Bill Gates showed a simulation by the Institute for Disease Modelling which found that a new flu similar to the one that killed approximately 50 million people in the 1918 Spanish flu pandemic would now most probably result in 30 million deaths within six months (Hoffower, 2020).

Bill Gates also stated that the prospect that such a disease would appear, continued to rise in today's interconnected world, and that such a disease could either originate naturally or be created as a weaponized disease. He further stated that sense of urgency was lacking in case of biological threats and stressed the world needs to prepare for pandemics with same seriousness it prepares for war (Hoffower, 2020).

In 2018, Dr. Luciana Borio of the former White House National Security Council (NSC) team responsible for pandemics had warned of a pandemic flu threat. According to CNN's Daniel Dale, in 2018, the intelligence community's Worldwide Threat Assessment cautioned that a "novel strain of a virulent microbe that is easily transmissible between humans continues to be a major threat. (Hoffower, 2020)."

Virologist and flu expert Robert G. Webster predicted an upcoming global influenza pandemic in his book entitled "Flu Hunter: Unlocking the secrets of a virus," that was published in 2018 (Webster, 2018).

However, while there had been talks about an impending pandemic, most of the countries did not have preparedness to deal with the COVID-19 pandemic.

Coronaviruses

There isn't just one coronavirus. Coronaviruses are a big family of viruses that are known to affect both humans and animals. Coronaviruses are not new; they have been in being for a long time. They cause respiratory illness in humans which can range from the common cold to more serious infections. Although symptoms of coronaviruses are often mild—the most common symptoms are fever and dry cough—in some cases they lead to more serious respiratory tract illness including pneumonia and bronchitis.

They are named coronaviruses because of their shape. The individual virus looks like a sphere encircled by a spiky crown (or corona), when seen through a microscope.

Coronaviruses are members of the subfamily *Coronavirinae* in the family *Coronaviridae* and the order *Nidovirales* [International Committee on Taxonomy of Viruses]. Based on their phylogenetic relationships and genomic structures, this subfamily consists of four genera (Cui et al., 2019) (as shown in Figure 4.1)

- Alphacoronavirus,
- Betacoronavirus,
- Gammacoronavirus, and
- Deltacoronavirus.

The alphacoronaviruses and betacoronaviruses cause infection in mammals only. The gammacoronaviruses and deltacoronaviruses cause infections in birds, but some of them can also cause infections in mammals. Alphacoronaviruses and betacoronaviruses typically cause respiratory disease in humans and gastroenteritis in animals (Cui et al., 2019; Woo et al., 2012).

Besides severe acute respiratory syndrome coronavirus 2 (SARS-CoV-2) a zoonotic virus which is the cause of the COVID-19 pandemic, six other coronaviruses are known to infect human beings.

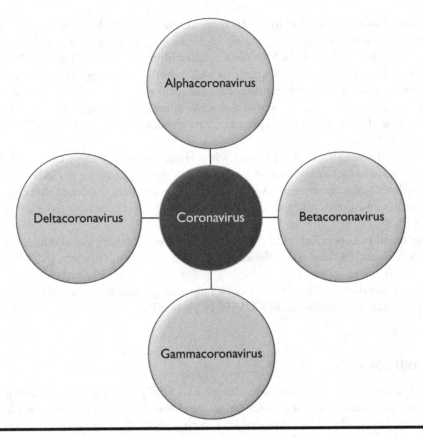

Figure 4.1 Four genera of coronaviruses.

The coronaviruses that can infect people are:

- 229E (alpha),
- NL63 (alpha),
- OC43 (beta),
- HKU1 (beta),
- MERS-CoV, a beta virus that causes Middle East respiratory syndrome (MERS),
- SARS-CoV, a beta virus that causes severe acute respiratory syndrome (SARS), and
- SARS-CoV-2, beta virus which causes COVID-19.

Of these seven coronaviruses, four coronaviruses (HKU1, NL63, OC43, and 229E) are mild and common, causing one third of colds. However, three of them are rare and severe, causing the diseases—MERS, the original SARS, and COVID-19. In addition, scientists have also identified about 500 other coronaviruses among China's many bat species (Andersen et al., 2020; Yong, 2020).

"There will be many more—I think it's safe to say tens of thousands," says Peter Daszak of the EcoHealth Alliance, who has led that work. Laboratory experiments show that some of these new viruses could potentially infect humans. SARS-CoV-2 likely came from a bat, too (Yong, 2020).

SARS-CoV-2 virus is closely related to the original SARS-CoV virus found in humans, bats, pangolins, and civets, and which caused the SARS epidemic in 2003 (Zhu et al., 2020). Even though there are many similarities between the SARS-CoV-2 that is the cause of COVID-19 pandemic and the SARS-CoV virus that caused the SARS epidemic, there are also differences resulting from changes in their genomes. This includes how they are passed from one individual to another, and the differing symptoms of coronaviruses (UKRI, 2020).

Genetic analysis has revealed that the SARS-CoV-2 coronavirus genetically clusters with the genus Betacoronavirus, in subgenus Sarbecovirus (lineage B) together with two bat-derived strains. From genomic perspective, the SARS-CoV-2 coronavirus has a 96% match with other bat corona-virus samples (BatCov RaTG13), and shares around 50% and 79% of its genetic sequence with the MERS-CoV and the SARS-CoV, respectively. Furthermore, SARS-CoV-2 shares a receptor-bind-ing domain structure with SARS-CoV (WHO, 2020e; Rathore and Ghosh, 2020; Ashour et al., 2020).

Coronaviruses are spherical in shape and layered with spikes of protein. While these spikes of protein help the virus bind to and infect healthy cells, these spikes also allow the immune system to "see" the virus. A layer of membrane can be found underneath these spikes. The virus' genetic mate-rial, that is, its genome, is inside the membrane. The genomes of some viruses like chickenpox and smallpox are made of DNA like humans, whereas those of coronaviruses are made of the closely related ribonucleic acid (RNA). From a molecular perspective, the SARS-CoV-2 is an enveloped, single-stranded, positive-sense RNA virus (Li et al., 2020). RNA viruses have small genomes which are subject to continuous change. These changes, called mutations, aid the virus to adapt to and cause diseases in new host species. It is thought that the new COVID-19 likely originated from bats but it is not yet known whether mutations allowed this jump from animals to humans (UKRI, 2020; Corman et al., 2018).

What Is COVID-19?

COVID-19 is a disease which is caused by a novel type of coronavirus. Common symptoms of the disease are fever, coughing, sore throat, and shortness of breath. The virus can spread from person to person. At the time when I am writing this book there is no treatment for COVID-19.

The disease was first reported as pneumonia of unknown cause, in the city of Wuhan (home to approximately 11 million people at the time), Hubei province in China to the WHO Country Office in China on December 31, 2019. This was consequently identified as a new virus in Janu-ary 2020 (WHO, 2020f).

The disease quickly spread globally and the number of cases continued to rise showing expo-nential growth worldwide. The outbreak was announced as a Public Health Emergency of Interna-tional Concern on January 30, 2020 (WHO, 2020g).

On February 11, 2020, WHO announced a formal name for the novel coronavirus disease: COVID-19. "Co" stands for coronavirus, "Vi" is for virus, and "D" is for disease and 19 stands for the year when the disease was first detected [Wiki-COVID-19].

It's widely accepted, together with the head of China's Center for Disease Control and Pre-vention that the virus originated in Hubei [The Guardian]. While the disease was first seen in Wuhan, Hubei province China and is considered to have originated in bats, as the origins of the virus became part of US-China diplomatic conflict, fueled by US officials calling the disease "Chi-nese coronavirus" or "Wuhan virus," health officials purposely avoid naming COVID-19 after a geographical location, animal or group of people, so as not to denounce locations, creatures or individuals (Prieto-Ramos et al., 2020).

Due to the rapid global rise in cases, WHO declared COVID-19 a pandemic on March 11, 2020 (WHO, 2020a, [STAT News]). As of March 13, 2020, over 132,000 cases and 5000 deaths had been reported to WHO from 123 countries and territories (WHO, 2020b). As of March 15, 2020, over 150,000 cases had been identified globally in 123 countries with over 5,000 fatalities (ECDPC, 2020). As of September 21, 2021, more than 229 million cases and 4.7 million deaths have been reported, making it one of the most lethal pandemics in history [Wiki-COVID-19].

Who Was Patient Zero in COVID-19?

The first confirmed case of the COVID-19 disease, caused by the SARS-CoV-2 virus, was traced back to a 55-year-old patient in Hubei province in China, and was reported in a Chinese newspaper on November 17, 2019 (The Economic Times, 2020; Walker, 2020). On the other hand, on March 27, 2020, news outlets, citing a government document, reported that a 57-year-old woman, who tested positive for the coronavirus disease on December 10, 2019, and described in The Wall Street Journal on March 6, 2020, may have been patient zero in what developed into a pandemic (Oliveira, 2020; Page et al., 2020). Hence, there has not been a definitive patient zero in case of COVID-19 pandemic.

COVID-19—From a Localized Outbreak into a Global Pandemic

In a very short period of time, a localized outbreak of COVID-19 evolved into a global pandemic with three defining characteristics (WHO, 2020d):

- Speed and scale: the COVID-19 disease has spread very fast across the globe, with its capacity for explosive spread having had an overwhelming effect on even the most robust health systems (Figure 4.1).
- Severity: in general, 20% of cases are severe or critical; the approximate clinical case fatality rate at over 3%, and rising in older age brackets and in individuals who have certain underlying health conditions.
- Societal and economic disruption: shocks to health and social care systems and measures taken to control transmission have had wide-ranging and profound socio-economic consequences.

COVID-19 Features

The outbreak of major public health incidents usually has the characteristics of suddenness, uncertainty, unpredictability, high hazard, high social concern, chain reaction, timely disposition, and evasive prevention (Wang, 2014). The explanation of these features of COVID-19 are shown in Table 4.1.

Spread and Impact of COVID-19—What Does the Data Say

COVID-19 is a highly infectious disease. Although its mortality rate is lower than SARS, its transmission rate (diagnosis rate of close contacts) is very high, resulting in a high number of infections.

Table 4.1 Characteristics of COVID-19 Incidents

Feature	Explanation	COVID-19
Sudden	The incident can suddenly erupt without prior notification or warning.	Sudden disease outbreak.
Uncertainty	Knowledge of new pathogens may be limited.	Unknown, new coronavirus.
Unpredictability	The impact and sustainability of the event cannot be predicted quickly and accurately.	Political, economic, social, health, cultural and other influences and impacts.
Highly hazardous	Harm to people's health and property.	More than 83 million cases have been diagnosed worldwide, and more than 1.8 million deaths [Johns Hopkins University].
High social attention	Stir extensive and in-depth public attention.	The Google trends index reached 100 (represents the hottest search) [Google Trends].
Chain reaction	The incident has a chain reaction spurring similar incidents, thus expanding the scope and area of its impact.	Spread quickly to 188 countries in the world.
Timely response	Governments respond quickly with strict controls.	A WHO Global Emergency [WHO].
Preventive measures	Preventive actions to minimize the pandemic loss, so that the pandemic is gradually controlled; resume work and production on the basis of establishing strict avoidance and prevention experience.	Strictly control the source of infection; cut off the route of infection; close borders and impose travel restriction; protect susceptible people; introduce quarantine, lockdown, social distancing, and ban on public gatherings.

Source: Adapted from [WHO], Qiong et al. (2020).

In the period between January 20, 2020 and March 8, 2020, a total of 80,735 accumulated confirmed cases were reported in China, with a total of 58,600 recoveries and 3119 deaths from COVID-19. A total of 674,760 close contacts were tracked during this period and the number of close contacts observed was 20,146 [WHO]. By August 18, 2020, there was an exponential increase in the number of cases, with a total of 21,826,342 accumulated confirmed cases being reported in the world, with 13,888,301 recoveries, and 773,152 fatalities from COVID-19 [WHO].

As of January 1, 2021, more than 83 million COVID-19 cases have been diagnosed worldwide, and there have been more than 1.8 million deaths [Johns Hopkins University].

Figure 4.2 shows the global monthly infections and deaths from COVID-19, January to October 2020.

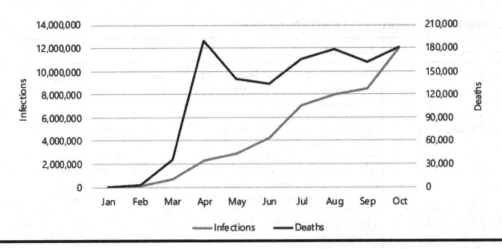

Figure 4.2   Global monthly infections and deaths from COVID-19, January to October 2020.

Source: Our World in Data, "Coronavirus Pandemic (COVID-19)," University of Oxford, accessed November 2, 2020

COVID-19 has had and continues to have a huge multi sectoral impact; that is, it not only has a health impact but also has social, political, economic, and business impacts. However, the scale of impact to various sectors varies from country to country, depending on the extent and severity of spread, and how well they have been able to respond to it.

As per a joint statement by ILO, FAO, IFAD, and WHO, in October, 2020, tens of millions of people are at risk of falling into extreme poverty, while the number of malnourished people, presently estimated at approximately 690 million, could rise by up to 132 million by the end of the year. Millions of businesses' very existence is threatened. Nearly half of the world's 3.3 billion global workforce are at risk of losing their livelihoods (WHO, 2020c).

In another report entitled "COVID-19 and the world of work: Impact and policy responses" by International Labour Organization, it was explained that the pandemic crisis has adversely impacted both the economic and labor market, and has affected not only supply (production of goods and services) but also demand (consumption and investment). This is because, shutting down, social distancing, strict restrictions on movements (including interstate, national, and international travel restrictions) are the only cost-effective tools available to prevent the spread of COVID-19. However, while these measures result in productivity loss on the one hand, on the other hand they cause a sharp drop in demand for goods and services by the consumers in the market, thus resulting in a collapse in economic activity (Ananya, 2020).

International Monetary Fund's (IMF) chief said that, "World is faced with extraordinary uncertainty about the depth and duration of this crisis, and it was the worst economic fallout since the Great Depression." The IMF projected the external funding requirements for emerging markets and developing economies in the order of trillions of dollars (Ananya, 2020).

Coronavirus pandemic demands coordinated fiscal and monetary policy measures to deal with it. The fiscal measures include paying the healthcare bill raised by the pandemic. Providing for masks, gloves, testing kits, personal protection equipment, ventilators, ICU beds, quarantine wards, medicines, and other equipment would mean a huge increase in healthcare spending (Ananya, 2020).

The COVID-19 pandemic has affected international relations. The pandemic has had an impact on the political systems of a large number of countries across the globe, triggering interruptions in legislative activities, isolation or deaths of multiple politicians and postponement of elections due to qualms of disease transmission and spread. The pandemic has also caused varied discussions about political issues such as the relative benefits of democracy and autocracy, how states respond to crises, politicization of beliefs about the virus, and the appropriateness of prevailing frameworks of international cooperation (Ang, 2020; Stasavage, 2020; Lipscy, 2020; Druckman and Klar, 2020; Fazal, 2020; [Wikipedia]).

The COVID-19 pandemic has adversely affected a large number of business sectors—hospitality, tours and travels (including the aviation industry), healthcare, retail, banks, hotels, real estate, education, health, IT, recreation, media, and others. The tourism industry has been the worst affected due to the COVID-19 crisis, internationally, due to travel bans, closing of public places, including travel attractions, museums and monuments, and government advice against travel. A lot of airlines have had to cancel flights due to lower demand, and British regional airline "Flybe" folded. The cruise line industry has also been hit hard by the pandemic, and several train stations and ferry ports have been closed. Millions of people associated with industry have lost their jobs (Ananya, 2020).

Concluding Thoughts

COVID-19 pandemic is the defining health crisis of the 21st century. It has far reaching impacts that will leave profound scars. It has spread to all continents across the globe.

COVID-19 pandemic has a multisectoral impact—hence every sector and every individual must be involved in the fighting and preventing the disease. A global collaborative effort and solidarity is needed to beat the COVID-19 pandemic. COVID-19 puts an enormous strain on countries. Different countries are facing different challenges in dealing with the disease such as lack of capacity and resources, misinformation, and public anxiety. All countries must strike an acceptable balance between protecting health, minimizing business, economic and social disruption, and respecting human rights (WHO, 2020a).

Data have occupied a center stage in understanding and fighting the COVID-19 pandemic. This is reinforced by Connecticut CDO Scott Gaul as he states (Jaiani and Audet, 2020):

> There has been unprecedented interest in data from citizens, advocacy groups and other researchers to understand the pandemic. This is something I have not seen before that has been sustained for months. We have received a lot of different questions about the numbers, people really want to understand what they mean.

The role of data in a pandemic, the data challenges and pandemic data analytic use cases will be discussed in the subsequent chapters in this book.

References

Ananya, V. (September 2020) Impact of COVID-19 on Society and Environment Readers Blog. *Times of India*, https://timesofindia.indiatimes.com/readersblog/myfantasies/impact-of-covid-19-on-society-and-environment-25587/

Andersen, K. G., Rambaut, A., Lipkin, W. I., Holmes, E. C., and Garry, R. F. (2020) The Proximal Origin of SARS-CoV-2. *Nature Medicine*. 26(4): 450–452. https://doi.org/10.1038/s41591-020-0820-9

Ang, Y. Y. (2020) When COVID-19 Meets Centralized, Personalized Power. *Nature Human Behavior*. 4(5): 445–447. doi:10.1038/s41562-020-0872-3. PMID 32273583. S2CID 215532797.

Ashour, H. M., Elkhatib, W. F., Rahman, M. M., and Elshabrawy, H. A. (2020) Insights into the Recent 2019 Novel Coronavirus (SARS-CoV-2) in Light of Past Human Coronavirus Outbreaks. *Pathogens.* 9: 186.

Browne, S. (2008) *End of Days: Predictions and Prophecies about the End of the World.* Dutton.

Corman, V. M, Muth, D., Niemeyer, D., and Drosten, C. (2018) Hosts and Sources of Endemic Human Coronaviruses. *Advances in Virus Research.* 100: 163–188. doi:10.1016/bs.aivir.2018.01.001.

Cui, J., Li, F., and Shi, Z. L. (March 2019) Origin and Evolution of Pathogenic Coronaviruses. *Nature Reviews. Microbiology.* 17(3): 181–192. doi:10.1038/s41579-018-0118-9.

Druckman, J., and Klar, S. (2020) How Affective Polarization Shapes Americans' Political Beliefs: A Study of Response to the COVID-19 Pandemic. *Journal of Experimental Political Science*: 1–12. doi:10.1017/XPS.2020.28. S2CID 222312130.

(ECDPC, 2020) European Centre for Disease Prevention and Control., Jump up↑ Situation Update Worldwide, as of 15 March 2020 08:00, Last accessed on March 15, 2020.

The Economic Times (March 13, 2020) First COVID-19 Case Can Be Traced Back to November 17 in China's Hubei Province: Report, https://economictimes.indiatimes.com//news/international/world-news/first-covid-19-case-can-be-traced-back-to-november-2017-in-chinas-hubei-province-report/articleshow/74608199.cms?utm_source=contentofinterest&utm_medium=text&utm_campaign=cppst.

Fazal, T. (2020) Health Diplomacy in Pandemical Times. *International Organization*: 1–20. doi:10.1017/S0020818320000326. S2CID 229265358.

[The Guardian], First Covid-19 Case Happened in November, China Government Records Show - Report. Last accessed on August 16, 2021 https://www.theguardian.com/world/2020/mar/13/first-covid-19-case-happened-in-november-china-government-records-show-report

[Google Trends], Last accessed on August 16, 2020, from https://trends.google.com/trends/explore?q=covid%2019.

Hoffower, H. (April 7, 2020) 6:29 AM. Bill Gates Has Been Warning of a Pandemic for Years, *Business Insider Australia.* www.businessinsider.com.au/people-who-seemingly-predicted-the-coronavirus-pandemic-2020-3?r=US&IR=T.

Jaiani, V., and Audet, D. (September 17, 2020) 8 Data Leaders on Leveraging Data During and After COVID-19. *GCN, Data Leaders Roundtable*, https://gcn.com/articles/2020/09/17/data-leaders-round-table.aspx.

[Johns Hopkins University], COVID-19 Map, Last accessed on January 1, 2021, from https://coronavirus.jhu.edu/map.html.

Kettley, S. (November 6, 2020) Coronavirus: Did the Psychic Sylvia Browne Predict COVID-19? Prophecy of Pneumonia in 2020, *Express.* Last accessed on March 20, 2021, from www.express.co.uk/news/weird/1256553/Coronavirus-Sylvia-Browne-prediction-COVID19-prophecy-pneumonia.

Li, X., Zai, J., Zhao, Q., Nie, Q., Li, Y., Foley, B. T., and Chaillon, A. (2020) Evolutionary History, Potential Intermediate Animal Host, and Cross-Species Analyses of SARS-CoV-2. *Journal of Medical Virology*, 92(6): 602–611. doi:10.1002/jmv.25731

Lipscy, P. (2020) COVID-19 and the Politics of Crisis. *International Organization*: 1–30. doi:10.1017/S0020818320000375. S2CID 225135699.

Mearns, E. (2020) A Stark Warning from the Book That Predicted the 2020 Pandemic, *CTGN*, https://newseu.cgtn.com/news/2020-08-21/A-stark-warning-from-the-book-that-predicted-the-2020-pandemic-T7cbOmRHi0/index.html

Oliveira, N. (March 27, 2020) Shrimp Vendor Identified as Possible Coronavirus 'Patient Zero,' Leaked Document Says. *New York Daily News*, Last accessed on March 27, 2020.

Page, J., Fan, W., and Khan, N. (March 6, 2020) How It All Started: China's Early Coronavirus Missteps. *The Wall Street Journal*, Last accessed on March 27, 2020.

Prieto-Ramos, F., Pei, J., and Cheng, L. (2020). Institutional and News Media Denominations of COVID-19 and Its Causative Virus: Between Naming Policies and Naming Politics. *Discourse & Communication*, 14(6), 635–652. https://doi.org/10.1177/1750481320938467

Qiong, J., Guo, Y., Wang, G., and Barne, S. J. (August 2020) Big Data Analytics in the Fight Against Major Public Health Incidents (Including COVID-19): A Conceptual Framework, August 2020. *International Journal of Environmental Research and Public Health*, 17(17): 6161. doi:10.3390/ijerph17176161

Rathore, J. S., and Ghosh, C. (August 25, 2020) Severe Acute Respiratory Syndrome Coronavirus-2 (SARS-CoV-2), a Newly Emerged Pathogen: An Overview. *Pathogens and Disease*, 78(6).

Saloman, L. (February 17, 2018) The Spanish Flu Pandemic 100 Years Later: Are We Ready for Another One? *Contagion Live*. 3(1), www.contagionlive.com/view/the-spanish-flu-pandemic-100-years-later-are-we-ready-for-another-one

Stasavage, D. (2020) Democracy, Autocracy, and Emergency Threats: Lessons for COVID-19 from the Last Thousand Years. *International Organization*: 1–17. doi:10.1017/S0020818320000338.

[STAT News], WHO Declares the Coronavirus Outbreak a Pandemic.

Smil, V. (2008) *Global Catastrophes and Trends*. The MIT Press.

UKRI (March 25, 2020) What Is Coronavirus? The Different Types of Coronaviruses. *Coronavirus: The Science Explained—UKRI*, Last accessed on November 14, 2020, from https://coronavirusexplained.ukri.org/en/article/cad0003/

Walker, J. (March 14, 2020) China Traces Cornovirus to First Confirmed Case, Nearly Identifying 'Patient Zero'. *Newsweek*, Last accessed on March 14, 2020.

Wang, J. (2014) Research on the Model and Effectiveness Evaluation of Emergency Plan System. Ph.D. Thesis, Dalian University of Technology, Dalian, China.

Webster, R. G. (2018) *Flu Hunter: Unlocking the Secrets of a Virus*. Otago University Press, 220 p, ISBN: 1988531314.

[WHO] World Health Organization, Coronavirus Disease (COVID-19) Outbreak, Last accessed on August 18, 2020, from https://covid19. who.int/.

WHO (March 11, 2020a) WHO Director-General's Opening Remarks at the Media Briefing on COVID-19–11 March 2020, www.who.int/director-general/speeches/detail/who-director-general-s-opening-remarks-at-the-media-briefing-on-covid-19–11-march-2020.

WHO (March 13, 2020b) WHO Director-General's Opening Remarks at the Media Briefing on COVID-19–13 March 2020, www.who.int/director-general/speeches/detail/who-director-general-s-opening-remarks-at-the-mission-briefing-on-covid-19–13-march-2020.

WHO (October 13, 2020c) Impact of COVID-19 on People's Livelihoods. Their Health and Our Food Systems, www.who.int/news/item/13-10-2020-impact-of-covid-19-on-people's-livelihoods-their-health-and-our-food-systems

WHO (April 14, 2020d) COVID-19 Strategy Update, Last accessed on December 3, 2020, from www.who.int/docs/default-source/coronaviruse/covid-strategy-update-14april2020.pdf?sfvrsn=29da3ba0_6

WHO (February 24, 2020e) Report of the WHO-China Joint Mission on Coronavirus Disease 2019 (COVID-19).

WHO (January 21, 2020f) Novel Coronavirus (2019-nCoV) Situation Report-1, Last accessed on December 3, 2020, from https://www.who.int/docs/default-source/coronaviruse/situation-reports/20200121-sitrep-1-2019-ncov.pdf

WHO (January 30, 2020g) Statement on the second meeting of the International Health Regulations (2005) Emergency Committee regarding the outbreak of novel coronavirus (2019-nCoV), Last accessed on December 3, 2020, from https://www.who.int/news/item/30-01-2020-statement-on-the-second-meeting-of-the-international-health-regulations-(2005)-emergency-committee-regarding-the-outbreak-of-novel-coronavirus-(2019-ncov)

[Wiki-COVID-19], COVID-19 Pandemic, Last accessed on September 21, 2021, from https://en.wikipedia.org/wiki/COVID-19_pandemic

[Wikipedia], Impact of the COVID-19 Pandemic on Politics, Last accessed on January 01, 2021, from https://en.wikipedia.org/wiki/Impact_of_the_COVID-19_pandemic_on_politics#cite_note-5.

Woo, P. C., et al. (2012) Discovery of Seven Novel Mammalian and Avian Coronaviruses in the Genus Deltacoronavirus Supports Bat Coronaviruses as the Gene Source of Alphacoronavirus and Betacoronavirus and Avian Coronaviruses as the Gene Source of Gammacoronavirus and Deltacoronavirus. *Journal of Virology*, 86: 3995–4008.

Yong, E. (April 19, 2020) Why the Coronavirus Is So Confusing, *The Atlantic*. Last accessed on November 12, 2020, from www.theatlantic.com/health/archive/2020/04/pandemic-confusing-uncertainty/610819/.

Zhu, N., Zhang, D., Wang, W., Li, X., Yang, B., Song, J. et al. (February 2020) A Novel Coronavirus from Patients with Pneumonia in China, 2019. *New England Journal of Medicine*, 382(8): 727–733. doi:10.1056/NEJMoa2001017.

Chapter 5

Data and Pandemic in the Digital World

"Data really powers everything that we do."

—Jeff Weiner

"If we make the right decisions now—informed by science, data and the experience of medical professionals—we can save lives and get the country back to work."

—Bill Gates, CEO and founder of Microsoft

"South Korea has "acted like an army." They brought data to fight the war."

—Lee Sang-won, an infectious diseases expert at the Korea Centers for Disease Control and Prevention

Data, Technology, Digital World, and Pandemic

The COVID-19 pandemic has resulted in the acceleration in the pace of digitization more than any other recent event. The increased restrictions placed on travel, the need for limiting interactions and social distancing to restrict and stop disease spread, has resulted in most organizations having their employees work from home and conduct their day-to-day operations digitally where possible, and consumers making purchases online. These online activities have resulted in a huge influx in data that organizations are able to capture and store. However, this data can be both a challenge and an opportunity.

We are currently living in a digital world and armed with sophisticated technology that can be used to leverage data and derive insights that can help in combating pandemic of a scale similar to COVID-19, in ways that was not possible in previous centuries. This is because the variety and amount of data available today and the technologies to leverage data to derive insights from them were not there in the previous centuries. As highlighted by Eric Schmidt, Executive Chairman of Google:

DOI: 10.4324/9781003270911-5

There were 5 exabytes of information created between the dawn of civilization through 2003, but that much information is now created every 2 days.

One of the reasons contributing to this exponential data growth is electronic data collection (EDC) through use of widely available, low-cost hardware (e.g., smartphones and tablets) as well as sensors and other electronic equipment, that can, when appropriately configured, consume little power and collect data offline, making them suitable for use in resource-poor settings (Polonsky et al., 2019; King et al., 2013). Also, with data storage available cheaply, it is possible to store massive amounts of data.

Data and technology have a critical role to play in managing a pandemic. It is important to be able to understand the nature of the contagion, as well as the measures that can help manage and prevent spread of the disease. It is also important to understand the wider impact to the economy and businesses such as changes in consumer behavior, supply chain impact, resourcing issues, and risks. Data sits at the heart of this exercise.

As stated by Tedros Adhanom Ghebreyesus, director-general of the World Health Organization (WHO, 2020): "You cannot fight a fire blindfolded." The right information in the hands of the right people can save lives in a time of crisis.

Insights into the nature of the contagion and spread of a disease can help countries respond more effectively to a pandemic. Data can not only help in understanding the impact of a pandemic across different geographies and forecast the spread of a disease, and help plan suitable response to controlling the spread as well as allocation of resources, understand and plan for meeting changing demands and consumer patterns, but also help in planning recovery from the impact of the pandemic. Being data driven along the lines of resilience, realignment, and recovery maximizes the organizations' and countries' chances to recover from the crisis brought about by a pandemic.

A pandemic is usually a global crisis and characterized by a great degree of uncertainty. Health leaders need to make quick and effective decisions to combat a pandemic and minimize damage. These decisions are critical as they influence the number of fatalities. Good quality data is the key to making informative decisions. Having good quality data related to population mobility, disease spread, location data (for contact tracing information), and medical data (such as confirmed cases, hospitalizations, critical cases, and deaths) can provide useful insights to design effective countermeasures as well as preventive measures for the pandemic.

COVID-19 pandemic has triggered increased use of data by organizations. As per statistics reported in the State of BI and Business Analytics Report, published by Sisense, 50% of survey respondents use data more often or much more often than before COVID-19. In the wake of COVID-19 pandemic, Sisense surveyed 500 data professionals in the US, which showed that as a result of COVID-19, 55% of businesses have started to use data to improve efficiency, 47% to support customers, and 45% to predict future outcomes (Noor, 2020; Sisense, 2020).

South Korea managed to effectively flatten the COVID-19 infection curve, by leveraging data to its maximum extent. This chapter discusses how data can help in managing a pandemic, the concept of traditional data and big data, and the challenges around traditional data and big data in managing a pandemic with special emphasis on the COVID-19 pandemic.

Types of Data from a Pandemic Analytics Perspective

Data is used in a pandemic is mainly used to drive decisions to combat pandemic impacts in different industry sectors, and can be categorized in two broad categories (Mahanti, 2021b):

- Traditional data—Traditional data is structured data (that is, data stored in a fixed format or fields).
- Big data—Big data is high-volume, high-velocity, and/or high-variety information assets that demand cost-effective, innovative forms of information processing that enable enhanced insight, decision-making, and process automation [Gartner Information Technology Glossary].

Role of Data in Pandemic

Data can be used strategically to address health and economic crises, and can enable informed decision-making. Pandemics are primarily a health crisis. However, pandemics generally have a widespread and cascading impact on several sectors. The COVID-19 pandemic is a "wake-up call" for the same.

A pandemic starts as an outbreak and data need to be collected at each of the three levels (Cori et al., 2017; Polonsky et al., 2019):

- individual level: detailed information about cases. This is also known as case data and includes dates of onset and admission, gender, age, location, exposure and contact tracing data, pathogen whole genome sequencing (WGS), and data pertaining to outbreak investigations (e.g., case—control and cohort study data).
- exposure level: detailed information about exposure events that may have led to spread of the disease.
- population level: characteristics of the population(s) in which the disease outbreak is spreading and the interventions carried out in the population(s). Background data record the inherent characteristics of the impacted populations. This includes demographic information (e.g., plots of population densities, age groups, and mixing patterns), movement data (e.g., borders, traveler movements, and relocation), health infrastructure (e.g., drug supplies, hospital facilities, and equipment) and epidemiological data themselves (e.g., levels of pre-existing immunity).

Some data such as pathogen whole genome sequencing, contact tracing, and exposure data are context-specific, and can be used for that particular disease event only. However, other data, specifically, the data at the population level, will be valuable for a wide range of epidemics and pandemics, and should be consistently, systematically and centrally collected, stored, and analyzed in preparation for the next disease outbreak (Cori et al., 2017).

A wide range of data can be helpful when dealing with a pandemic situation. The uses of data go beyond health sector in characterizing disease outbreak and designing appropriate health response strategies to other industry sectors too. Some examples of how data can help during a pandemic crisis are summarized as follows:

- Data held by the tech and telecom sectors can be helpful to track people's movements, predict the spread of the pathogen, identify vulnerable populations and anticipate public health needs. Surveillance data are crucial for understanding the pattern of transmission to plan appropriate response activities, following the subsequent roll-out of interventions, continued evaluation to detect reductions in transmission, and assess the relative impact of different interventions (Cori et al., 2017).

■ Data held by financial service organizations such as banks and insurance companies, and payment processors can assist in making the most efficient decisions to rebuild the economy.

■ Point of sale (POS) data held by retail grocery stores can be used in understanding consumer behavior and buying trends and facilitating in making decisions related to supply chain management.

■ Genome data can facilitate clinical advancements in risk prediction, diagnosis, treatment options, and outcomes.

■ Clinical data can facilitate understanding the severity of the disease, build clinical case definition, assess pharmaceutical interventions, and monitor consequences of the disease (Salje et al., 2020; Kraemer et al., 2021).

■ Serological data are essential in illustrating immunity, antibody responses and how they may link to clinical outcomes (Kucharski et al., 2020; Kraemer et al., 2021).

■ Metadata associated with individual epidemiological cases can be crucial to comprehend early disease dynamics and crucial transitions from imported infections to those locally acquired (Kraemer et al., 2020; Kraemer et al., 2021).

■ Disease data that contain demographic information can be and have been used widely to figure out population level attack rates (Rodriguez-Barraquer et al., 2019; Kraemer et al., 2021).

Big Data Sources and Pandemic Management

Sophisticated analysis tools and technologies have enabled the use of big data sources to assist pandemic prevention. Examples of these sources and examples of usage of data in the COVID-19 pandemic are as follows (Qiong et al., 2020):

■ Internet of Things (IoT) data—The Internet of Things (IoT) refers to a large number of devices embedded with sensors and people connected to the internet all collecting and sharing information. These devices include radio frequency identification (RFID), infrared sensors, global positioning systems, laser scanners, motion sensors, smart meters, and other information sensing devices. By exchange and transmission of information, IoT can be used for the intelligent identification, placement, tracing, monitoring, and management of goods (Atzori et al., 2017). Sensors can transmit a large amount of static and dynamic data in real-time (Li et al., 2013). These data include real-time status data, location data, personal data, and user feedback data. With respect to the COVID-19 pandemic, in the medical environment, real-time status data regarding patients, medical staff, and hospitals will generate a large amount of real-time data (Qiong et al., 2020).

To identify disease cases of COVID-19 in the community, IoT can also collect facial recognition data and conduct accurate infrared thermal imaging screening to check if people wear masks or not and body temperature so as to provide early warning [Xinzhixun]. Personalized behavior data and user feedback data that come from the contactless retail data of unmanned superstores supported by the IoT technology, also provides a data source for analyzing consumer behaviors during the COVID-19 pandemic (Qiong et al., 2020).

■ Mobile device data—Mobile device data mainly refer to data generated through mobile phones, and it can be used track people's movements. GPS coordinates obtained from mobile phone data assist professionals to trace whether individuals have been in contact with already infected individuals. This helps identify and isolate these people and test them in advance and treat them in case they have got infected. The mobile data of the infected population not only helps to understand the overall situation during the outbreak, but it also helps us predict how the disease will spread in future outbreaks and understand which interventions are the most effective (Wesolowski et al., 2016).

■ Social media data—The development of social media platforms such as Facebook, Twitter, Weibo, and WeChat provide a new stream of big data to carry out disease prevention and control (Althouse et al., 2015). Crowdsourced social media data can influence intermediations, inferences, and decisions of the authorities during a pandemic (Yigitcanlar et al., 2020).

■ Navigation search engine and e-commerce data—Navigation and search engine data are not directly related to medical treatment or disease diagnosis, but their potential information can reflect the development of the disease and can capture people's attention toward some diseases, and hence are an important source of disease prevention and control (Qiong et al., 2020).

■ Large scale genetic data—Efficient genome sequencing methods can amass enormous amounts of data to assist in-depth analysis of mutant micro-organisms in real time (Zhou et al., 2020). The genetic data from pathogens play a vital role in the discovery of the source of the pathogen, development of drug and vaccine, and medical diagnosis.

One constraint and challenge of big data and related data collection is that the misrepresentation of complicated social realities can result in hazardous consequences for public health and human rights. This means that while technology may facilitate the collection and analysis of digital data, an absence of access to the information behind these trends can lead to bad decisions (Qiong et al., 2020). For example, the 2014 to 2016 Ebola epidemic in West Africa demonstrated miscalculation using big data, with inappropriate assumptions on people's movements from call records [Toh]. Therefore, big data applications for preventing diseases must use careful research design and technologies from skilled and experienced professionals (Qiong et al., 2020).

Use of External Data and Data Sharing in a Pandemic

The COVID-19 pandemic has shown by example how quickly an organization's internal data (that is data generated/captured within an organization) can become obsolete. It has also shown the relevance and use of external data (that is, third-party data, or data that has been generated/captured, processed, and provisioned from outside the organization) in dealing with the impacts of the pandemic. Organizations consider external data "very valuable," particularly during uncertain market conditions (Explorium, 2021).

The COVID-19 pandemic has brought significant and rapid changes. For example, consumer behavior such as product preferences and purchasing patterns have changed drastically. This has resulted in rendering pre-existing consumer research, forecasts, and predictive models obsolete. Also, the internal data that these models and research were based on are of little value as they do not reflect these new patterns (Aaser and McElhaney, 2021).

However, every cloud has a silver lining. There is a wealth of external data that can help organizations plan and respond at a granular level (Aaser and McElhaney, 2021). Companies are using a large variety of external data such as foot traffic, product placement, pricing data, firmographics, technographics, and other marketing and financial attributes to improve their predictive models. Third-party data is used to strengthen analytical and machine learning models which predict demand, understand consumer behavior, improve conversion rates, assess risk, and detect fraud (Explorium, 2021).

Sharing data about both the pathogen and the disease allows the scientific and academic communities, and professionals from all disciplines, to assess, compare, and test new hypotheses as the disease progresses. The information and knowledge are also key to reducing uncertainty and making sure that more and more people take the essential precautions. In case of COVID-19 pandemic, Johns Hopkins University's global map, built with data reported daily by each country, is a good example of how to visualize data to make it easily understandable. Sharing data is a critical resource for scientists, doctors, researchers, and big data experts battling against time to help limit the spread of the disease (Straface, 2020).

External data sources have massive potential. However, there are numerous challenges associated with them. Gaining a fundamental understanding of what data is available requires substantial effort. This is because the external data environment is fragmented and growing rapidly. Thousands of data products can be acquired through a variety of channels, such as data brokers, data aggregators, and analytics platforms. Analysis of the quality and determination of economic value of data products can be tough. The effective usage and operationalization of external data may need changes in the organization's existing data environment, including changes to systems and infrastructure. Companies also need to be aware of privacy concerns and consumer scrutiny when they use certain types of external data and need adequate data governance processes around ingesting, maintaining, and using these data (Aaser and McElhaney, 2021).

Data partnerships can be formed to share data. However, these partnerships must come with boundaries. What data is shared with which entity and how long the entity should have access to the data should be defined, and data sharing should not be done at the cost of violation of security and/or privacy. Even if a data partnership is built around crisis response, the stakeholders should hold each other accountable for using data for mutually agreed upon goals, including maintaining proper governance and controls (Compton, 2020).

Data Challenges in a Pandemic—COVID-19 as an Example

While data can help manage a pandemic, there are challenges associated with data collected and used to manage the crisis as shown in Figure 5.1.

Data Collection

Data collection comprises data collected through electronic devices (such as sensors and mobile devices), IoT as well as manual data collection.

Electronic devices and IoT has resulted in the generation of huge volumes of data at unprecedented rates, and availability of high capacity storage at low cost has enabled capture and storage of these large volumes of data on a daily basis. These vast volumes of data are produced from a large number of sources. It is important to ascertain the credibility of the data sources and to use data only from authoritative sources. Also, it is necessary to understand how and when the data was captured, the metadata, and whether the data were transformed in some way before storing them. It might also be needed to filter out the noise before using the data for analysis purposes. This is reinforced by Matt Holzapfel, solutions lead at Tamr, when he states (Woodie, 2020):

> "With so much COVID-19 data flying around, it's best to take the data with a grain of salt, especially at this stage of the crisis. . . . I think there are enough sources of data to see the ranges of predictions and use those ranges in order to establish some level of

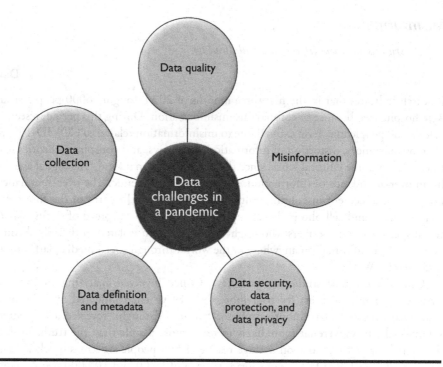

Figure 5.1   Data challenges in a pandemic.

confidence in what the range should be. I think trying to use the data to come up with absolute claims is a wasted exercise." . . . "Skeptical data consumers could learn from enterprise in how they approach new data sets. In that respect, COVID-19 data is no different than any other piece of data that an enterprise is used to dealing with."

Matt Holzapfel continues (Woodie, 2020):

"If someone gives you a data set, one of your first questions is where did you get it from and what did you do to it," . . . "I think we need much more transparency with regard to this [COVID-19] data to understand it. If people are taking out things that they consider outliers, we should know that, because the raw data is very powerful."

In public health, critical surveillance systems remain chiefly based on manually collected and coded data, which are slow to collect and hard to distribute. Traditional health surveillance systems are notorious for severe time lags and lack of spatial resolution, and there is critical need for robust systems that can collect and disseminate data in a timely fashion (Bansal et al., 2016).

The pandemic presents an unprecedented opportunity to leverage diverse, real-world data sources to inform medical and regulatory responses to the public health emergency. However, using this type of real-world data may not be simple. It requires high-quality data collection and appropriate procedural considerations. There are established guidelines on how best to plan, execute, and report observational studies in a way that ensures the validity and relevance of the evidence gathered (Berger et al., 2017). Yet researchers and clinicians can sometimes disregard those guidelines, specifically during a health crisis in which the rush to publish has given birth to some dubious research practices, according to some observers. However, the necessity for speed should not come at the cost of procedural rigor and detail (Dolgin, 2020).

Misinformation

"The truth is out there (if only if I could find it)."

—**Dana Mckay**

Research indicates that in the first three months of 2020, roughly 6000 people around the globe were hospitalized because of coronavirus misinformation. During this period, researchers state that at least 800 people may have expired due to misinformation related to COVID-19*(WHO, 2021).

Gossip, rumors, distortion of information, fake news, and conspiracy theories have been intricately woven in the cultural fabric since the beginning of mankind. The digital age is characterized by an over-abundance of information, also called an infodemic. The over-abundance of information and advancement in communication technologies in the form of the Internet, social media and telephone and cell phones have amplified the problem of spread of misinformation at exceptional speed. Rumor-mongers who might once have been isolated in their local communities can now propagate information anywhere in the world, through social media platforms and the world wide web (WWW).

One of the largest studies on fake news (which involved analyzing around 126,000 stories tweeted by 3 million users for over more than 10 years), conducted by MIT professors Sinan Aral, Deb Roy, and Darthmouth professor Soroush Vosoughi, revealed a very interesting observation—false news were far more likely to reach more people than the truth. In their study, they discovered that a false story on average reaches 1,500 people six times quicker than a true story, and that the top 1% of false news spreads to around 1,000 and 100,000 people while a true story seldom reaches more than 1,000 people (Carballido et al., 2021).

One of the downsides of the digital age is that infodemics spread like wildfire. They trigger uncertainty and insecurity, which in turn promote skepticism and distrust. This results in an environment, where negativity, fear, anxiety, finger-pointing, stigma, violent aggression, and dismissal of proven public health measures are rife—which can lead to loss of life (WHO, 2021).

With the COVID-19 pandemic, more people are working from home or being isolated. This has resulted in further amplification of the spread of misinformation as people are spending more time on the Internet and social media. With a lot of credible information, partisan bias, disinformation, and misinformation (see Figure 5.2), people are facing the problem of information overload and finding it difficult to distinguish fact from fiction.

Misinformation vs. Disinformation

These two terms that are merely one letter apart, are often used interchangeably. Both are wrong information, the only distinguishing factor being the intent.

Misinformation is false information that is spread, regardless of intent to mislead.

Disinformation is intentionally misleading or biased information; manipulated narrative or facts; propaganda. Hence, disinformation is intentionally spreading misinformation (Dictionary.com).

People tend to share misinformation without validating, with countless number of people, compounding the problem and creating a viral effect. Misinformation, disinformation, and propaganda are shared on social networks and diffuse rapidly across all media types using automation technologies such as social bots and organized activities coordinated by malicious entities. Misinformation and disinformation circulating on the internet and social media and going viral, form one of the major challenges to combating the COVID-19 pandemic. In fact, the spread of misinformation has become the second pandemic. The World Health Organization (WHO) has warned that the world is fighting a viral pandemic as well as an "infodemic."

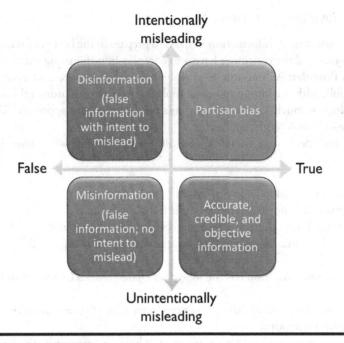

Figure 5.2 Different types of information.

Source: Adapted from Butcher (2021)

Misinformation and disinformation range from misinterpreted understandings of the disease itself, wishful thinking about miracle cures and preventive medicines, and fanciful implications drawn on how the spread of the virus will play out. Some of the misinformation with regard to COVID-19 are as follows (Samios, 2020; Newman, 2020):

■ Make sure that your mouth and throat are continuously moist.
■ Stomach acid can kill coronavirus.
■ It is just the flu.
■ 5G network caused COVID-19.
■ Drinking hot drinks in large quantities stops COVID-19.
■ Drinking alcohol reduces the risk of infection.
■ China created COVID-19 as a biological weapon.
■ At least 60 percent of the population needs to be exposed to the virus, to build up "necessary resistance" to it.
■ Chloroquine is a cure for COVID-19.
■ Anyone who contracts COVID-19 will die.
■ Children are immune to COVID-19.
■ Spraying chlorine or alcohol on the skin kills viruses in the body.
■ Coronavirus can be killed by hand dryers.
■ Flu and pneumonia vaccines can give protection against COVID-19.
■ Coronavirus can be killed by antibiotics.
■ Garlic protects against coronaviruses.
■ The virus will get killed, when temperatures increase in the spring.
■ Injecting or consuming bleach or disinfectant kills coronavirus.
■ Vaccines can alter human DNA.

What Could Have Been Done Better

It is important to have correct information in hand to prepare in the best possible manner. Both the information provider and the consumer have a role to play in minimizing information overload.

Information Provider: An important approach to limiting the spread of a contagious disease is to provide the public with the information and tools, so that they can protect themselves effectively. However, providing as much information as possible isn't the best approach. The 19th century proverbial phrase—"Less is more" applies here.

Information providers need to think carefully along the following lines before providing information:

■ How will the information be useful in combating the disease?
■ How to convey the information in a simple but clear fashion?
■ Who does the information apply to; that is, who is the recipient of the information?
■ Under what circumstances, when, and what action items are expected?

The most effective communication has the following characteristics (as shown in Figure 5.3):

1. Completeness—omission of information can impact the effectiveness of the information and trigger incorrect decisions.
2. Accuracy—the message should accurate and not based on assumptions.

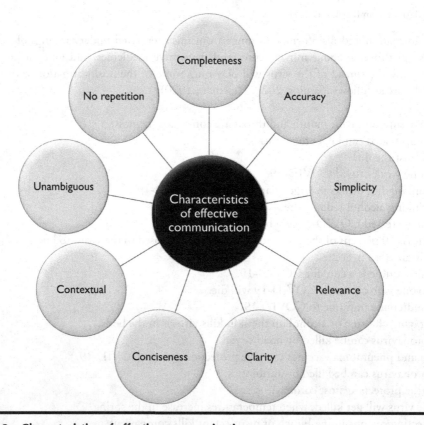

Figure 5.3 Characteristics of effective communication.

3. Simplicity—the message should be simple.
4. Relevance—the message should be relevant.
5. Conciseness—the message should be crisp.
6. Clarity—the message should be clear.
7. Contextual—there should be context associated with the message.
8. Free of ambiguity.
9. No repetition.

Consumer: Consumers should process and consume information sensibly (McKay, 2020).

Consumers should resist forwarding every message or email that they get. They should look at the source of information and determine the trustworthiness of the source before accepting it.

Consumer need to thoughtful and consider about how much information they consume and when, and whether the information increases or decreases their anxiety.

Fake news sites can be spotted with the help of tools such as Hoaxy. Hoaxy is an online tool, which is accessible to everyone and that helps people visualize the spread of claims and fact-checking online. Many Chrome extensions have been built with an ability to alert and assist in the filtration of fake news. Popular websites like Snopes and FactCheck.org can also help detect the most egregious fake stories (Marr, 2017).

Data Quality

Pandemic brings with it a world of chaos and uncertainty. While data can provide a good base to fight a pandemic, collection of data in chaotic and uncertain times that are brought about by a pandemic, is fraught with challenges around different dimensions of data quality such as accuracy, completeness (missing data), validity, consistency, data coverage, relevance, timeliness, and reliability as shown in Figure 5.4. Data entered by human beings are subject to error, resulting in missing, biased, invalid (data that does not conform to defined format or definition standards), and/or inaccurate data. There is also a risk of manipulation of data. The risk of bad data being entered increases where resource strength is low or resources making the entry are not data savvy and/or do not understand the context. Also, data collection might not be standardized; hence, data sets holding the same information may not be consistent with respect to format and structure. Hence, combining data sets for analysis and modeling purposes is difficult.

For example, COVID-19 data that have been reported, differs pointedly from country to country, and even from state to state. Some reports include possible positives in their numbers, while others do not. Many reports classify COVID-19 cases by severity or demographics, but do not use the same parameters to do so. Change in computation methodologies half-way through results in discrepancies within the same data set. The equivalence of the data may also be impacted by divergent testing approaches.

Data manipulation has been identified as a key marker of COVID-19 corruption, with some statistics, having been massaged to reveal a rosier version of reality (Buguzi et al., 2021). In the absence of a consistent reporting standard, the underlying data points that support COVID-19 projection models aren't necessarily reliable. Effective data governance is a must to ensure that process of capturing, processing, and reporting data is standardized across entities.

Data sets should have appropriate coverage, that is they must include data of a sufficient number of people to make it representative and reliable, to avoid biased or inaccurate results. However, a pandemic is an emergency situation, and data are usually collected without proper planning. Hence, the data set might not be a true representative of the pandemic and might not have sufficient

Figure 5.4   Data quality challenges in a pandemic.

coverage to draw correct inferences. Also, the data set might not contain all the relevant information necessary for analysis.

The trustworthiness of big data has always been highly controversial due to data completeness, accuracy, credibility, consistency, and validity problems. The big data sources for the control of COVID-19 also have these drawbacks and seldom capture the complexity of all social dynamics everywhere. Massive amounts of data are generated online with the incessant spreading of the disease, but the value is buried under the noise in the data. Therefore, the raw data needs to be pre-processed to remove the noise, before it can be used.

Data smoothing or removing noise from the data needs to be done correctly; smoothing done incorrectly introduces error in the data. In his article—"5 Wrong Ways to Do COVID-19 Data Smoothing", Steve McConnell states that one common mistake when doing data smoothing is that, in many cases, states dump weeks or months' worth of corrections into the data pool on one day resulting in a sudden spike on that particular day, which is not correct. The recommendation is to have smoothing period of 7 days (McConnell, 2020).

Ungoverned data need considerably more time and effort to prepare for analysis. When the insights are only needed for a crisis scenario and are one-off, a complete data governance refit is impractical, so it is best to prioritize pre-processing the source data that is needed to meet specific project requirements. However, if the organizational data governance maturity level is low, data are not treated as an asset, the data are critical, and uses of data go beyond crisis scenario, this should be taken as an opportunity to develop a business case and strategy to institute effective data governance in the organization.

Pre-processing includes data cleaning, data linking, matching, consolidation, transformation, and the reduction of missing and noisy data is necessary (Petrov, 2020). However, this is a cost-intensive exercise, and before investing in this work, organizations should also identify the areas where big data could provide value for controlling the disease, confirm the reputation of the data sources, estimate the quality of the data and impact of poor-quality data, and determine the investment amount. Accountable and authoritative institutions may rather provide cleaned and reliable data directly. For example, the public Github repository maintained by the Johns Hopkins University Center for Systems Science and Engineering has developed to become a standard resource for individuals (Qiong et al., 2020).

With reference to the COVID-19 pandemic, Phaik Yeong Cheah, Associate Professor at the University of Oxford, Head of the Department of Bioethics and Engagement at the Bangkok-based Mahidol Oxford Tropical Medicine Research Unit, makes the following statement (Slaughter, 2020):

> Data quality is a huge issue in COVID-19 because it is such a new disease. People collect data very, very differently because it's not a disease that everybody understands.

With reference to the COVID-19 pandemic, visual journalist Davide Mancino during a webinar with Stella Roque, ICFJ's Director of Community Engagement, as part of ICFJ's Global Health Crisis Reporting Forum stated (Dorroh, 2020):

> Exact figures on those infected don't exist, and during this rapidly unfolding crisis, even solid estimates are tough to come by.

Other conversations around COVID-19 data are as follows (Dorroh, 2020; Henderson, 2020):

- "In an ideal world we would test anybody to see who is infected, but we can't do that because there is no infrastructure in place anywhere in the world. Even if we could, one-time tests would not be enough. People can always be infected later. They would need to get tested several times over until a vaccine or a cure is found. Tests are never 100% accurate".
- "Healthcare systems in some countries have been overrun by the outbreak, and could not keep track of everybody even if they wanted to".
- "Since COVID-19 emerged late last year, there's been an enormous amount of research produced on this novel coronavirus disease. But the content publicly available for this data and the format in which it's presented lack consistency across different countries' national public health institutes, greatly limiting its usefulness, Children's National Hospital scientists report in a new study".
- "The prospects of finding the same types of formats that would allow us to aggregate information, or even the same types of information across different sites, was pretty dismal"—Dr. Emmanuèle Délot, Ph.D., Research Faculty at Children's National Research Institute.

These conversations highlight some of the issues around accuracy, completeness, and consistency of data collected to manage the COVID-19 pandemic.

For the discussion of missing data challenges due to the COVID-19 complications, it is worth revisiting the definition of missing data according to the ICH E9 addendum (ICH, 2019): "Data that would be meaningful for the analysis . . . but were not collected. They should be distinguished from data that do not exist or data that are not considered meaningful because of an intercurrent event." It is of importance that missing data relates to data that would be meaningful if it had been collected. Missing data not only leads to loss of information, but it can also introduce selection bias. Therefore, appropriate missing data handling approaches aligned with the plausible sensitivity analyses need to be specified (Akacha et al., 2020).

There is poor data on testing availability, and testing results are too often incorrect, delayed, or not counted (Davenport et al., 2020). While a lot of data are being collected from different data sources for COVID-19 research, the quality of the data is questionable. This is reinforced by Chris Moore, Director of Solution Engineering at Trifacta when he states (Woodie, 2020):

> It's been great to see the growing number of datasets that have been made available for COVID research and response efforts. Unfortunately, a lot of this data has questionable quality and underlying structural issues. It's also critical to have a solid understanding around the context of the data—how it was assembled, metadata around each feature, when it was last updated, etc.

Chris Moore continues (Woodie, 2020):

> With so much data flying around that's of questionable quality, decision-makers should approach the data carefully. It's especially important to investigate the data's quality if it's going to be used for machine learning purposes.

The importance of collecting quality data related to the pandemic is not to be taken lightly as at the heart of analytics is good data. Absence of quality data can put data integrity, trial integrity and clinical trial interpretability at risk, and most likely impact future submissions (Akacha et al., 2020). Data integrity is defined as the extent to which all trial data are complete, consistent, accurate, trustworthy, and reliable throughout the data lifecycle (WHO, 2019).

It is also important to understand the context in which the data are to be used. Data suitable for one purpose might not be suitable for another purpose. It is also recommended to compare data sets containing same data elements and similar information from different sources. If the data across different data sets are not consistent, the accuracy of the data sets becomes questionable. In case one data set for a source contains data significantly different for other similar data sets from other sources, then the accuracy and validity of that one data set becomes questionable. This is reinforced by Chris Moore in his email to *Datanami* (Woodie, 2020):

> Decision-makers should make sure that they understand the context of the data they're using before they can confidently make decisions off of it. I also recommend that people try to compare datasets provided by different outlets. If there's a dataset that shows trends that massively differ from multiple others that contain similar information then it might put into question the validity of that dataset.

Data Definition and Metadata

While a lot of data have been collected and continues to be collected from different sources to fight the COVID-19 pandemic, one of the major issues is the lack of clarity and consistency of data definitions, which can result in reporting and formatting discrepancies. For example, in the US, basic data on numbers of cases and "death due to coronavirus" are reported in a different manner by different states. Some states report presumed cases and deaths, while others do not. Some states report on cases and deaths of non-residents that occur in the state or in long-term care facilities, prisons, and business sites—and others do not (Davenport et al., 2020). This is because the definitions of what constitutes a case and what constitutes a death in relation to COVID-19 is not consistent or not clear. It is very important to have an international agency that defines data definition standards and data definition for collection of different data elements in relation to a new disease and pandemic. This will ensure that data collected all over the world in relation to a new disease and pandemic will be consistent.

It is also extremely important to have a record of what the data are about, that is, metadata to be able to make the best use of data. However, metadata is not always collected, limiting the reusability of the data. Asked whether there are "low-hanging fruit" to improve the response to the pandemic, Max Roser, Program Director of the research program at the University of Oxford, "Our World in Data" (which maintains a global database on testing for COVID-19) stated: "for all those who publish original data, provide a clear description of your data" (@MaxCRoser: 1:39 am · April 12, 2020 · Twitter Web App) (Schriml et al., 2020).

For example, with COVID-19, describing the WHO, WHAT, HOW, WHERE, and WHEN of genomic data makes possible comparative analysis, informs public health responses, drives assessment of outbreak progression and reveals variation in the host-specificity, modes of transmission, and sample collection protocols. The cost of imperfectly defining information about the human host and collection procedure from genomic studies is more than just the missing fields in a biological sample or nucleotide sequence record. Loss of critical genomics data reduces the short-term as well as long-term utility of the data and hampers clinical advancements in risk prediction, diagnosis, treatment options, and outcomes (Schriml et al., 2020).

It is crucial to create and use guidelines that help standardization of the dataset as well as the metadata associated with it (Ferguson et al., 2014; Callahan et al., 2017; Rafael et al., 2020). This need has led to the creation of the Findable, Accessible, Interoperable, and Reusable (FAIR) principles (Wilkinson, 2016), which are a set of guidelines capable of regulating both data and metadata regardless of area of study, with the main focus of enhancing the reusability of data (Rafael et al., 2020).

In the Global.health initiative, a standardized format for epidemiological data (Xu et al., 2020) has been decided on by different regional working groups after conferring with a number of individuals, groups, and organizations such as public health agencies, academic research groups, and health policy experts. The intent of conducting these interviews was to identify a format that could house most use cases, empower rapid decision-making, and decrease time needed to clean data. This included undertaking a data mapping exercise where data were mapped to a common geographic reference frame. International partnerships, as well as sharing of testing protocols and local expertise, were crucial to define a standard. Since standards would continue to evolve with time, these partnerships must continue in the future to ensure that there are usable standards available for the community. A standardized format was also developed with extensibility in mind, although this needs to be revised in a timely manner, to ensure that the resources in place can include pathogen-specific information from other infectious diseases (Kraemer et al., 2021).

Data Security, Data Protection, and Data Privacy

Before we delve into this topic, we will distinguish between the closely related terms data security, data protection, and data privacy.

Data security is the process of protecting data from any kind of action that can compromise the data such as unauthorized access, corruption, theft, and distribution (Mahanti, 2021a).

The term data protection is often used interchangeably with data security. It can be considered as the same as data security, in the context of protecting the data from being accessed by unauthorized users. On the other hand, data protection may also be used for protecting the data from viewpoint of authorized users, so that these data can be accessed easily later (Difference Between, 2019; Mahanti, 2021a).

Data privacy is often confused with data security. Data privacy and data security are very closely interconnected, so much so that they are often thought of as being the same. Data security is more of a technical issue, whereas data privacy is a legal one. While data can be protected by means of technology, the protected data still may not be suitably private (Mahanti, 2021a).

Occurrences of data breaches, phishing scams, ransomware attacks, fake news, and scams targeting government, health care, and individuals significantly increased in early 2020, when the COVID-19 pandemic spread rapidly and went out of control (Interpol, 2020). In the initial days of COVID-19, there was a 400% increase in cyberattacks reported to the FBI (MonsterCloud, 2020).

With the pandemic leading to an increase in the amount of data being collected about various aspects of people such as health, finances, and locations, people are growing increasingly wary of how secure their information is, who has access to it, and how it is used. A study uncovered that 79% of individuals want to be notified when their data is shared (Kerry and Morris, 2019).

Data governance helps establishing processes to determine the need and usage of the data, who is accountable and responsible for the data, what are security concerns around the data and implementing processes and controls throughout the life cycle of the data to capture, process, manage, secure, access, distribute, and archive/purge the data. These activities can ensure more effective and ethical use of data even during crisis situations such as a pandemic. For example, in the COVID-19 app of the UK National Health Service (NHS), the Department of Health and Social Care, NHS England, and NHS Improvement are the authorized data controllers that determine the intent of data collection, whether data should be further shared, the period for which the app can hold the data, and more [NHS England].

It is also important to be transparent about data collection and their usage with an option for citizens to be able to control both what data are collected and how they are used. Such transparency increases trust and enables citizens to decide how much data they are willing to share and for what purposes (Eggers et al., 2020). Widespread collection of personal data to combat and contain COVID-19 spread has also brought to attention the urgent need for stronger data privacy laws. For example, the federal COVID-19 privacy bill—the Public Health Emergency Privacy Act was introduced in the US Congress to help ensure transparency of data collection after user consent, and restriction on data usage (Schwartz, 2020).

Data governance needs to be deployed across the entire business to ensure that data is appropriated managed and secured while protecting individuals' privacy. After the mandatory privacy controls are incorporated, and the data have been evaluated by the right teams, external data can then be ingested into the organization and be used to assist in prediction of behaviors (Dard, 2021)

While technologies such as artificial intelligence (AI), big data and Internet of Things (IoT) appear to be the best possible tools for assessing, controlling, and mitigating a pandemic, researchers can't always have access to the data needed to build these models due to data privacy restrictions.

This is reinforced by James Hendler, the Tetherless World Professor of Computer, Web, and Cognitive Science at Rensselaer Polytechnic Institute (RPI) and Director of the Rensselaer Institute for Data Exploration and Applications (IDEA), told HealthITAnalytics in his statements in relation to data access issues in relation to managing the COVID-19 pandemic (Kent, 2020):

The ideal data is hospital data that would tell us who is experiencing certain impacts from the virus. For example, one project we'd love to do would be to correlate environmental or genomic factors to the people who are getting advanced respiratory problems, which is what's killing most people with this disease. Is there a genetic component to that? Is it something where environmental factors are some kind of comorbidity? But can we can't get that kind of data because of HIPAA restrictions.

With the COVID-19 pandemic, governments and organizations have been compelled to change their ways of operation. They have had to align their actions not only to secure their own business operations but also to assist public authorities' decision-making, policy creation/modification, developing mandates, and emergency response activities with the help of relevant technologies, tools, resources, and personal data. Personal data are usually sensitive in nature, and need to be protected and used appropriately. Quite a lot of these activities have data privacy and data protection consequences and there have been concerns around the usage of data that are sensitive. Organizations have had to evaluate and quickly decide how to pursue new and beneficial uses of data, consistent with applicable data protection requirements, and ensure ethical usage of data. One common approach to protect privacy is by anonymizing data by encrypting, eliminating, or substituting sensitive data elements within the data sets, while still preserving the fundamental nature of the data set (Eggers et al., 2020).

In the pre-COVID-19 world and times, accessing and using data that have data privacy and data protection consequences would have been a time taking endeavor, requiring preceding assessments, reviews, and approvals by multiple stakeholders as well as by Data Protection Authorities (DPAs). DPAs have issued guidance on some COVID-19-related matters. However, there is no general or holistic guide for organizations to effectively adapt their interpretations of applicable data privacy and protection requirements to new data uses during times of crisis. Traditional analyses and interpretations of legal requirements, as well as specific data protection tools and measures, will still have to be adapted and updated (during the pandemic and after) to enable these new and beneficial data uses (CIPL, 2020).

In today's age of globalization, multinational organizations have offices and employees working in several countries that have different data privacy and protection regulations. An added, common challenge that these organizations face has been the need to ensure consistent and reliable rules and processes in battling COVID-19 for all of their global entities and workforce, when applicable privacy laws and data protection rules and regulations differ from country to country, or when the understanding of these laws, rules, and regulations is not consistent across the countries.

This challenge has become even more obvious as employees across the globe expect and demand organizations to take proactive measures to ensure their health and well-being in the midst of COVID-19 crisis. Organizations have struggled to decide on the most appropriate choice of legal basis for processing of employees' personal data, specifically in scenarios, when data privacy and protection laws require a legal base to process personal data. This is especially true when the relevant DPA interpretation of the legal basis has been constricted. This problem is aggravated when the data is considered "sensitive" and subject to additional restrictions that may obstruct certain usage and processing that may be necessary for health or employment purposes. Thus, organizations are under pressure to identify the suitable grounds for using and processing sensitive data when such grounds are very limited and interpreted narrowly by DPAs (CIPL, 2020).

A pandemic needs cross-jurisdictional as well as international harmonization to combat it. However, while some DPAs have taken a realistic stand in enabling the use of personal data for fighting the COVID-19 pandemic, other DPAs have not. For instance, some DPAs have taken conservative views on the use of employee personal data in the context of COVID-19. Some DPAs have even expressed concerns over the usage and sharing of anonymous data under the pretext that such data always presents a risk of re-identification. Such inconsistent approaches between global DPAs cause tension and confusion, in particular for multinational organizations that operate across multiple jurisdictions and countries and create uncertainties as to how data privacy laws apply to certain scenarios, such as contact tracing in cases involving multiple jurisdictions and the use of health data without explicit consent (CIPL, 2020).

The COVID-19 crisis highlights the need to further consider the balance between individual and collective interests and the relationship between competing rights, with respect to global data privacy and protection laws (CIPL, 2020). DPAs should confirm that when data privacy and protection laws allow scientific research to be exempted from some of the data protection law requirements (such as Article 89 of the GDPR), this exemption encompasses all organizations for data analytics, research and algorithmic training purposes (CIPL, 2020). Also, all the DPAs worldwide should get together and adopt a united approach with regard to sharing, processing, and usage of data to combat a pandemic crisis.

Appropriate governance policies, processes, standards, and controls need to set in relation to usage of data. It is also important to ensure that health surveillance measures and new technologies used to collect, disseminate, and use data in order to support the fight against the pandemic, does not prevail beyond the extreme circumstances created by the pandemic, so that people do not feel they are losing their privacy in a new world order (Zaimova, 2020). Michael Ryan, a key advisor for the World Health Organization (WHO), observed during a briefing on March 26, 2020, that there is a lot of excitement for using digital technologies, but cautioned that there are serious data-protection and human-rights principles involved in the collection and uses of information on citizens or tracing their movements, and that entities must never step beyond the principles of individual freedoms and rights (Nature.com, 2020).

Independent ethical boards or data trusts can be instituted for creation of data governance processes to find an appropriate balance between competing public interests, while protecting individual privacy. This will ensure that data are used ethically. Such data governance processes include setting up clear guidelines on the purpose of use of data and a definite timeline for the use of the data, defining policies, processes, guidelines, and rules for the access, usage, distribution, processing, retention, archiving, purging, and termination of use of personal data at the end of the crisis (Zaimova, 2020). Only legitimate entities should be allowed to collect and use the data, so long as their purpose is temporary, legitimate, and specific, and their processing of data meets the tests of need and balance.

With respect to data, constant monitoring by governments, citizens, and the private sector is necessary to ensure legal and ethical use of data while also addressing and resolving privacy concerns. For example, Estonia uses a contact-tracing app that protects citizen privacy according to guidelines from the European Data Protection Board. The private sector assisted in creation of this app (Numa, 2020). The Global Privacy Assembly, which consists of 30 data protection regulators across countries, launched a COVID-19 taskforce to attend to privacy concerns of governments as well as help foster innovation through data to fight the pandemic (Global Privacy Assembly, 2020; Eggers et al., 2020)

Concluding Thoughts

Data can be at the core of a pandemic response; it can enable rapid pandemic responses and this has been evident in the COVID-19 pandemic crisis. For example, the State of BI and Business

Analytics Report from Sisense shows that 45% of companies are using data to predict future outcomes in their COVID-19 response (Noor, 2020; Sisense, 2020).

While a pandemic is essentially a health crisis, the key data that need to collected and stitched together during a public health investigation for infectious disease management are not restricted to demographic and clinical data. Other important data may be serological data, pathogen genomic data, or non-epidemiological, spatial data that help illustrate the drivers of transmission which are generally, socio-economic, demographic, and ecological. The underlying process and standards of data capture or generation, the granularity of data across these different data sources and data types, and understanding the data, the context of usage, the data's feasibility and suitability for a particular study, the linkages and integrating them rationally, is a key for improving infectious disease research (Kraemer et al., 2021).

Data help driving the point home on where we are and what we should do. Good data leveraged by robust analytics can serve as a base for (but not limited to) socio-economic as well as political strategic planning for governments and business model development and resource planning for organizations.

Pandemic presents an exceptional prospect to leverage disparate, real-world data sources to prepare medical and regulatory responses to the public health emergency situation created by the pandemic. However, the need for speed should not be at the cost of not validating data sources and absence of methodological rigor in collection of data. This is reinforced by Almut Winterstein, a pharmacoepidemiologist from the University of Florida in Gainesville, when he states (Dolgin, 2020):

> That's [the] balance that needs to be maintained. On the one hand, you need real-world data in order to have complete evidence for decision making. But at the same token, you have to follow proper epidemiological methods and consider and address the biases in the data before making any causal inferences.

The globalized world connected with internet can rapidly generate and share a vast amount of data about a global crisis situation, as seen in the case of COVID-19. The rapid spread and life threatening consequences of COVID-19 pandemic and technological advancements have contributed to the breaking down of silos between research institutions, provider organizations, pharmaceutical companies, government agencies, and other healthcare bodies. However, whether the new surge in data sharing will become permanent is yet to be seen (Mixson, 2021).

With vast number of data sources and the large amount data, the quality of the data is a key differentiator. While good data can be converted into lifesaving knowledge through expertise, transparency, and application of analytics, bad data might lead to bad decisions.

Collecting certain data, such as detailed demographic characteristics of cases and contacts, costs money, time, and trained personnel. However, these three "resources" are usually limited even during normal circumstances, and even more so during a pandemic, and hence insights drawn and decision driven by the data should outweigh the costs to justify data collection.

While pandemic has wrought a lot of changes, resulting in the production of a lot of unusual data such as sudden spike in demand or disappearing demand, organizations should not totally disregard data from the pandemic period. These data can be used for forecasting similar disastrous events occur in the future. In the words of Thomas H. Davenport (Brown, 2021),

> I don't think you should throw that data away. But you should put the data and the resulting models on the shelf and say, "Okay, when something bad like this happens, let's bring them out again."

Walmart, the retail giant, which is known for its supply chain preparation during catastrophic situations, is already doing things like this (Brown, 2021).

One pressing need surfaced by the pandemic is digitization of services which will in turn provide even more data that needs to be analyzed at scale (Jaiani and Audet, 2020). While data provides a base to make informed decisions, it is the insights that are drawn from the data that help direct a path forward.

Data analytics is the analysis and consolidation of data of data from a number of heterogeneous sources to derive insights. Henke et al. (2020), in a McKinsey's report, suggest that such data analytics capabilities could offer between $9.5 trillion and $15.4 trillion in annual economic value to organizations. The next chapter discusses the role of data analytics in a pandemic.

References

Aaser, M., and McElhaney, D. (February 3, 2021) Harnessing the Power of External Data, *McKinsey Digital*, www.mckinsey.com/business-functions/mckinsey-digital/our-insights/harnessing-the-power-of-external-data

Althouse, B. M., Scarpino, S. V., Meyers, L. A., Ayers, J. W., Bargsten, M., Baumbach, J., Brownstein, J. S., Castro, L., Clapham, H., Cummings, D. A. T., et al. (2015) Enhancing Disease Surveillance With Novel Data Streams: Challenges and Opportunities. *EPJ Data Science*, 4, 17.

Akacha, M., Branson, J., Bretz, F., Dharan, B., Gallo, P., Gathmann, I., Hemmings, R., Jones, J., Xi, D., and Zuber, E. (2020) Challenges in Assessing the Impact of the COVID-19 Pandemic on the Integrity and Interpretability of Clinical Trials, *Statistics in Biopharmaceutical Research*, 12(4), 419–426, DOI: 10.1080/19466315.2020.1788984

Atzori, L., Iera, A., Morabito, G. (2017) Understanding the Internet of Things: Definition, Potentials, and Societal Role of a Fast Evolving Paradigm. *Ad Hoc Networks*, 56, 122–140.

Bansal, S., Chowell, G., Simonsen, L., Vesipignani, A., and Viboud, C. (December 2016) Big Data for Infectious Disease Surveillance and Modelling, *Journal of Infectious Diseases*, 214, S375–S379.

Berger, M. L., et al. (2017) Good Practices for Real-world Data Studies of Treatment and/or Comparative Effectiveness: Recommendations from the Joint ISPOR-ISPE Special Task Force on Real-world Evidence in Health Care Decision Making. *Pharmacoepidemiology and Drug Safety*, 26, 1033–1039.

Brown, S. (January 5, 2021) How COVID-19 is Disrupting Data Analytics Strategies, *MIT Sloan School of Management*, https://mitsloan.mit.edu/ideas-made-to-matter/how-covid-19-disrupting-data-analytics-strategies

Buguzi, S., Broom, F., Adriano, J., and Rueda, A. (April 2021) COVID-19, Lies and Statistics: Corruption and the Pandemic, *Phys.org provided by SciDev.Net*, Last accessed on September 30, 2021, https://phys.org/news/2021-04-covid-lies-statistics-corruption-pandemic.html

Butcher, P. (2021) COVID-19 as a Turning Point in the Fight Against Disinformation. *Nature Electron*, 4, 7–9, Last accessed on September 17, 2021, from https://doi.org/10.1038/s41928-020-00532-2.

Callahan, A., Anderson, K. D., Beattie, M. S., et al. (September 2017) Developing a Data Sharing Community for Spinal Cord Injury Research. *Experimental Neurology*, 295, 135–143.

Carballido, A., Yáñez Soria, I., and Ortiz, S. (February 2, 2021) Fighting Misinformation with Big Data and Artificial Intelligence, *Data-Pop Alliance—Links We Like*, Last accessed on May 17, 2021, from https://datapopalliance.org/lwl-24-fighting-misinformation-with-big-data-and-artificial-intelligence/.

CIPL (June 2, 2020) Looking Beyond COVID-19: Future Impacts on Data Protection and the Role of the Data Protection Authorities, last accessed on November, 20, 2020, from www.informationpolicycentre.com/uploads/5/7/1/0/57104281/cipl_remarks_-_looking_beyond_covid-19_-_future_impacts_on_data_protection_and_the_role_of_data_protection_authorities__2_june_2020_.pdf

Compton, J. (December 30, 2020) How the Pandemic Has Underscored the Value of External Data, *Forbes*, www.forbes.com/sites/tableau/2020/12/16/data-sharing-in-the-covid-era/?sh=73662e13db21

Cori, A., et al. (2017) Key Data for Outbreak Evaluation: Building on the Ebola Experience. *Philosophical Transactions of the Royal Society*, 372, 20160371, DOI: 10.1098/rstb.2016.0371.

Dard, N. (June 11, 2021) Five Ways the Pandemic Changed Data Analytics for Good, *Privitar*, www.privitar.com/blog/five-ways-the-pandemic-changed-data-analytics-for-good/

Davenport, T. H., Godfrey, A. B., and Redman, T. C. (August 25, 2020) To Fight Pandemics, We Need Better Data, *MIT Sloan Management Review*, Last accessed on November, 20, 2020, from https://sloanreview.mit.edu/article/to-fight-pandemics-we-need-better-data/

Difference Between (2019) Difference Between Data Protection and Data Security, Last accessed on May 1, 2020, from www.differencebetween.info/difference-between-data-protection-and-data-security.

Dolgin, E. (November 2020) Core Concept: The Pandemic is Prompting Widespread Use—and Misuse—of Real-World Data, *Proceedings of the National Academy of Sciences*, 117(45), 27754–27758, DOI: 10.1073/pnas.2020930117, www.pnas.org/content/117/45/27754

Dorroh, J. (April 22, 2020) Key Quotes: A Story of Uncertainty: How to Deal with COVID-19 and Data, *The International Center for Journalists (ICFJ)*, Last accessed on November, 20, 2020, from www.icfj.org/news/key-quotes-story-uncertainty-how-deal-covid-19-and-data

Eggers, W. D., Chew, B., Nunes, N.-M., Davis, A., and Rodrigues, G. (2020) Seven Lessons COVID-19 Has Taught Us about Data Strategy, *Deloitte*, Last accessed on May 17, 2021, from https://www2.deloitte.com/us/en/insights/economy/covid-19/government-data-management-lessons.html.

Explorium (April 1, 2021) Seeking Context, Organizations Struggle with Fragmented External Data Market, *Yahoo Finance*, https://in.finance.yahoo.com/news/seeking-context-organizations-struggle-fragmented-150000241.html

Ferguson, A. R., Nielson, J. L., Cragin, M. H., et al. (November 2014) Big Data from Small Data: Data-sharing in the 'Long Tail' of Neuroscience. *Nat Neurosci*, 17(11), 1442–1447.

[Gartner Information Technology Glossary], *Big Data*, Last accessed on June 20, 2021, from www.gartner.com/en/information-technology/glossary/big-data.

Global Privacy Assembly (May 27, 2020) Global Privacy Assembly Launches COVID-19 Taskforce, https://globalprivacyassembly.org/global-privacy-assembly-launches-covid-19-taskforce/

Henderson, E. (August 20, 2020) Lack of Consistency in COVID-19-related Data could Harm Prevention Efforts, *News Medical Life Sciences*. www.news-medical.net/news/20200820/Lack-of-consistency-in-COVID-19-related-data-could-harm-prevention-efforts.aspx

Henke, N., Puri, A., and Saleh, T. (May 21, 2020) *Accelerating Analytics to Navigate COVID-19 and the Next Normal*, McKinsey & Company, Last accessed on May 17, 2020, from www.mckinsey.com/business-functions/mckinsey-analytics/our-insights/accelerating-analytics-to-navigate-covid-19-and-the-next-normal.

ICH (2019) Topic E9(R1) on Estimands and Sensitivity Analysis in Clinical Trials to the Guideline on Statistical Principles for Clinical Trials, Last accessed on November 20, 2020, from www.ich.org.

Interpol (August 4, 2020) Interpol Report Shows Alarming Rate of Cyberattacks during COVID-19. Last accessed on October 17, 2020, https://www.interpol.int/en/News-and-Events/News/2020/INTERPOL-report-shows-alarming-rate-of-cyberattacks-during-COVID-19

Jaiani, V., and Audet, R. (September 17, 2020) 8 Data Leaders on Leveraging Data During and After COVID-19, *GCN, Data Leaders Roundtable*, https://gcn.com/articles/2020/09/17/data-leaders-roundtable.aspx

Kent, J. (April 2, 2020) Understanding the COVID-19 Pandemic as a Big Data Analytics Issue, *Health IT Analytics*, Last accessed on 24 August 2020, from https://healthitanalytics.com/news/understanding-the-covid-19-pandemic-as-a-big-data-analytics-issue

Kerry, C. F., and Morris, J. B. (June 26, 2019) Why Data Ownership is the Wrong Approach to Protecting Privacy, *Brookings*. Last accessed on 24 August 2020, from https://www.brookings.edu/blog/techtank/2019/06/26/why-data-ownership-is-the-wrong-approach-to-protecting-privacy/

King, J. D., et al. (2013) A Novel Electronic Data Collection System for Large-Scale Surveys of Neglected Tropical Diseases. *PLOS ONE*, 8, e74570, DOI: 10.1371/journal. pone.0074570.

Kraemer, M. U. G., et al. (2020) The Effect of Human Mobility and Control Measures on the COVID-19 Epidemic in China. *Science*, 368, 493–497.

Kraemer, M. U. G., Scarpino, S. V., Marivate, V., et al. (2021) Data Curation During a Pandemic and Lessons Learned from COVID-19. *Nature Computational Science*, 1, 9–10. https://doi.org/10.1038/s43588-020-00015-6

Kucharski, A. J., and Nilles, E. J. (2020) Using Serological Data to Understand Unobserved SARS-CoV-2 Risk in Health-Care Settings. *Lancet Infectious Diseases*, 20, 1351–1352.

Li, X. L., Zhang, L., Li, K., Wang, Y. Y. (2013) A Data Allocation Strategy for Sensor of Internet of Things. *Computer Science Research and Development*, 50, 297–305.

Mahanti, R. (2021a) *Data Governance and Compliance: Evolving to Our Current High Stakes Environment*, Springer, number 978-981-33-6877-4

Mahanti, R. (2021b) *Data Governance and Data Management Contextualizing Data Governance Drivers, Technologies, and Tools*. Springer Book. DOI: 10.1007/978-981-16-3583-0; Print ISBN—978-981-16-3582-3

Marr, B. (March 1, 2017) Fake News: How Big Data and AI Can Help, *Forbes*, Last accessed on May 17, 2021, from www.forbes.com/sites/bernardmarr/2017/03/01/fake-news-how-big-data-and-ai-can-help/?sh=1d25aee270d5.

McConnell, S. (October 1, 2020) 5 Wrong Ways to Do Covid-19 Data Smoothing, *towards data science*, Last accessed on September 12, 2021, from https://towardsdatascience.com/five-wrong-ways-to-do-covid-19-data-smoothing-1538db6ff182

McKay, D. (2020) The Truth Is Out There (if only if I could find it), *Pursuit*, Last accessed on July 03, 2020, from https://pursuit.unimelb.edu.au/articles/the-truth-is-out-there-if-only-i-could-find-it

Mixson, E. (April 27, 2021) 3 Ways AI and Advanced Analytics are Being Used to Combat Covid-19, *AI Data and Analytics Network*. Last accessed on May 17, 2021, from www.aidataanalytics.network/data-science-ai/articles/3-ways-ai-and-advanced-analytics-are-being-used-to-combat-covid-19.

MonsterCloud (August 11, 2020) Top Cyber Security Experts Report: 4,000 Cyber Attacks a Day Since Covid-19 Pandemic, *PR Newswire*.

Nature.com (2020) Pandemic Data Challenges. *Nature Machine Intelligence*, 2, 193, https://doi.org/10.1038/s42256-020-0172-7, Last accessed on November 20, 2020, from www.nature.com/articles/s42256-020-0172-7

Newman, T. (November 8, 2020), Coronavirus Myths Explored, *Medical News Today*, Last accessed on September 2021, from www.medicalnewstoday.com/articles/coronavirus-myths-explored

[NHS England], NHS COVID-19 Data Store, Last accessed on September 9, 2020.

Noor, M. (September 2, 2020) Different Ways Business Analytics are Used in a Pandemic, *W University of Washington FOSTER Blog*. Michael G. Foster School of Business, University of Washington, Last accessed on November 20, 2020, from https://blog.foster.uw.edu/different-ways-business-analytics-used-pandemic/

Numa, A. (April 2020) How Do You Trace Covid-19 While Respecting Privacy? *E-estonia*.

Petrov, C. (2020) Big Data Satistics, Last accessed on February 17, 2020, from *Techjury*. https://techjury.net/stats-about/big-data-statistics/.

Qiong, J., Guo, Y., Wang, G., and Barne, S. J. (August 2020) Big Data Analytics in the Fight Against Major Public Health Incidents (Including COVID-19): A Conceptual Framework, August 2020. *International Journal of Environmental Research and Public Health*, 17(17): 6161. doi:10.3390/ijerph17176161

Polonsky, J. A., et al. (2019) Outbreak Analytics: A Developing Data Science for Informing the Response to Emerging Pathogens. *Philosophical Transactions of the Royal Society B*, 374, 20180276, http://dx.doi.org/10.1098/rstb.2018.0276

Rafael, S. R., Kenneth, I. Z., and Ming-Hua, Z. (2020) Data Sharing During COVID-19 Pandemic: What to Take Away. *Expert Review of Gastroenterology & Hepatology*, 14(12), 1125–1130, DOI: 10.1080/17474124.2020.1815533

Rodriguez-Barraquer, I., Salje, H., and Cummings, D. A. (2019) Opportunities for Improved Surveillance and Control of Dengue from Age-Specific Case Data, *eLife*, 8, e45474.

Salje, H., Tran Kiem, C., Lefrancq, N., Courtejoie, N., Bosetti, P., Paireau, J., Andronico, A., Hozé, N., Richet, J., Dubost, C.-L., Le Strat, Y., Lessler, J., Levy-Bruhl, D., Fontanet, A., Opatowski, L., Boelle, P.-Y., and Cauchemez, S. (2020) Estimating the Burden of SARS-CoV-2 in France. *Science*. 2020 Jul 10;369(6500):208-211. doi: 10.1126/science.abc3517. Epub 2020 May 13. Erratum in: Science. 2020 Jun 26;368(6498): PMID: 32404476; PMCID: PMC7223792.

Samios, Z. (March 23, 2020) The Other Viral Problem in the COVID-19 Pandemic: Online Misinformation, *The Sydney Morning Herald*, www.smh.com.au/business/companies/the-other-viral-problem-in-the-covid-19-pandemic-online-misinformation-20200318-p54bd3.html

Schriml, L. M., Chuvochina, M., Davies, N., et al. (2020) COVID-19 Pandemic Reveals the Peril of Ignoring Metadata Standards. *Scientific Data*, 7, 188, https://doi.org/10.1038/s41597-020-0524-5

Schwartz, A. (May 28, 2020) Two Federal COVID-19 Privacy Bills: A Good Start and a Misstep, *Electronic Frontier Foundation*.

Sisense (2020) State of BI and Business Analytics Report, Last accessed on January 17, 2021, www.sisense.com/whitepapers/state-of-bi-analytics-report-2020/.

Slaughter, L. S. (26 September, 2020) AI Acceleration of Vaccine Research Hinges on Data Quality, *University World News*, Last accessed on November, 20, 2020 www.universityworldnews.com/post.php?story=20200925161214927

Straface, F. (September 24, 2020) COVID-19: How Open Data Can Help Us Beat the Pandemic, *World Economic Forum*, Last accessed on November 20, 2020, from www.weforum.org/agenda/2020/09/covid-19-how-open-data-can-help-us-beat-the-pandemic/

[Toh] Toh, A., Big Data Could Undermine the COVID-19 Response, *Wired*, Last accessed on August 15, 2020, from www.wired.com/story/big-data-could-undermine-the-covid-19-response/

Wesolowski, A., Buckee, C. O., Engø-Monsen, K., and Metcalf, C. J. E. (2016) Connecting Mobility to Infectious Diseases: The Promise and Limits of Mobile Phone Data. *The Journal of Infectious Diseases*, 214, S414–S420.

WHO (2019) Guideline on Data Integrity—Working Document QAS/19.819, Last accessed on November, 20, 2020, from www.who.int/.

WHO (March 16, 2020) WHO Director-General's opening remarks at the media briefing on COVID-19 - 16 March 2020. Last accessed on July 1, 2021, from https://www.who.int/director-general/speeches/detail/who-director-general-s-opening-remarks-at-the-media-briefing-on-covid-19---16-march-2020

WHO (April 27, 2021) Fighting Misinformation in the Time of COVID-19, One Click at a Time, Last accessed on May 17, 2021, from www.who.int/news-room/feature-stories/detail/fighting-misinformation-in-the-time-of-covid-19-one-click-at-a-time.

Wilkinson, M. D., Dumontier, M., Aalbersberg, I. J., et al. (March 2016) The FAIR Guiding Principles for Scientific Data Management and Stewardship. *Scientific Data*, 15(3), 160018.

Woodie, A. (April 2020) Coming to Grips with COVID-19's Data Quality Challenges, *Datanami*, www.datanami.com/2020/04/21/coming-to-grips-with-covid-19s-data-quality-challenges/

[Xinzhixun], Why Does the "War Epidemic" Weapon Continue to be in Short Supply? Depth Analysis of Infrared Thermography Body Temperature Detection Industry Chain, Last accessed on February 10, 2020, from https://baijiahao. baidu.com/s?id=1658122236080361101&wfr=spider&for=pc.

Xu, B., Gutierrez, B., Mekaru, S., et al. (2020) Epidemiological Data from the COVID-19 Outbreak, Real-Time Case Information. *Scientific Data*, 7, 106. https://doi.org/10.1038/s41597-020-0448-0

Yigitcanlar, T., Kankanamge, N., Preston, A., et al. (2020) How Can Social Media Analytics Assist Authorities in Pandemic-Related Policy Decisions? Insights from Australian States and Territories. *Health Information Science and Systems*, 8(37), https://doi.org/10.1007/s13755-020-00121-9

Zaimova, R. (March 31, 2020) How Data Can Help Fight a Health Crisis Like the Coronavirus, *World Economic Forum*, last accessed on November 20, 2020, from www.weforum.org/agenda/2020/03/role-data-fight-coronavirus-epidemic/

Zhou, P., Yang, X. L., Wang, X. G., Hu, B., Zhang, L., Zhang, W., Si, H. R., Zhu, Y., Li, B., Huang, C. L., et al. (2020) A Pneumonia Outbreak Associated with a New Coronavirus of Probable Bat Origin. *Nature*, 579, 270–273.

Chapter 6

Data Analytics and Pandemic

"Hiding within those mounds of data is knowledge that could change the life of a patient, or change the world."

—Atul Butte

"Information is the oil of the 21st century, and analytics is the combustion engine."

—Peter Sondergaard

Pandemics and Data Analytics

Pandemics have attacked mankind since ancient ages, though the scale of impact has varied, with the density of population, the extent of globalization, and connectivity being the major influencers. The 1918 Spanish influenza pandemic, the most terrible pandemic in the 20th century, infected one-third of the world's population, and killed roughly 50 million people, recording more mortalities than World War I. Till the 20th century, manual tracing, investigator records, and hospital records were typically used to pinpoint outbreaks (The Economist, 2017, [National Center for Biotechnology Information]). However, these approaches are slow and not very efficient in predicting progress of infectious diseases.

In the early 1850s, as London fought a widespread increase in the number of cholera cases, John Snow—the founder of modern epidemiology—discerned cluster patterns of cholera cases around water pumps. This finding led scientists to combat pandemics by leveraging data for the first time, driving their efforts toward quantifying the risk, isolating and understanding the root cause, and formulating appropriate mitigation and response strategies (Sogn, 2020). We are presently in the 21st century which is the digital age and there has been a lot of technology advances since 1920s. The ability to collect, store, and process vast amounts of diversified data in a short time period, the availability of sophisticated technology to leverage data, and other technological advances are the main differences in fighting a pandemic in the present digital age from fighting pandemics that occured in the non-digital age, for example, the Spanish flu in the early 20th century and cholera outbreak in the 19th century.

DOI: 10.4324/9781003270911-6

On December 21, 2019, an artificial intelligence (AI) system operated by a Toronto-based startup called BlueDot spotted the earliest anomalies related to a mysterious pneumonia strain (that is, the COVID-19 disease) in Wuhan, China. The AI system examined more than one million articles in 65 languages and spotted a similarity to the 2003 SARS outbreak. On December 30, 2019, that is, only nine days later, the WHO alerted the wider public about the emergence of the new disease—COVID-19 (Sogn, 2020).

Taiwan leveraged big data analytics and communication technologies to foresee and proactively guide their citizens in the wake of the COVID-19 pandemic. They joined the data from the national health insurance database and the data from immigration and customs database to get real-time alerts about possibly infected individuals, and trace the spread of the COVID-19 infection (Verma, 2020).

Lorcan Malone, Analytics Institute Chief Executive, highlights the important role played by data analytics in a pandemic crisis. Lorcan Malone says:

> Data analytics have been brought front and centre because of the pandemic; we're all analysts now, because decision making based on guesswork won't cut it in a life or death situation. People are now demanding data-driven decisions, and data-driven decision making (O'Brien, 2020).

When the COVID-19 pandemic hit Qatar, leaders at Hamad Medical Corporation (HMC) relied comprehensively on data and analytics to make informed decisions on a whole lot of things such as capacity management, founding field hospitals, contact tracing, and even catering services. Ali Latif, MD, Executive Director, business intelligence, HMC, said (Cerner Corporation, 2020):

> Without the analytics, I think we would have been blind. We would have been in big trouble in terms of preparedness. The analytics told our leaders how much we needed to expand services, and I think it was crucial in responding well to the pandemic.

Quick and accurate data analytics backed by good quality data that can locate outbreaks and forecast progression of a disease is a key to fighting infectious diseases. As per response of an Economist Intelligence Unit survey, sponsored by SAS, 73% believed that data analytics will help prevent future pandemics. In addition, approaches such as mobile-phone tracking and data mining of search engines and social media can help deliver a faster, more refined picture of where diseases are unfolding and might head to next (The Economist, 2017). When asked by the Economist what technology would have the biggest impact on their recovery from the impacts of the COVID-19 pandemic, Canadian executives identified digital data collection (46 percent) and the use of analytics to inform decisions (42 percent) (Baker, 2020).

One similarity across companies who are surviving the pandemic is a mature analytics foundation (Baker, 2020; [Farrell]). The COVID-19 pandemic has proved data analytics as a must-have capability for organizations. According to the Retail and Consumer Goods Analytics Study, COVID-19 has had a substantial impact on analytics usage in both small and large companies with 52 percent stating their analytic resources shifted or changed so that they could react more quickly or analyze faster (Ganji, 2020).

Data analytics can help businesses design their investment portfolio by determining the products, services, capital projects, markets, and people to invest in; determine which disruptive events might necessitate a modification in strategy, monitor for irregularities and patterns that may reveal a threat or opportunity, and determine the best actions to take if these disruptive events occur (RS&F, 2020).

Analytics or data analytics is the analysis and consolidation of data from a number of heterogeneous sources, with the aid of specialized applications, systems, tools, technology, and software to derive insights. When used to study and fight global outbreaks, it is called pandemic analytics. Pandemic analytics is a modern way to combat a problem as old as humanity itself: the proliferation of disease (Sogn, 2020).

A new rapidly spreading disease like the COVID-19 pandemic has a large number of unknowns; scientists, doctors, and researchers struggle to even begin understanding the basics of the disease. Data analytics can help in the understanding of a disease. This is reinforced by Najat Khan, chief data science officer and global head of strategy and operations for Janssen Research & Development when she states (Park, 2021):

> Data science and machine learning can be used to augment scientific understanding of a disease. For Covid-19, these tools became even more important because our knowledge was rather limited. There was no hypothesis at the time. We were developing an unbiased understanding of the disease based on real-world data using sophisticated AI/ML algorithms.

However, the use cases of data analytics during a pandemic are not restricted to the proliferation of the disease only. Results of a survey conducted by Sisense in the wake of COVID-19 to understand the use of data analytics during the crisis revealed that small businesses are using data analytics in multiple business areas, with 68% using analytics in operations, 56% in finance, 50% in sales, and 45% in product (Sisense, 2020).

The significance of data analytics in pandemics lies in its abilities to process large data sets from heterogeneous sources, if required on a real-time basis constantly, deliver granular infection and immunity rates, make projections that present ideal disease testing locations, predict consumer behavior and spending patterns, and evaluate decisions regarding entire product and service lines (Shah and Jiles, 2020).

In this chapter, data analytics use cases in a pandemic, data visualization, and its role in a pandemic, with special reference to COVID-19, are discussed.

Data Analytics Use Cases in the Pandemic

While a pandemic is a health crisis, it has a cascading impact on various industry sectors other than the healthcare sector. There are data analytics use cases in several industry sectors to combat the pandemic and related issues.

Pandemics are characterized by different degrees of uncertainty and unpredictability, a fact reinforced by the COVID-19 pandemic. Organizations should look at the pandemic as an opportunity to leverage data and data analytics to deal with these factors. In this section, we discuss the application areas and examples of data analytics with regard to pandemic in general, as well as in relation to the COVID-19 pandemic.

The widespread of COVID-19 and the lockdown restrictions imposed in different countries to stem and possibly stop its spread, have made a considerable difference in the way people conduct their life and how most businesses operate and interact with customers through different channels. For example, digital channel of interaction driven by technology has become the preferred channel over physical interactions which was the preferred option prior to COVID-19. Digital channel of interaction generates huge amounts of data, which can be collected, stored, and analyzed using a combination of analytical approaches to improve the digital experience.

In general, data analytics can help during a pandemic by enabling automation, optimization of resources, enhance responses, and provide better service. Analytics can help decide which products and services, capital projects, and markets, to invest in during the pandemic, determine which disruptive events might require a change in strategy, and monitor for anomalies and patterns that may indicate a threat or opportunity (BDO, 2020) and determine responsive strategies for responding to the threat or opportunity.

Using big data analytics to track cases can help to spot regions that may experience disease outbreaks in the near future. Data analytics can project how much policy measures—such as stay at home ordinates, restrictions on public gatherings, the closure of non-essential businesses, or mask mandates—will reduce the spread of the disease and flatten the curve. These insights can assist the government at different levels, to determine the proper timing and strategy, to reopen the economy without unnecessarily risking a resurgence in illness (BDO, 2020).

South Korea has leveraged big data to find the number of test kits that needs to be produced to meet demands during the COVID-19 pandemic. In a report in the *Journal of the American Medical Association* in early March 2020, Taiwan's success in handing the COVID-19 crisis has been partly attributed to big data analytics (Biswas, 2021).

Descriptive analytics, predictive analytics, and prescriptive analytics can be used to understand what the changes in market, workplace, lifestyle, and consumer behavior mean for their business, risk appetite, and employees, and how to provide better service. Mobility analysis and telecom data can be used to assess the effective execution of social distancing restrictions as well as highlighting high-risk suburbs.

Pandemics put an enormous stress on the healthcare industry. Descriptive analytics can be used to report confirmed cases, deaths, and recoveries by geography. Diagnostic and predictive analytics can be used predict infection and its severity, recovery, drug development, and mortality rates of the disease. Through automation, analytics can not only help cope with the rising diagnostics workloads but also free up valuable resources to focus on treating patients.

Data-driven forecasting can be used to optimize allocation of personnel and resources in advance of potential local outbreaks. Predictive analytics supported by machine learning algorithms can offer predictive insights based on all accessible data about the spread of the disease, such as confirmed cases, deaths, test results, contact tracing, population density, demographics, migration flow, availability of medical resources, and drug supplies. With the right analytics capabilities, healthcare professionals can answer questions such as where the next cluster of disease cases is most expected to happen, which demographic is most vulnerable, and how the pathogen may mutate over time.

In this digital age dominated by internet and social media, there is a lot of information and misinformation being posted. Analytics can also be used to separate reliable and authoritative sources from unreliable ones to reduce the spread of misinformation regarding the disease and how it is contracted. Social media data can help governments to capture community perceptions within a shorter time period without reaching the people directly/physically (Kankanamge et al., 2020). This characteristic of social media analytics makes it fit to be used to make community friendly decisions during pandemic situations (Yigitcanlar et al., 2020).

The ongoing COVID-19 pandemic has put an enormous stress on the healthcare industry, and there is shortage of resources to fight the disease. Data analytics has helped in the following areas (Shah and Jiles, 2020; Vivekanandarajah, 2021):

- predicting virus spread,
- medical imaging,
- new drug development,
- modelling infection severity,
- combating misleading information, and
- vaccine development, management, and distribution.

Predicting Virus Spread

A multitude of entities—governments, academic, and health care institutions—have developed models to predict the virus spread. For example, the US Department of Homeland Security's National Biodefense Analysis and Countermeasures Center developed a predictive modeling tool to assess the natural decay of the virus on surfaces. The center designed and implemented an online calculator to evaluate the decay of the virus with a combination of environmental factors such as relative humidity, UV index, and temperature (Eggers et al., 2020).

Medical Imaging

Huawei Cloud, Lanwon Technology, and Huazhong University of Science and Technology, in a collaborative effort, leveraged computer-vision AI-based imaging analysis techniques to accurately and repeatedly produce CT quantification results in seconds, decreasing the diagnosis time from CT scan results from about 5 minutes to 20 seconds. These techniques helped resolve the crisis created by the shortage of qualified imaging doctors in China in the early days of the COVID-19 pandemic (Shah and Jiles, 2020; Sogn, 2020).

New Drug Development

Since COVID-19 is a new disease, there is no pre-established drug for treating the disease. Research for a drug is still ongoing and data and analytics have a critical role to play in drug discovery.

In April 2020, Excelra, a leading global data and analytics company, released the COVID-19 Drug Repurposing Database. Excelra has a Global Repurposing Integrated Platform (GRIP) which drives drug repurposing at Excelra. This platform syndicates proprietary repurposing databases, algorithms, analytics tools, and a visualization engine. The GRIP database is constructed by collecting huge amounts of chemical data, biological data, and clinical data, which together contribute to more than ten million relationships among "drug-disease-target" trios. The COVID-19 Drug Repurposing Database is an open-access database which characterizes a landscape of "Approved" small molecules and biologics with known preclinical, pharmacokinetic, pharmacodynamic, and toxicity profiles; these may be used directly in clinical settings against COVID-19. The database also contains information on hopeful drug candidates that are in various stages of drug discovery and development (Excelra, 2020).

Dr. Nandu Gattu, Senior Vice President, Pharma Analytics, Excelra, said (Excelra, 2020):

> The COVID-19 DR database aims to provide critical insights into SARS-CoV-2 biology and mechanism of COVID-19 disease pathogenesis. It's a compilation of crucial data that is dispersed across numerous publications, reports, databases and knowledge-repositories along with referenced literature covering the drug, disease, target,

and mechanism of action. Our endeavour is in support to the ongoing global scientific efforts for identifying safe and effective therapeutic options to treat the novel coronavirus disease.

Machine learning models are being used to determine whether a drug will be effective in fighting the COVID-19 virus. Examples of inputs to these models are historical data for COVID-19, and data conveying the effectiveness of drugs in fighting other diseases (Shah and Jiles, 2020).

Modeling Infection Severity

Because there weren't enough resources for everyone to get tested regularly for COVID-19, it became critically important to gain more information about the possible outcomes of the spread of the disease (as to the infection risk, severity risk, and outcome risk), so as to be able to make the best effort at allocating medical resources appropriately. Data analytics have been used to predict the infection risk, severity risk, and outcome risk.

- Infection risk is the possibility of an individual being exposed to COVID-19.
- Severity risk is the likelihood that, if diseased, the individual might require hospitalization, intensive care, or a ventilator.
- Outcome risk is the probability of an infected person dying from COVID-19-related complications (Shah and Jiles, 2020).

Healthcare providers are leveraging data from countries that were affected earlier by the COVID-19 pandemic to predict requirements for capacity planning, facilities, and equipment such hospital beds, masks, PPE, and ventilators (Shcwenk, 2020). For example, with concerns of huge numbers of patients needing care, HMC's business intelligence team began compiling data to provide leaders with direction on creation of new isolation and quarantine facilities. Using analytics, the team presented existing occupancy at HMC's regular health facilities and field hospitals, and how much each facility needed to expand capacity for the surge in demand. Predictive models developed in partnership with a local university facilitated calculation of expected everyday admissions and forecast when the health system would possibly discharge people (Cerner Corporation, 2020).

Combating Misleading Information

Graham Stroman, vice president of sales, U.S. State, and Local Government at Tableau Software states (Kosaraju, 2021):

> Transparency matters, and data and analytics will combat disinformation, providing the source of truth when citizens need it most.

Social media companies, for example, Twitter used a deep learning algorithm to distinguish trustworthy and authoritative data sources from untrustworthy and unauthoritative data sources, to diminish the distribution of misinformation regarding COVID-19 and how it is contracted (Shah and Jiles, 2020).

Sentiment analysis through the mining of social media data provided useful insights to help design appropriate health messaging for the public.

Vaccine Development, Management, and Distribution

"COVID-19 vaccine—A ray of hope in an otherwise dark moonless night."

—Rupa Mahanti

One distinguishing difference between the non-digital age pandemic—Spanish flu and the digital age pandemic—COVID-19—is the stride at which pharmaceutical companies have been able to develop vaccines.

The minimum vaccine development timeline is 10 years, before the vaccine gets approved by regulatory authorities in charge of widespread manufacturing and distribution. The time taken to develop vaccines for the diseases such as human papillomavirus, shingles, and pneumococcal infections ranged between 9 and 13 years (Agrawal et al., 2021). The quickest any vaccine had previously been developed prior to COVID-19 vaccine, from viral sampling to approval, was four years, for mumps in the 1960s (Ball, 2020).

The reason behind the long vaccine development timeline is—the development of a vaccine for any disease requires pharmaceutical companies to conduct a series of rigorous experiments and clinical trials involving a large number of participants, to prove the effectiveness of a vaccine against the pathogen (Vivekanandarajah, 2021).

On December 30, 2019, the WHO had alerted the wider public about the emergence of the new disease—COVID-19. Less than a year later, on December 2, 2020, a vaccine made by Pfizer (a leading research-based biopharmaceutical company) with German biotech firm BioNTech became the first fully tested immunization to be approved for emergency use for COVID-19 (Ball, 2020). As of July 2021, at least 13 different vaccines have been administered. Some of these are Oxford/AstraZeneca, Moderna, Pfizer/BioNTech, Johnson & Johnson, Sputnik V, Sinopharm/Beijing, and Sinovac.

Data and analytics have had critical roles to play in the success and speed of vaccine development and distribution in case of COVID-19. For example, Pfizer was able to cut down the time required to review clinical data from one month to 22 days, using a machine learning tool called Smart Data Query (SDQ). SDQ also reduced the cycle time to identify and call out a query by 50% within the COVID-19 vaccine trial and, over a period of four months, fine-tuned and reconciled more than 103 million combinations of clinical data points to spot discrepancies and trigger queries (Mixson, 2021).

During the clinical trials phase, Moderna's scientists relied on Amazon Redshift AWS's fully managed data warehousing service to consolidate and evaluate results from dozens of parallel experiments. This aided them to make better and faster clinical decisions, which was not possible earlier (Mixson, 2021).

Design of experiments (DOE) was used in the development of the COVID-19 vaccine. Design of experiments (DOE) is a tool that helps prepare a set of representative experiments in which all factors under investigation are varied simultaneously and systematically. A model can be derived from a set of experiments. This model captures the relationship between the factors (settings) and the experimental results (responses). DOE capitalizes on the information content while minimizing the number of experiments.

In many cases, when running experiments, there is need to determine which factors are critical and have an effect on the outcome, and how these parameters might interact with or affect each other. Data analytics through regression modelling provides an efficient means of determining which factors will have any effect on key performance indicators.

In case of COVID-19 vaccine development, DOE improved the effectiveness of preclinical and clinical experiments to reach conclusions, while lessening the number of experiments otherwise required, thereby reducing the time, and in the long run, also reducing the overall cost of experimentation. DOE helped companies design experiments methodically, enabling them to recognize and control the effects of different factors on the outcome of clinical experiments (Vivekanandarajah, 2021).

Data analytics tools like predictive analytics and multivariate analytics helped companies to forecast vaccine demand to scale production up, as well as to lessen the number of batches needed to demonstrate the effectiveness of the vaccine (Vivekanandarajah, 2021).

Vaccine distribution is another segment, where data analytics was used to predict and handle fluctuations in vaccine supply due to various factors—political, economic, and logistics. Vaccine distribution has several parameters associated with it, right from its procurement to storage, and then distribution and administration. Data and analytics can help public health agencies identify people most in need of the COVID-19 vaccine; that is, the most vulnerable locations and population segments, and tailor outreach to them—block by block (Vivekanandarajah, 2021; Kassler, 2021).

Many countries, for example, have been prioritizing vaccination based on the following criteria:

- existing medical conditions,
- exposure risk,
- job role (for example, targeting health care workers and frontline staff first), or,
- age (for example, target population whose age is above 60 or 65).

The population segment that was considered, the most vulnerable to the virus were prioritized for vaccination. Governments also used data analytics to spot virus transmission patterns to find out probable outbreak spots and avert them by vaccinating the residents in and around that geographical area.

COVID-19 vaccine administration and management are a multifaceted, evolving process with no one size fits all approach, owing the following factors (Kassler, 2021):

- large population to be immunized;
- multiple vaccines coming out;
- requirements to keep the vaccines cold;
- a limited supply of vaccines;
- shelf life of the vaccines;
- dealing with new contractors;
- two doses required;
- timing between doses different for different vaccines;
- dissemination in locations outside the medical system; and
- the diverse beliefs of different groups of people.

A PULSE® Health Poll conducted in 2020 found the following results (see Figure 6.1) ([Survey Results]; Kassler, 2021):

- 35% of all respondents said they would get the COVID-19 vaccine as soon as it becomes available.
- 41% said they would wait before deciding. The most common reasons given for waiting were concerns about safety (36%) and concerns about side effects (25%).
- Of the 24% of respondents who said they would not get the vaccine at all, 34% cited concerns about safety and 12% said they simply did not need it.

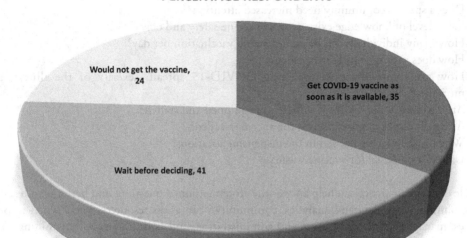

Figure 6.1 2020 PULSE® Health Poll survey results on public attitude toward COVID-19 vaccination.

As stated by Srinivas Kosaraju, in his Forbes article, "Vaccine Management Analytics: Will It Be The Next 2021 Data Story?":

> Effective management of any vaccine distribution program requires a holistic picture of the vaccine supply chain, the populations being prioritized, the success rate in reaching those populations, and the strengths and weaknesses of the metrics used to measure progress and performance.

Allocating vaccine supply is based on a range of complex, interrelated factors that include populations being administered, the availability of different vaccines, providers' capability for storing and refrigeration, and meeting the timing requirement between two doses. Optimizing these distribution strategies while facing fluctuating supplies, evolving need driven by dynamic nature of disease outbreaks and high-risk zones, and changing provider registrations require a strong data-driven and analytic approach.

Some of the questions that need to be addressed for the effective management of COVID-19 vaccine are (Kosaraju, 2021):

■ Where is the highest vaccine reluctance based on rate of spread and case count?
■ What are the reasons behind vaccine reluctance?
■ Is additional marketing, public outreach, and communications needed to overcome vaccine reluctance?
■ How do we prioritize population groups for immunization and at the same preserve parity?

- What are the locations and concentrations of priority populations?
- Does a specific community need increased attention?
- What level of knowledge exists around vaccine safety and efficacy?
- How many individuals can be administered vaccination per day?
- How does vaccine supply match demand?
- How are immunizations impacting COVID-19 spread, severity of the illness, and mortality?
- Are vaccine sites known and sufficiently equipped and staffed?
- At which dispensing locations is the vaccine needed?
- When is the vaccine needed in the dispensing locations?
- Is there a potential for vaccine waste?

Reliable data and analytics can help answer the aforementioned questions and better plan response and resolution. With data and analytics, communities can assess resources, know when to order supplies, manage vaccine distribution and administration, and assist leaders in determining where to focus their efforts (Kosaraju, 2021). Data analytics can rapidly and accurately model vaccination schedules, estimate vaccine supply needs, identify and resolve quality/safety concerns, and produce requisite regulatory reports.

Pandemics, Analytics, and Retail

Pandemic can have a huge impact on consumer spending, needs, and behavior, and descriptive analytics can be used to analyze transaction data to understand the same. With the COVID-19 pandemic, there have been changes in the consumer needs as well as spending patterns. An example of analytics use case in relation of spending pattern changes during COVID-19 is New York City's use of geographic spending pattern changes (by neighborhood) to estimate the impact of consumer spending on the city's sales tax revenue, resulting in more data-driven budgetary adjustments (Shah and Jiles, 2020).

Descriptive analytics using point-of-sale (POS) data help distributors identify and ship the items most important to their customers. Different regions have had varying levels of demand, depending upon the stage of their recovery and analytics have been used to get a much more concise view of the demand at a regional level to understand how the demand patterns have shifted and will continue to shift in the days, weeks and months to come (Baker, 2020).

An Asian country by analyzing transaction data found that the consumer spending growth had crashed from double-digit year-on-year to minus 15 percent within a month of the economy being shuttered as a result of lockdown. It analyzed the consumer expenditure by breaking down into different slices like online and offline spending, discretionary versus non-discretionary and spending by segments like groceries, dining out, travel, and entertainment. Changing consumption patterns indicated the segments that had been most affected and also provided a base for framing effective response strategies (DQIndiaOnline, 2020).

Pandemics, Analytics, and Finance

During the COVID-19 pandemic, the finance department in organizations throughout the world has had a critical role to play in their respective organization's recovery. Insights derived from application of data analytics using financial as well as non-financial data have been used to drive informed business decisions in relation to better management of cash flow, identification of top products, forecast demand, assessment of employment levels, and evaluation of financing and investment options (Shah and Jiles, 2020).

COVID-19—Examples of Data Analytics Application in Different Industry Sectors

Some other examples of application of data and data analytics in different industry sectors and business functions to deal with uncertainties created by COVID-19 are as follows:

- Telecommunication companies are analyzing network traffic data to monitor and manage network capacity, develop predictive capacity models, detect bottlenecks, and prioritize and plan network expansion decisions (Shcwenk, 2020).
- In the public sector, SAS is working with a provincial justice department to manage the stock pile of court cases that accumulated during the COVID-19 pandemic lockdown period. Analytics is being used to organize and prioritize cases to make sure that trials take place within the required time limits, as well as develop a plan to provide appropriate personal protective equipment to their frontline staff (Baker, 2020).
- HR analytics can be used to aid the recovery process by leveraging data to help decide when and how to reopen offices, and what needs to be done to protect employees (Baker, 2020).
- Financial models such as scenario analysis have been used in the area of cash and working capital management during the COVID-19 pandemic. Overall present and future cash inflows and outflows have been analyzed to determine the effect of a multitude of cost and revenue drivers, such as manufacturing a new product that is in higher demand than existing products, an increased cost of raw materials, curbing certain marketing activities, or offering free or extremely discounted services. This analysis enlightens the business, of how much cash is needed to maintain restricted, or amplified operations, offers guidance on the possible need to secure supplementary funds, and predicts cash implications of pulling other operational or business levers (Shah and Jiles, 2020).
- Scenario analysis has also been used to make employment decisions during the COVID-19 pandemic such as number of individuals to lay off or additional persons needed to be hired to meet unprecedented surges in demand (Shah and Jiles, 2020).
- In financial services businesses, utility companies, manufacturing organizations, consulting firms, and finance teams, predictive analytics has been used to assess accounts receivables and customer account history to recognize those presenting the greatest risk of delinquency (Shah and Jiles, 2020).
- HCL, a multinational IT company, has leveraged predictive analytics to evaluate the possible impact of COVID-19 pandemic on their customers, as well as the markets where the organization services them. The organization has used techniques such as statistics, control theory, simulation modelling, and natural language processing (NLP) to track the situation quantitatively and qualitatively to understand its magnitude and responding using a mathematical model of the situation (using robust and contextual variables) as a proxy for the actual pandemic (Sogn, 2020).

Data Visualization and Its Role in a Pandemic

"A picture is worth a thousand words."

"The human brain processes images 60,000 times faster than it does text."

—William D. Eggers and Amrita Datar

"Show, don't just tell."

—William D. Eggers and Amrita Datar

Human beings' brains are equipped to process visual data such as maps better than other forms of data such as text. For example, public health data depicted on a map might be substantially more meaningful and accessible to citizens than a spreadsheet or document with the same information. According to the Social Science Research Network, 65% of people are visual learners. Hence, one of the best means to drive the message home is via visual content (Gillet, 2014; Eggers and Datar, 2018).

Visualizations can be very helpful from a pandemic perspective, as it can assist both individuals who are aggressively working on solutions to fight the disease, as well as the general public who are trying to figure out the disease and gauge their own personal risks. This is important in case of the COVID-19 pandemic, as everyone needs to see the extent of impact of COVID-19 on the different geographies across the globe.

The first, and arguably one of the most important steps in data analysis is exploration, where visualization plays a central role, completed with informative summary statistics (Wickham, 2016; Polonsky et al., 2019; Crawley, 2012).

Raw data is impossible to interpret without analytical methods or technology, and even summarized data can be difficult to interpret without visualization, specifically for the average person. Numbers do communicate, but a visual heat map or a graph can be more effective and sometimes, communicate better (Ayers, 2020).

In the past, it was hard to inform the public using data because specialized knowledge was needed for the same, and it was not easy to communicate and share visualizations with a bigger audience (Ayers, 2020). However, in today's digital age, with the Internet and availability of strong data visualization tools, public knowledge is growing rapidly. Public are getting a better comprehension of the types of data, as well as, how to construe visualizations (Ayers, 2020). For example, the Washington State Department of Health presents important COVID-19 data using visualization tools and metrics on its website for a better understanding of citizens and policymakers (Washington State Department of Health, 2020; Eggers et al., 2020).

However, at the heart of reliable visualization is good quality data; hence, this should be kept in mind when using the data to create visualizations. The raw data need to be pre-processed to remove the noise, before it can be used. Data smoothing or removing noise from the data needs to be done correctly; smoothing done incorrectly introduces error in the data. In his article—"5 Wrong Ways to Do COVID-19 Data Smoothing", Steve McConnell—states that one common mistake when data smoothing is that in many cases, states dump weeks or months worth of corrections into the data pool all on one day resulting in a sudden spike on that particular day, which is not correct. The recommendation is to have smoothing period of 7 days (McConnell, 2020).

Visualizations on the following parameters have helped give a better picture of the COVID-19 disease impact:

- Total number of cases so far: Number of people infected with the disease including those currently suffering (that is, active cases), deaths, and recoveries till date.
- Number of new cases: Number of new infections reported on a particular day (the most recent date).
- Total number of deaths: Number of people who have died from the disease till date.
- Number of new deaths: Number of people who have died from the disease on a particular date (the most recent date).
- Total number of recoveries: Number of people who have recovered from the disease till date.
- Total number of new recoveries: Number of people recovered from the disease on a particular date (the most recent date).
- Number of active cases: Number of people currently suffering from the disease.
- Number of critical cases: Number of people who are critically ill.
- Total number of tests: Total number of people tested for the disease till date.
- Total number of hospitalizations: Total number of people hospitalized till date.
- Total number of new hospitalizations: Number of people hospitalized on a particular date (the most recent date).

Dashboards have been built to report the aforementioned parameters at a global level, with drill down facilities available by geographies, countries, regions, states, and so on. Governments of all countries have been using visual analyses of big data for the real-time visualization of key COVID-19 indicators such as case data, epidemic distribution, epidemic situation trends, and hot spot reports (Qiong et al., 2020).

The accessibility of data from trusted sources has led to unprecedented sharing of information and visualizations to educate the public and increase awareness about COVID-19. Some common examples of COVID-19 data visualization (that showed/shows the viral spread in humans over a period of time) include:

- Flattening the curve function (see Figure 6.2),
- the Johns Hopkins COVID-19 tracker (see Figure 6.3) [Johns Hopkins University],
- the Washington Post's animated-dots simulation (see Figure 6.4)
- WHO coronavirus (COVID-19) dashboard (see Figure 6.5)
- the COVID-19 Healthcare Coalition's COVID-19 decision support dashboard (C19HCC DSD) (see Figure 6.6)

The first type of graphics needed for rapid assessment of ongoing dynamics is the epidemic curve (epicurves) (Polonsky et al., 2019), which visualizes the onset and progression of a disease outbreak. Cumulative case counts, sometimes used in the absence of a raw line list, are best avoided in epicurves, as they tend to obscure ongoing dynamics and create statistical dependencies in data points that will result in biases and lead to under-estimating uncertainty in downstream modelling (King et al., 2015; Polonsky et al., 2019). Flattening the curve function as shown in Figure 6.2 (and discussed in detail in Chapter 3) is spreading out the number of infected cases over a greater period time (as shown by the yellow/greyish epidemic curve in Figure 6.2) so that the number of cases is lower and healthcare is not overwhelmed. This can be accomplished by taking appropriate steps to slow down the transmission in absence of which, the epidemic curve would be steep, with rapid spread of infection and a large number of infected cases in relatively short period of time as shown by navy blue/dark coloured curve with a high peak in Figure 6.2.

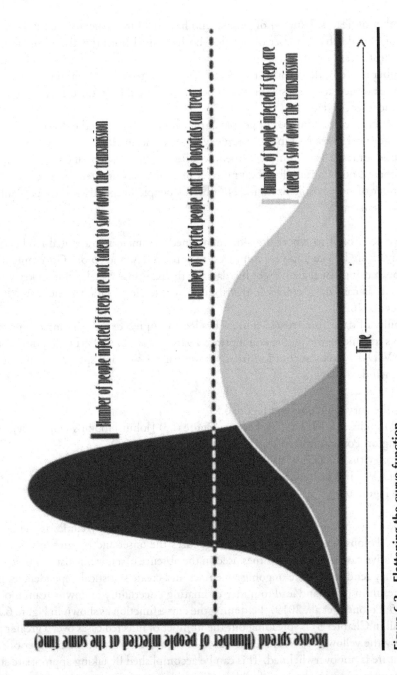

Figure 6.2   Flattening the curve function.

Source: Adapted from Yigitcanlar et al. (2020), Gavin (2020)

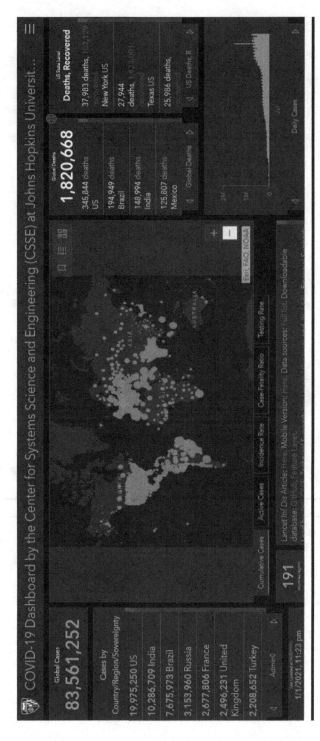

Figure 6.3 Visualization of the global development of the COVID-19 pandemic as of January 1, 2021.

Source: [Johns Hopkins University]

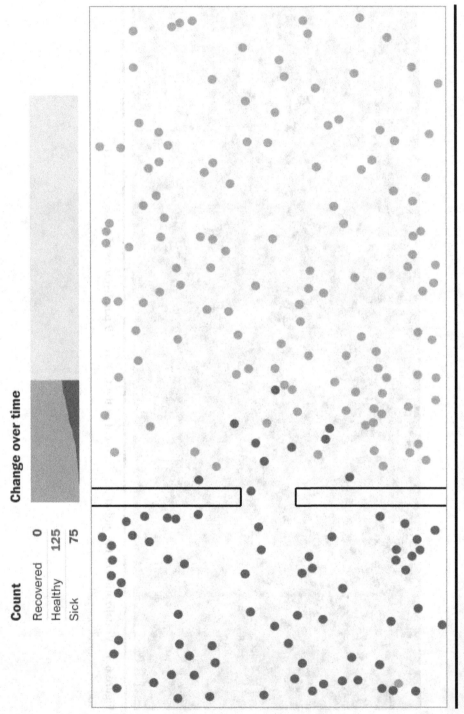

Figure 6.4 The *Washington Post*'s animated-dots simulation screenshot.

Source: Washington Post; Stevens (2020)

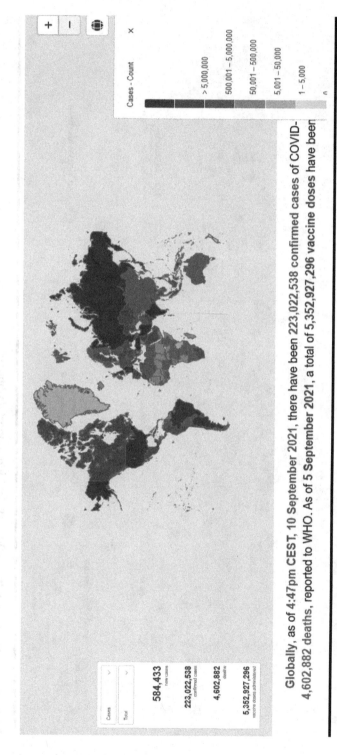

Figure 6.5   Screenshot of the WHO coronavirus (COVID-19) dashboard.

Source: https://covid19.who.int/

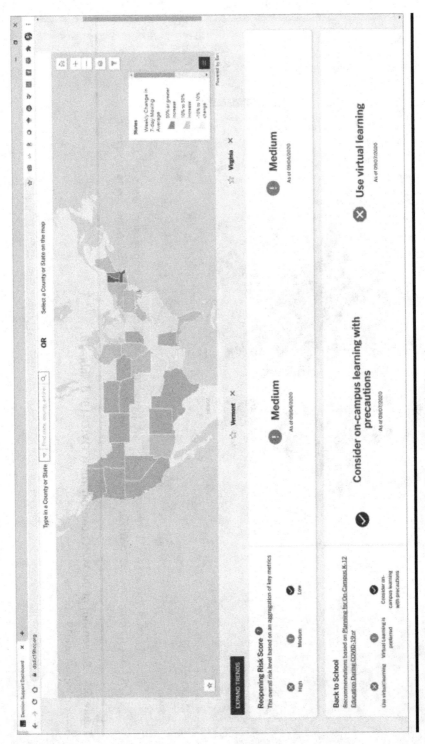

Figure 6.6 Screenshot of the COVID-19 decision support dashboard.

Source: https://dsd.c19hcc.org/ (initial screen)

Maps are typically used to visualize the distribution of disease (Wertheim et al., 2012), for representing the "ecological niche" of infectious diseases at large scales (Messina et al., 2016; Pigott et al., 2014; Nunes et al., 2015) and for assessing the spatial dynamics of an outbreak and strategizing interventions (WHO Ebola Response Team, 2014; WHO Ebola Response Team et al., 2015).

For example, visualizations such as the dynamic world map (see Figure 6.3) created by Johns Hopkins' Center for Systems Science and Engineering and brilliantly simple yet enlightening animations from the Washington Post are quickly teaching the public about how viruses spread, and which individual actions can help or hinder that spread.

The Washington Post's animated-dots simulation (see screenshot in Figure 6.4) assisted Americans in understanding the importance of social distancing in slowing the spread of COVID-19 (Stevens, 2020; Makulec, 2020). Such simulations are dynamic, and allow the public to experience data differently from static graphics or video explanations of complex concepts. Rather than passively consuming information, they are immersed in the outcomes, without ever seeing the math or complex logic running in the back end which can help build an intuitive understanding of a disease outbreak. This is reinforced by Harry Stevens, graphic reporter at Washington Post in his statement as follows (Stevens, 2020; Makulec, 2020):

> It's hard to develop an intuitive understanding of dynamic systems like epidemics. Simulations help readers build up their intuition about how diseases work in a way that words and even static charts cannot.

Interestingly, the data that are used in these simulations is not explicit to COVID-19. A demonstrative fast-spreading disease with similar characteristics is used in the simulations rather than the real characteristics of COVID-19. There are a lot of uncertainties around COVID-19, which make creating an accurate forecast tough.

Researchers at Johns Hopkins University also maintain a dashboard that gives a summary of the current number of COVID-19 cases, demises, and recuperations on a per country basis. Figure 6.3 provides an example of an online GIS supplied by Johns Hopkins University, with COVID-19 data from January 1, 2021.

The World Health Organization publishes daily situation reports detailing the number of confirmed COVID-19 cases and deaths per country. They also run a situation dashboard which is updated three times per day (see Figure 6.5).

The COVID-19 Healthcare Coalition's COVID-19 Decision Support Dashboard (C19HCC DSD) was first developed in April 2020 (Figure 6.6) and organizes a large amount of vital, complex data into red, yellow, and green risk indicators (RYG risk indicators) that guide reopening strategies for governments and businesses. The report identifies key metrics and analytic questions that must be resolved before a state or location can take actions to return to normalcy. The power of the DSD is that it can display data with different pedigrees side-by-side for comparison. This allows also to show the results of different model forecasts and prognoses side by side. Additionally, it provides users with drill down facilities into data with higher resolution, starting on the state level and going down to counties, and place names or cities, if these data are available. It should be emphasized that higher resolution does not always equal higher fidelity, as data can be updated in various degrees of accuracy as well as frequency, to tailor their search to focus regions, facilitating comparison and enabling insights on how areas are coping and the effects of policy changes over time (Eggers et al., 2020; Tolk et al., 2021).

The team of Max Roser collects and syndicates all available data about the COVID-19 pandemic on one single page. This exceptional summary provides interactive charts on many different topics ranging from the number of cases to symptoms, incubation period, and fatality rate (Eeckhout, 2020).

As of August 2021, there are a number of COVID-19 vaccines available. Data dashboards provide an overall view of vaccination records, such as which country has the highest vaccinated people, what are the different types of vaccines offered, and which vaccine is used in various countries.

Covax is a global initiative run by the World Health Organization (WHO). It also involves the Global Vaccine Alliance (Gavi) and the Coalition for Epidemic Preparedness Innovations (Cepi). According to this scheme, 98 more affluent countries will dispense vaccines to 92 poorer countries. The program aims to deliver two billion doses of vaccine to people in less than a year (Beatrice, 2021).

Data dashboards are used as a go-to public resource for up-to-date statistics on the world's COVID-19 vaccine market and the Covax facilities deliveries. The data dashboard presents a comprehensive view of vaccine development and progresses toward vaccine approvals, global vaccine production capacity, manufacturing agreements, bilateral and multilateral supply agreements, and vaccine prices. It also provides an outlook on total daily Covax vaccine deliveries, doses allocated, and doses ordered (Beatrice, 2021).

Several key takeaways have emerged from leading examples of COVID-19-related data visualization (Eggers et al., 2020), and can be applied in normal business setup as well as other crisis situations. They are:

- Show and tell: Visualizations are more meaningful, and easier for human brain to process than text.
- Keep it simple, yet effective: Visualizations should be designed keeping the audience in mind, and should be simple and quick to understand, but at the same time be powerful, and convey the desired message clearly to the prospective audience.
- Provide information at different levels of granularity: Visualizations should provide bird's eye view of the situation and also allow drill down facility to get detailed view of a specific area.
- Take actions, make decisions: The end goal of data presentation is to improve decision-making and take action. (COVID-19 Healthcare Coalition, 2020). The value of data does not lie in the data by itself, but by the message conveyed, insights extracted, decisions made, and actions taken (Eggers et al., 2020).
- Be straightforward about design choices, assumptions, and uncertainties, and provide a clear explanation about your data.

Concluding Thoughts

The COVID-19 pandemic started in the end of 2019, and it has affected all continents across the globe in 2020, with Antarctica being the last continent to be affected in December 2020. The pandemic is still ongoing (as of September, 2021) with the virus having undergone several mutations with several strains of coronavirus infecting people, with some strains being more life threatening than other strains. It has been labeled as "once in a century health crisis" and is similar to the Spanish flu along the lines of a definitive cure being absent and public health measures like quarantine, social distancing, hand hygiene, isolation, and vaccination being the only prevention alternatives. However, what is different between these two health crises that are set apart by a century is the availability of sophisticated tools and technology to assess the crisis and plan response strategies in different business functions and industry sectors as well as speed the development of preventive strategies such as vaccines.

The State of BI and Business Analytics Report from Sisense shows that small businesses are leveraging data analytics in the business areas of operations, finance, sales, and product (Noor, 2020; Sisense, 2020) to combat the impact of the COVID-19 pandemic.

The democratization of data and analytics tools, combined with mass capability to share information via the internet, has enabled people to perceive the remarkable power of data (Sogn, 2020).

Owing to a multisector impact and interdisciplinary nature of the problem, a multi-stakeholder collaboration is essential to handle a disease outbreak. Data analytics to track pandemics requires collaborative effort of diversely skilled individuals. Also, there is no single silver bullet or a "one size fits all" approach that can be used to tackle a pandemic crisis. As the pandemic progresses, depending upon the gravity of the situation, a combination of different strategies, tools and technologies needs to be applied to combat the crisis and mitigate the impacts.

According to Quantzig's healthcare analytics experts (Business Wire, 2020):

> Developing healthcare solutions for a global pandemic is a huge challenge, since it revolves around analyzing data at a standardized scale, and this is where pandemic analytics can play a crucial role. With the right mix of analytics and healthcare insights applied in the right direction, we have the potential to minimize the impact of diseases.

It is essential to remember that data lies at the heart of any analytics exercise and hence the data used for analytics needs to be of good quality. This is reinforced by Steve Holder, Head of Strategy and Innovation at SAS Canada when he states (Baker, 2020):

> I think organizations need to start by getting their data right.

Another trend that has gained momentum in the COVID-19 pandemic is the usage of external data. This is because internal data about past activities is no longer a good predictor of the future. However, while internal data is not good predictor of future by itself, McKinsey & Company has discovered that existing data from pre-COVID-19 times can still furnish organizations with constructive insights, if the organizations supplement data with appropriate assumptions and add their own human parameters to it afterward (Noor, 2020).

Organizations are using external data to figure out what's going on, particularly about consumer behavior and demand. In the words of Thomas H. Davenport (Brown, 2021):

> One of the big problems that we've had with data and analytics in a lot of organizations is they've been too internally focused. Switching to figuring out what's going on in the outside world, with people who aren't our customers—what people think about us, what's happening with our suppliers and their suppliers, and so on, are all good things to do.

While data analytics cannot solve every problem, it will continue to be a force for good as it helps us navigate the complexities and uncertainties of public health crises—today and in the future (Vivekanandarajah, 2021). However, given the complexities and uncertainties, one has to keep in mind that data analytics will not be able to predict with 100% accuracy, and the analytics solutions are not fool proof. For example, there is always some margin of error when using analytics to predict spread of diseases. However, data analytics can definitely assist in dealing with complex and uncertain situations more efficiently and quickly.

References

Agrawal, G., Hermann, R., Møller, M., Poetes, R., and Steinmann, M. (May 13, 2021) Fast-forward: Will the Speed of COVID-19 Vaccine Development Reset Industry Norms? *McKinsey & Company*, Last accessed on June 10, 2021, from www.mckinsey.com/industries/pharmaceuticals-and-medical-products/our-insights/fast-forward-will-the-speed-of-covid-19-vaccine-development-reset-industry-norms

Ayers, R. (October 2, 2020) Data Visualization and the Pandemic Spread, *Big Data Made Simple*, Last accessed on December 14, 2020, from, https://bigdata-madesimple.com/data-visualization-and-the-pandemic-spread/

Baker, C. (August 4, 2020) Why Data Analytics is Essential to Your Organization's Pandemic Recovery, *IT World Canada*, Last accessed on November 14, 2020, from www.itworldcanada.com/article/why-data-analytics-is-essential-to-your-organizations-pandemic-recovery/434011

Ball, P. (December 18, 2020) The Lightning-Fast Quest for COVID Vaccines—and What it Means for other Diseases, *Nature*, Last accessed on June 10, 2021, from www.nature.com/articles/d41586-020-03626-1

BDO (June 2020) The Data Analytics War Room: Lessons Learned from the COVID-19 Pandemic, *BDO Digital*, Last accessed on November 14, 2020, from www.bdo.com/insights/business-financial-advisory/bdo-digital/the-data-analytics-war-room-lessons-learned-from-t

Beatrice, A. (April 8, 2021) Big Data Analytics: The Secret Tool Behind Covax and Vaccine Passport, *Analytics Insight*, Last accessed on June 2, 2021, from www.analyticsinsight.net/big-data-analytics-the-secret-tool-behind-covax-and-vaccine-passport/

Biswas, A. (January 1, 2021) Five Reasons Why the Covid-19 Pandemic is a Failure of Big Data Analytics, *BW Business World*, Last accessed on January 1, 2021, from www.businessworld.in/article/Five-reasons-why-the-Covid-19-pandemic-is-a-failure-of-Big-Data-Analytics/03-11-2020-339005/

Brown, S. (Jan 5, 2021). How COVID-19 is Disrupting Data Analytics Strategies. *MIT Management Sloan School*, Last accessed on June 2, 2021, from https://mitsloan.mit.edu/ideas-made-to-matter/how-covid-19-disrupting-data-analytics-strategies

Business Wire. (2020) Quantzig's Analytics Experts Answer 3 FAQs on Pandemic Analytics, *BioSpace*, Last accessed on June 10, 2021, from www.biospace.com/article/releases/quantzig-s-analytics-experts-answer-3-faqs-on-pandemic-analytics-learn-more/

Cerner Corporation (July 7, 2020) Analytics Help Data-driven Decision-making During Pandemic, Last accessed on December 14, 2020, from www.cerner.com/perspectives/analytics-help-data-driven-decision-making-during-pandemic

COVID-19 Healthcare Coalition (May 29, 2020) COVID-19 Healthcare Coalition Launches COVID-19 Decision Support Dashboard, *Newswise*.

Crawley, M. J. (2012) *The R Book*. Hoboken, NJ: John Wiley & Sons.

DQIndiaOnline (September 24, 2020) Data Analytics Will Drive Financial Innovation and Business Growth in a Post-COVID World, *Data Quest*, Last accessed on November 14, 2020, from www.dqindia.com/data-analytics-will-drive-financial-innovation-business-growth-post-covid-world/

The Economist (2017) From Chaos to Coherence: Managing Pandemics with Data, Last accessed on November 14, 2020, from https://expectexceptional.economist.com/managing-pandemics-with-data.html

Eeckhout, Van den K. (March 2020) Data Visualization in a Time of Pandemic, *Medium*, https://medium.com/@koenvandeneeckhout/data-visualization-in-a-time-of-pandemic-5c8c45d4b147

Eggers, W. D., Chew, B., Nunes, N.-M., Davis, A., and Rodrigues, G. (2020) Seven Lessons COVID-19 Has Taught us about Data Strategy, *Deloitte*, Last accessed on May 17, 2021, from https://www2.deloitte.com/us/en/insights/economy/covid-19/government-data-management-lessons.html

Eggers, W. D., and Datar, A. (May 29, 2018) Connecting Data to Residents Through Data Storytelling, *Deloitte Insights*, Last accessed on May 17, 2021, from https://www2.deloitte.com/us/en/insights/industry/public-sector/chief-data-officer-government-playbook/open-data-success-stories.html.

Excelra (April 8, 2020) Excelra Releases COVID-19 Drug Repurposing Database to Support Global Drug Development Efforts against Novel Coronavirus, Last accessed on June 10, 2021, from www.excelra.com/newsroom/excelra-covid19-drug-repurposing-database/

[Farrell] Farrell, A. Five Ways Your Organization Can Enhance Resilience for Years to Come, Last accessed on November 14, 2020, from www.sas.com/en_in/insights/articles/analytics/five-ways-your-organization-can-enhance-resilience-for-years-to-.html#/

Ganji, M. (October 8, 2020) Data Must Go Viral, *Blue Notes*, Last accessed on November 14, 2020, from https://bluenotes.anz.com/posts/2020/10/data-pandemic-analytics-business

Gavin, K. (March 11, 2020) Flattening the Curve for COVID-19: What Does It Mean and How Can You Help? *Michigan Health*. Last accessed on June 25, 2020, from https://healthblog.uofmhealth.org/wellness-prevention/flattening-curve-for-covid-19-what-does-it-mean-and-how-can-you-help

Gillet, R. (September 18, 2014) Why We're More Likely to Remember Content with Images and Video (Infographic), *Fast Company*, Last accessed on May 17, 2021, from www.fastcompany.com/3035856/why-were-more-likely-to-remember-content-with-images-and-video-infogr.

[Johns Hopkins University], COVID-19 Map, Last accessed on January 1, 2021, from https://coronavirus.jhu.edu/map.html

Kankanamge, N., Yigitcanlar, T., Goonetilleke, A., and Kamruzzaman, M. (2020) How Can Gamification Be Incorporated into Disaster Emergency Planning? A Systematic Review of the Literature. *International Journal of Disaster Resilience in the Built Environment* 11(4): 481–506.

Kassler, W. J. (January 4, 2021) Vaccine Distribution: Targeted Analytics Can Help Prioritize Critical Populations, *IBM Blog*. Last accessed on June 10, 2021, from www.ibm.com/blogs/watson-health/vaccine-distribution-critical-populations/

King, A. A., Domenech de Celle's, M., Magpantay, F. M. G., and Rohani, P. (2015) Avoidable Errors in the Modelling of Outbreaks of Emerging Pathogens, with Special Reference to Ebola. *Proceedings of the Royal Society B* 282: 20150347. http://dx.doi.org/10.1098/rspb.2015.0347

Kosaraju, S. (April 6, 2021) Vaccine Management Analytics: Will It Be the Next 2021 Data Story? *Forbes*, Last accessed on June 10, 2021, from www.forbes.com/sites/tableau/2021/04/06/vaccine-management-analytics-will-it-be-the-next-2021-data-story/?sh=77f261980d0e

Makulec, A. (June 1, 2020) Move Over, Data Visualization. The Era of 'Data Simulation' is Here, *Fast Company*.

McConnell, S. (October 1, 2020), 5 Wrong Ways To Do Covid-19 Data Smoothing, towards data science, Last accessed on September 12, 2021, from https://towardsdatascience.com/five-wrong-ways-to-do-covid-19-data-smoothing-1538db6ff182.

Messina, J. P. et al. (2016) Mapping Global Environmental Suitability for Zika Virus. *Elife* 5: e15272. http://dx.doi.org/10.7554/eLife.15272

Mixson, E. (April 27, 2021) 3 Ways AI and Advanced Analytics are Being Used to Combat Covid-19, *AI Data Analytics and Network*, Last accessed on May 17, 2021, from www.aidataanalytics.network/data-science-ai/articles/3-ways-ai-and-advanced-analytics-are-being-used-to-combat-covid-19

[National Center for Biotechnology Information], "1918 Influenza: The Mother of All Pandemics."

Noor, M. (September 2, 2020) *Different Ways Business Analytics are Used in a Pandemic, Master of Science in Business Analytics*, Michael G. Foster School of Business, University of Washington, Last accessed on November 14, 2020, from https://blog.foster.uw.edu/different-ways-business-analytics-used-pandemic/

Nunes, M. R. T. et al. (2015) Emergence and Potential for Spread of Chikungunya Virus in Brazil. *BMC Medicine* 13: 102. http://dx.doi.org/10.1186/s12916-015-0348-x

O'Brien, C. (December 10, 2020) Coronavirus Pandemic Moves Data Analytics Front and Centre, *The Irish Times*, Last accessed on December 14, 2020, from www.irishtimes.com/business/technology/coronavirus-pandemic-moves-data-analytics-front-and-centre-1.4430982

Park, T. (May 18, 2021) Behind Covid-19 Vaccine Development, *MIT News*, Last accessed on July 12, 2021, from https://news.mit.edu/2021/behind-covid-19-vaccine-development-0518

Pigott, D. M. et al. (2014) Mapping the Zoonotic Niche of Ebola Virus Disease in Africa. *Elife* 3: e04395. http://dx.doi.org/10.7554/eLife.04395.

Polonsky, J. A. et al. (2019) Outbreak Analytics: A Developing Data Science for Informing the Response to Emerging Pathogens. *Philosophical Transactions of the Royal Society B* 374: 20180276. http://dx.doi.org/10.1098/rstb.2018.0276

Qiong, J., Guo, Y., Wang, G., and Barne, S. J. (August 2020) Big Data Analytics in the Fight Against Major Public Health Incidents (Including COVID-19): A Conceptual Framework, August 2020. *International Journal of Environmental Research and Public Health*, 17(17): 6161. doi:10.3390/ijerph17176161

RS&F (2020) The Data Analytics War Room: Lessons Learned from the Covid-19 Pandemic, Last accessed on May 17, 2021, from www.rsandf.com/news/2020/06/the-data-analytics-war-room-lessons-learned-from-the-covid-19-pandemic/.

Shah, H., and Jiles, L. (September 1, 2020) A Data-driven Approach to the Pandemic, *SF Magazine*, Last accessed on November 14, 2020, from https://sfmagazine.com/post-entry/september-2020-a-data-driven-approach-to-the-pandemic

Shcwenk, H.(May 18, 2020), How Data and Analytics Can Recover Businesses after the Pandemic, *Dataconomy*, Last accessed on November 14, 2020. from https://dataconomy.com/2020/05/how-data-analytics-can-recover-businesses-after-the-pandemic/

Sisense (2020) State of BI and Business Analytics Report, Last accessed on January 17, 2021, from www.sisense.com/whitepapers/state-of-bi-analytics-report-2020/.

Sogn, D. (March 31, 2020) Pandemic Analytics: How Data is Helping Us Combat COVID-19, *HCLTech Blog*, Last accessed on November 14, 2020, from www.hcltech.com/blogs/pandemic-analytics-how-data-and-analytics-can-help-us-combat-covid-19

Stevens, H. (March 14, 2020) Why Outbreaks Like Coronavirus Spread Exponentially, and How to "Flatten the Curve", *The Washington Post*, Last accessed on May 17, 2021, from www.washingtonpost.com/graphics/2020/world/corona-simulator/

[Survey Results], Results Represent Responses from 3,008 Survey Participants Interviewed from November 1–14, 2020, with a margin of error of +/—1.8%.

Tolk, A., Glazner, C., and Ungerleider, J. (January–February 1, 2021) Computational Decision Support for the COVID-19 Healthcare Coalition, *Computing in Science & Engineering*, 23(1), 17–24. http://dx.doi.org/10.1109/MCSE.2020.3036586

Verma, N. (May, 2020) Big Data Analytics and the COVID-19 Pandemic, *SG Analytics*, Last accessed on November 14, 2020, from www.sganalytics.com/blog/covid/big-data-analytics-and-the-covid-19-pandemic/

Vivekanandarajah, A. (March 31, 2021) How Data Analytics Supported the Development and Distribution of COVID-19 Vaccines, *Selerity*, Last accessed on June 1, 2021, from https://seleritysas.com/blog/2021/03/31/how-data-analytics-supported-the-development-and-distribution-of-covid-19-vaccines/

Washington State Department of Health (April 3, 2020) New Dashboards Make COVID-19 Data Visual, *Press Release*, Last accessed on May 17, 2021.

Wertheim, H. F. L., Horby, P., and Woodall, J. P. (2012) *Atlas of Human Infectious Diseases*. Hoboken, NJ: John Wiley & Sons.

WHO Ebola Response Team (2014) Ebola Virus Disease in West Africa—the First 9 Months of the Epidemic and Forward Projections. *New England Journal of Medicine* 371: 1481–1495. http://dx.doi.org/10.1056/NEJMoa1411100.

WHO Ebola Response Team et al. (2015) West African Ebola Epidemic after One Year—Slowing But Not Yet Under Control. *New England Journal of Medicine* 372: 584–587. http://dx.doi.org/10.1056/NEJMc1414992.

Wickham, H. (2016) *Ggplot2: Elegant Graphics for Data Analysis*. Berlin, Germany: Springer.

Yigitcanlar, T., Kankanamge, N., Preston, A. et al. (2020) How Can Social Media Analytics Assist Authorities in Pandemic-related Policy Decisions? Insights from Australian States and Territories. *Health Information Science and Systems* 8(37) https://doi.org/10.1007/s13755-020-00121-9

Chapter 7

Disease and Pandemic Potential

"The environment is changing and so are the viruses."

—Steven Magee

A pandemic is a crisis situation that results in destruction of human life, disruption, as well as economic turmoil. The COVID-19 pandemic which is caused by a zoonotic virus is an example of an emerging infectious disease that has created unprecedented challenges, shown exponential growth, and has had adverse impacts of a scale that have not been faced earlier by mankind. In Chapter 4, we discussed the COVID-19 pandemic and coronaviruses, the family of viruses which SARS-CoV-2 belongs to and causes the COVID-19 disease.

Pandemics are not new. They have been hitting mankind since ancient ages. However, what is new and different are the demography, infrastructure, technology, connectivity, and culture, and the role these factors play in how a disease can spread and take the shape of a pandemic. For example, the 1918–1919 Spanish flu pandemic, which killed up to 50 million people, occurred at a time when the world population was lower and international travel was not that common. Hence, events diffused more slowly in some parts of the world. The Spanish flu pandemic affected less than half of the countries across the world (Liang et al., 2021). However, in today's age with international travel being more common, the global impact of COVID-19 occured at a much greater speed, with almost all countries across the world being impacted within a span of few months.

Aviation tracker Flightradar24 followed an average of 188,901 flights per day criss-crossing the globe, in 2019. COVID-19 was first officially reported at the end of 2019. Three months down line, in March 2020, the average daily number had only dropped to around 145,000. Modern transport networks can proficiently spread a pathogen a few hundreds or thousands of miles within hours, thus making every flight a vessel for COVID-19 infection (Mearns and Parkinson, 2020).

There are a lot of pathogens and a lot of these infect humans. It is important to be able to answer the following questions with respect to pathogens and diseases:

What is risk factor associated with these pathogens infecting humans as well as the effectiveness of human-to-human transmission?

Will an infectious disease scale into a pandemic?

DOI: 10.4324/9781003270911-7

What are the factors that determine the pandemic potential of a disease?

In this chapter, we discuss some of the pathogens, their pandemic potential, and the factors determining the pandemic potential of a disease.

Pathogens and Pandemic Potential

There are millions of pathogens and thousands of diseases. Not all of them have caused a pandemic or will cause a pandemic. The key question is:

What pathogens are likely to cause a pandemic?

As reported by Anthony King in 2020 in his article, "Characteristics that Give Viruses Pandemic Potential," virologists lean toward to rank influenza, coronaviruses, and paramyxoviruses as the biggest pandemic threats. Table 7.1 summarizes and compares these viruses along the following dimensions or characteristics:

- Animal reservoirs,
- Spill over history,
- Case fatality rate,
- Transmission, and
- Animals affected.

While prior to COVID-19, most virologists regarded influenza as the biggest pandemic threat, with the ongoing COVID-19 pandemic, some researchers rank coronaviruses as the biggest threat. This is reinforced by Steve Luby, an epidemiologist at Stanford University, when he says, "I'd put coronavirus ahead of flu. It demonstrated higher case fatality—not with SARS-CoV-2, but we have seen it with SARS and MERS. . . . Our immediate highest risk is coronaviruses. (King, 2020)." Coronaviruses has been discussed in Chapter 3.

One characteristic that signals pandemic potential in a virus is, the virus containing an RNA, rather than DNA genome. The reason behind this is that the process of copying RNA typically doesn't include a proof-reader like the process of DNA replication does. Hence, RNA viruses have higher mutation rates than the DNA viruses. "This means they can change and become more adaptable to human infection and human transmission," says Steve Luby, an epidemiologist at Stanford University (King, 2020).

"An RNA virus that causes respiratory tract infections can evolve into something we haven't seen before and spread rapidly," says Ralph Baric, a virologist at the University of North Carolina, Chapel Hill (King, 2020).

Influenza is an RNA virus which can mutate. While not all influenza viruses infect humans, some of the viruses with killer features might undergo transformation in a manner that allows them to spread more easily, from one individual to another individual. Influenza virus can shapeshift in a drastic fashion. Its RNA genome is divided into eight segments. When two different subtypes of virus (whether, avian or mammalian strains), are in one cell, viral segments can be transposed to create completely new strains. "Pigs carry similar receptors to humans, and they can be infected by avian and mammalian viruses," says virologist Kanta Subbarao, Director of the World Health Organization (WHO) Collaborating Centre for Reference and Research on Influenza in Melbourne (King, 2020).

Table 7.1 Viruses that Are Considered as Topmost Pandemic Threats

Characteristics	Coronaviruses	Influenza	Paramyxoviruses (Henipaviruses)
Animal reservoirs	Huge diversity in insectivorous bats and fruit-eating bats. Horseshoe bats (genus *Rhinolophus*) in Southeast Asia harbor SARS—like coronaviruses.	Water birds, poultry, and domestic pigs. Some outbreaks in dogs and horses.	Some family members abundant in fruit bats.
Spillover history	Four "common cold" coronaviruses may have origins in bats, possibly in last few centuries. SARS caused an outbreak during 2003–04. MERS continues to infect people, presumably jumping from camels.	Numerous pandemics throughout human history were likely due to flu. Confirmed flu pandemics include the devastating 1918 pandemic, as well as pandemics in 1957–58, 1969, and 2009.	Hendra virus infected horses and people first in 1994. Nipah virus first recorded in pigs and humans in 1998.
Case fatality rate	Varies hugely. COVID-19 possibly around 1 percent. SARS is thought to be closer to 15 percent. MERS has proved fatal in about 35 percent of patients.	In the case of the 1918 pandemic, the case fatality rate was around 2.5 percent globally.	Some of the deadliest known pathogens. Hendra virus rarely infects humans, but when it does, the fatality rate is around 50 percent. The case fatality rate for Nipah is even higher, ranging from 50 percent to 100 percent in some outbreaks.
Transmission	Contact and airborne (droplets and aerosols)	Contact and airborne (droplets and aerosols)	Mostly urine and saliva from bats contaminating food of domestic animals and humans. Close contact between people for Nipah
Animals affected	Dogs, pigs, cats, cattle, camels, and others	Pigs, horses, ferrets, dogs, and poultry	Hendra virus infects horses and dogs. Nipah virus infects pigs (and lab animals such as hamsters and ferrets)

Source: From King (2020)

The 1957 and 1968 flu pandemics were caused by viruses, with some gene segments from avian influenza viruses and other segments from circulating human flu viruses. It is long proposed that the mixing of gene segments took place in an intermediate host, probably pigs. (King, 2020).

Another matter of concern is when the H protein in bird flu viruses gains the ability to infect human cells. This lets the virus to jump to humans, introducing them to a new strain with avian proteins to which they have little or no immunity and hence are easily susceptible.

Paramyxoviruses is a large family of viruses that includes mumps and respiratory syncytial virus (RSV), as well as Nipah virus. Nipah virus has a fatality rate between 50 percent and 100 percent, and hence, it is matter of great concern (King, 2020).

While Nipah virus has not yet caused extensive outbreaks in people, other paramyxoviruses, such as measles and mumps, have caused extensive outbreak as they spread more efficiently. "Some of these viruses spread really well," says Rebecca Dutch, a molecular biologist at the University of Kentucky. If Nipah moved efficiently from one person to another, perhaps mutating so it transmits before making someone really sick, "this would be devastating," says Steve Luby, "more like the Black Plague (King, 2020)."

Scientists are also paying attention to filoviruses such as Ebola and Marburg virus, which cause hemorrhagic fever and can infect apes, monkeys, and bats, in addition to humans. However, since Ebola requires blood or body fluids to be transmitted, it is harder to transmit, hence is less likely to evolve into a pandemic (King, 2020).

Factors Determining Pandemic Potential

Not every new disease or known disease caused by new strains of pathogen evolves into a human pandemic and nobody knows whether a disease will evolve into a human pandemic. Human beings are necessarily not susceptible to all diseases that infect other species. It could, probably, remain largely restricted to animal or bird population or species or only spread to a limited human population for a limited time, and then never resurface, and be forgotten eventually.

However, little stands between the best-case scenarios and worst-case scenarios. If the pathogen does mutate into a form that transmits easily from individual to individual, it could evolve into a pandemic. Because of the globally connected world, pandemic would likely infect a large population simultaneously in different locations across the globe, with well-connected thickly populated cities worse impacted.

The mode of transmission, effectiveness and pace of transmission, length of asymptomatic (that is, without symptoms) infectious periods, probability of detection and containment, and the rate of spread of infection are important considerations to gauge the possible scale of impact in terms of both severity and timeframe as shown in Figure 7.1. Collection, analysis, and sharing of these data can help predict the impact. Data-driven decisions can help leaders take correct steps to stop, or at the least, mitigate disease spread.

Not all pathogens have the potential to cause severe pandemics. If the effectiveness of transmission is low, rate of spread of infection is low, length of asymptomatic infectious periods is low and there is high probability of detection and containment, the risk of the disease taking the shape of a global pandemic is low.

On the other hand, if the effectiveness of transmission is high, rate of spread of infection is high, length of asymptomatic infectious periods is high which causes the disease to go undetected in infected individuals and transmission to others, and there is low probability of detection and containment, the risk of the disease taking the shape of a global pandemic is very high.

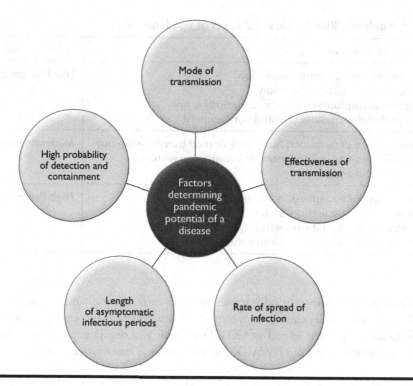

Figure 7.1   Factors determining pandemic potential of a disease.

The mode of transmission can play a significant role in the spread of the pathogen and disease. The most alarming situation is when a pathogen can spread through respiratory droplets, allowing it to jump from person to person through close contact, as seen in the case of seasonal flu and SARS-CoV-2 (that causes COVID-19).

Capturing the rate of spread of infection by testing people and storing test data results, using mobile location data and digital contact tracing to detect and measure infection spread, capturing data for the different epidemiological parameters discussed in Chapter 3, and designing good models using the data can certainly help drive decisions that help tackle disease. However, at the heart of this exercise is good quality data and no amount of sophisticated modelling or analytics can make up for inadequate measurement or other data quality issues like incompleteness, inadequate coverage, timeliness issues, and inconsistencies.

Table 7.2 shows the pandemic risk factors and the level of pandemic risk.

If the pathogens do not demonstrate sustained human-to-human transmission but could become transmitted more efficiently as a result of mutations and adaptation, there is a moderate risk of the disease taking the shape of a pandemic (Jamison et al., 2017). For example, swine flu is a viral disease that is common in pigs, but not in human beings. This, however, changed once an antigenic shift occurred. Other viruses that are a matter of concern along similar lines are the viruses that are linked to camels (Middle East Respiratory Syndrome, or MERS-CoV) and monkeys (Ebola) (Felman, 2020).

The effectiveness of transmission and rate of spread of infection for contagious diseases such as COVID-19 can be reduced by strategies such as implementing appropriate response strategies (e.g., travel restrictions, shutting down of effective areas, quarantine high-risk area, level of restrictions on social gatherings, school and workplace closure policies, and criteria for testing), practice of good hygiene, use of face masks, compliance with social distancing, and availability of non-

Table 7.2 Pandemic Risk Factors and Level of Pandemic Risk

Pandemic Risk Factors	Level of Pandemic Risk
• Effectiveness of transmission are low • Rate of spread of infection is low • Length of asymptomatic infectious periods is low • High probability of detection and containment	**Low Pandemic Risk**
• Non-existence of sustained human-to-human transmission but could become transmitted more efficiently as a result of mutations and adaptation	**Moderate Pandemic Risk**
• Effectiveness of transmission are high • Rate of spread of infection is high • Length of asymptomatic infectious periods is high • Low probability of detection and containment	**High Pandemic Risk**

pharmaceutical and pharmaceutical interventions. However, the individual strategies might differ from disease to disease depending on the mode of transmission. For example, while face masks would help restrict/prevent spread of COVID-19 with is a respiratory disease, it would not be helpful in restricting spread of HIV/AIDS, which is sexually transmitted disease.

Concluding Thoughts

Pandemic pathogens are uncommon, and are by their nature not easy to foresee. Hence, they tend to catch humankind unaware, when the disaster strikes. In this chapter, we discussed some of the pathogens that have pandemic potential and the factors to look out for when gauging the pandemic potential of a disease. Collection, analysis, and sharing of data related to these factors can help leaders to understand the risks and make informed decisions as to how to tackle a disease.

The number of emerging infectious diseases (EID) events has increased over time, with zoonoses comprised the majority of EID events. While not all these events were pandemics, pandemics are not going to go away. There will be more in the future too. For example, the coronavirus that causes COVID-19 is the third virus in the past two decades to jump from animals to humans. The likelihood of pandemics has increased over the past century because of increased global connectivity and travel, urbanization, changes in land use, and greater exploitation of the natural environment (Jones et al., 2008; Morse, 1995). It is a terrifying trend, one that's expected to continue.

References

Felman, A. (March 30, 2020) What to Know about Pandemics, *Medical News Today*. Last accessed on December 3, 2020, from https://www.medicalnewstoday.com/articles/148945

Jamison, D. T., Gelband, H., Horton, S., et al. (eds) (November 27, 2017) *Disease Control Priorities: Improving Health and Reducing Poverty*, 3rd ed., Washington, DC: The International Bank for Reconstruction and Development/The World Bank.

Jones, K. E., Patel, N. G., Levy, M. A., Storeygard, A., Balk, D., and others (2008) Global Trends in Emerging Infectious Diseases, *Nature* 451 (7181): 990–993.

King, A. (August 17, 2020) Characteristics that Give Viruses Pandemic Potential, *The Scientist*, Last accessed on December 3, 2020, from www.the-scientist.com/feature/characteristics-that-give-viruses-pandemic-potential-67822

Liang, S. T., Liang, L. T., and Rosen, J. M. (2021) COVID-19: A Comparison to the 1918 Influenza and How We Can Defeat It, *Postgraduate Medical Journal* 97: 273–274.

Mearns, E., and Parkinson, G. (2020) The Pandemic Playbook: Successful Strategies That Save Lives, *CGTN*, Last accessed on July 3, 2020, from https://newseu.cgtn.com/news/2020-04-29/The-Pandemic-Playbook-Successful-strategies-that-save-lives-PIKqCFMHEk/index.html

Morse, S. S. (1995) Factors in the Emergence of Infectious Diseases, *Emerging Infectious Diseases* 1 (1): 7–15.

Chapter 8

Pandemic and Critical Success Factors

"We live in an interconnected world, in an interconnected time, and we need holistic solutions."

—Naomi Klein

An Introduction to Pandemic Myths and Critical Success Factors

Pandemic is a period of great uncertainty with a multisector impact. Given the havoc that a pandemic can wreak, it is necessary to prepare for a pandemic and understand the different myths in relation to pandemics and the critical success factors in preparing for a pandemic and managing a disease outbreak.

Critical success factors (CSFs) are the specific elements that are vital for an initiative or program to be successful. D. Ronald Daniel of McKinsey & Company developed the concept of "success factors" in 1961 (Daniel, 1961). The refinement into critical success factors by John F. Rockart took place between 1979 (Rockart, 1979) and 1981 (Rockart, 1986). In 1995, James A. Johnson and Michael Friesen applied the concept of critical success factors to numerous industry sector settings, including healthcare (Johnson and Friesen, 1995). CSFs are those factors which are critical to the success of any organization, in the sense that, if intents connected with the factors are not accomplished, the organization will fail, perhaps catastrophically so (Rockart, 1979; Mahanti, 2019).

In this chapter, we discuss the various myths pertaining to pandemics and the different critical success factors in preparing for a pandemic and managing a disease outbreak.

Pandemic Myths

"I'm always interested in debunking myths if they are untrue. But it's also important to identify myths and how they function, what value they may have."

—Neal Ascherson

DOI: 10.4324/9781003270911-8

Myths are widely held misconceptions, false beliefs or ideas. Myths have been in vogue since ancient times and have been an important part of the cultural fabric and traditions throughout human history, which people invented to make something appear more interesting or awesome than it actually was. In other cases, they were exaggerations, misunderstandings, and Chinese Whispers that gained credence and became common knowledge over times.

Pandemic is a crisis situation. While each disease pandemic will have its own unique myths centered around the specific disease and related pathogen, some common myths associated with pandemics are as follows (see Figure 8.1).

Myth 1. Pandemics Are Public Health Problem Only

New diseases and pandemics are perceived as public health problem only, that is they have a health impact only. However, this is not true. Pandemics have far-reaching and multi-sector impact— political, social, economic, and business impacts.

Pandemics can be very expensive. The costs of SARS to the global economy was estimated by BioERA at >$30–$50 billion, and as per data, the past decade of outbreaks has been responsible for hundreds of $US billions in losses (Karesh and Machalaba, 2013). As per the semi-annual Global Economic Prospects report released by the World Bank in early 2021, the world economy probably shrank by 4.3% in 2020, a setback matched only by the Great Depression and the two world wars (The Economist, 2021).

Myth 2. Pandemics Are Extremely Rare and Have Short-Term Impacts

While novel disease outbreaks occur infrequently, they appear to be increasing because of increase in human–animal contact, due to disruption of natural habitat (caused by urbanization) and consumption and farming of wild animals. They have massive adverse impacts at local, regional, and global scales. Just because an outbreak starts suddenly, it does not mean it always ends rapidly as well; it may re-emerge in humans (as seen with Ebola), or become global and last for years (as seen with Cholera and COVID-19).

Most of the infectious human diseases have emerged from animals and transmitted to humans at some point in time; and they now account for over one million deaths and more than one billion illnesses annually (Karesh and Machalaba, 2013).

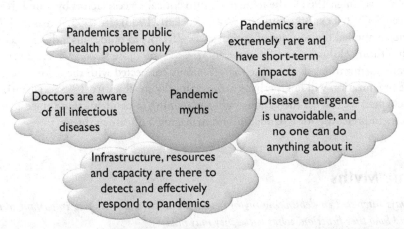

Figure 8.1   Pandemic myths.

Myth 3. Doctors Are Aware of All the Infectious Diseases

Doctors do not have knowledge of all of the infectious diseases. The WHO uses the term, "disease X" to acknowledge that a serious epidemic could be caused by a pathogen currently unknown to cause human disease (King, 2020).

Medical science has identified and named more than 1,400 infectious disease-causing agents. However, this is only the tip of the iceberg (Karesh and Machalaba, 2013). There are a number of undiscovered viruses in animals, birds, and reptiles, and some of these can jump from animals to humans.

Research needs to be undertaken to track and study these undiscovered pathogens. However, research needs funding, and getting funding is not easy. This is reinforced by Rebecca Dutch, a molecular biologist at the University of Kentucky, when she says (King, 2020):

> Until SARS emerged in 2002, those who study coronaviruses had trouble getting anyone to fund their research. There certainly could be things out there we don't know about.

Many new diseases originate in developing countries that do not have the resources for early detection, prevention or research, thus delaying opportunities for proactive discovery and intervention and preventing or slowing down the spread (Karesh and Machalaba, 2013).

Also, disease detection is not always as forthright. There are deterrents to detection of diseases, such as impacts on tourism and trade as people would avoid the affected areas (Karesh and Machalaba, 2013).

Myth 4. Infrastructure, Resources, and Capacity Are There to Detect and Effectively Respond to Pandemics

This misconception is rooted in the belief that new disease has short-term impacts and countries have the infrastructure, resources, and capacity to detect and respond to them effectively. While developed countries have capacity to detect and respond to common diseases, developing countries might barely or not have that capacity. The COVID-19 pandemic has exposed the strain that health systems have been under, and has certainly dispelled the myth that countries have adequate infrastructure, resources, and capacity to detect and respond to pandemics efficiently.

A 2009 World Bank/UN study estimated that an over $2 billion/year investment was needed through 2020 to get nations up to speed on diseases commonly shared between animals and people. That price tag seems steep, but pales in comparison to the costs of pandemic. Also there are potential cost-savings from tackling novel diseases in tandem across sectors through a "One Health" approach that considers links between humans, animals, and the environment (Karesh and Machalaba, 2013).

Myth 5. Disease Emergence Is Unavoidable, and No One Can Do Anything About It

While disease emergence is not avoidable, the root causes and spread of new diseases are not without reason. Rapid urbanization, and human beings' incursion into forest lands and deforestation have resulted in many species losing their habitat. This has created a new interface between humans and wildlife; and exposed humans to unfamiliar organisms often involving the consumption of exotic wildlife and subsequently creating a prolific ground for the propagation of zoonotic viruses. Preventive measures need to put in place to protect wildlife and nature, so that conditions for viral spill over events are minimized, if not eradicated.

Another way of dealing with disease emergence is to look for them before outbreaks occur, and in what species. USAID's Emerging Pandemic Threats program has invested in integrated disease surveillance and detection programs in developing countries that are "hotspots" for disease emergence. The WHO has a group of national labs to keep a look out for emerging strains of flu. It works in partnership with the World Organisation for Animal Health. This will help find new viruses, learn more about their risks to humans, and work with local governments to take actions to reduce risks of emergence (King, 2020; Karesh and Machalaba, 2013).

Critical Success Factors to Manage a Pandemic

From a perspective of preparing for and managing a pandemic, critical success factors (CSFs) would be elements that play a role in successfully fighting the disease. Figure 8.2 illustrate the critical success factors for managing a disease outbreak and pandemic, and each factor has been discussed as follows.

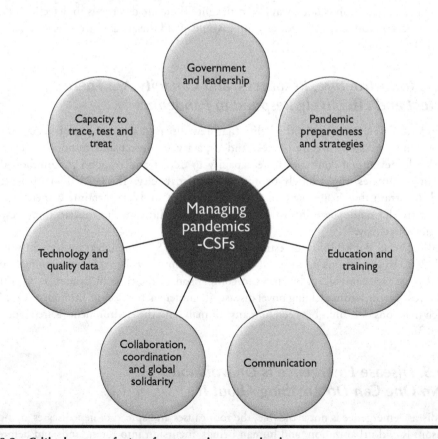

Figure 8.2 Critical success factors for managing a pandemic.

Government and Leadership

Only governments have the power to ensure that

- cases of infectious disease are reported promptly and accurately,
- policies are in place for preventive care,
- treatments are available,
- good public health practices are widely known and followed, and
- budget for funding in research in prevention of pandemic such as research of pathogens that can have a pandemic potential are available and assigned.

When and after a disease outbreak of an epidemic or pandemic level happens, power as well as authority are required to help a population return quickly to some semblance of normality (Brilliant, 2006).

Leadership plays a critical role in handling any crisis situation and pandemic is no different. Any crisis—including a pandemic—requires leaders to make sense of a fast changing and extremely uncertain state of affairs that threatens their societies' fundamental values (Boin et al., 2005). Key organizational and psychological determinants of crisis decision-making include, for example, leaders' beliefs (Brummer, 2016; Swinkels, 2020), different personalities in crisis recognition (Jong, 2017; van Esch and Swinkels, 2015), or opportunities for reform (Boin and 't Hart, 2003).

When contending with a crisis like the ongoing pandemic, it is easy for leaders to fall into the traps of waiting for the situation to make clear how to act and toning down the threat in order to reassure the public. However, this is not the right approach. Leaders are required to act in an urgent, honest, and iterative fashion, acknowledging that blunders are unavoidable and correcting course. Two examples of where leaders acted with urgency early on during the COVID-19 pandemic are as follows (Kerrissey and Edmondson, 2020).

1. Adam Silver, the commissioner of the National Basketball Association (NBA), on March 11, 2020 (the day that the World Health Organization formally designated the coronavirus a pandemic) took the then-surprising step of suspending the professional basketball league for the season. His decision was one of the earliest high-profile responses to COVID-19 outside China and at a time of great uncertainty, but a decision that changed the course of the virus by protecting million fans from probable exposure at games.
2. New Zealand Prime Minister Jacinda Ardern's response to the COVID-19 pandemic was bold and stimulated public support. On March 21, 2020, she released an eight-minute televised statement to the state, in which, she declared a four-level COVID-19 alert system. Modeled on fire risk systems already in use in New Zealand, this well-known approach set well-defined guidelines as to how the government would step up its response as well as what would be asked of citizens as infection rates increased. At that time, New Zealand had only 52 confirmed cases, the alert level was set at two, restricting some travel and pressing people to restrict contact. However, when cases grew to 205 four days later, the alert system was elevated to level four, activating a nationwide lockdown, which helped control the spread of the disease.

Predominantly in the initial stages of a crisis, sense-making and decision-making are at the heart of effective leadership (Boin et al., 2005). Sense-making describes the task of recognizing the existence (and severity) of a crisis and comprehending its origins. Unless the existence of a problem is acknowledged, steps to solve the problem cannot be devised. Recognizing the existence of a problem is subject to individual biases and institutional hurdles. Consequently, during the COVID-19 pandemic world leaders differed widely in their sense-making of COVID-19 (Glenn et al., 2021). Second, decision-making requires leaders to evaluate and adopt policies to mitigate the crisis at a time of considerable uncertainty (Boin et al., 2005). Decision-making is greatly influenced by leaders' ability to coordinate diverse groups of policymakers and stakeholders. During COVID-19, national and local governments' decision-making varied widely, and some of that variation has been ascribed to the leaders enabling these decisions (Al Saidi et al., 2020; Dirani et al., 2020; Reicher and Stott, 2020).

In the early stages of a crisis, leaders need to separate signal from noise and create a comprehensible story to facilitate crisis response (Boin et al., 2005). Those leaders whose countries were exposed to COVID-19 early, faced "first-mover disadvantages" (Lipscy, 2020, pp. 14–15; Plümper and Neumayer, 2020) because of the substantial uncertainty surrounding the severity and nature of the virus (that is too many unknowns) and the need to take unprecedented steps to mitigate it. Thus, such first-mover disadvantages rendered sense-making challenging and decisions needed to be taken based on little available data at the time (Forster and Heinzel, 2020).

In order to implement any strategy aimed to manage a pandemic and sustain its economy, countries need leadership at different levels that centralizes and coordinates actions. Leaders must be able to create flexible plans in the face of uncertain and fast changing situations, communicate clearly, and lead with compassion, clarity, and empathy. They also need to speak frequently, clearly, and with a consistent tone and message to their public. Leaders are responsible for the coordination of responses, across the health sector public, private sectors, and non-government organizations (Ahern and Loh, 2020).

Pandemic is a crisis, which is reigned by unfamiliarity and uncertainty. Hence, effective responses from leadership need to be improvised to a great extent (Howitt and Leonard, 2009). From business perspective, response strategies might involve a wide range of short-term and long-term actions: not just temporary moves (for example, instituting work-from-home policies) but also adjustments to ongoing business practices (such as the adoption of new tools to aid collaboration), which can be beneficial to maintain even after the crisis has passed, as well clear and ongoing communication. Another critical part of the leader's role, specifically in the emotional, tense, uncertain, and insecure environment that characterizes a pandemic crisis, is offering psychological support and promoting psychological safety so that the public can openly discuss ideas, questions, and concerns without fear of repercussions. This allows the network of teams to have brainstorming sessions to better understand the situation, and figure out how to best handle it (D'Auria and De Smet, 2020).

Leadership decisions should be driven by data rather than intuition. The exceptional disaster triggered by the COVID-19 pandemic elevated the importance of data-driven decisions in different industry sector to help manage the pandemic and assist economic recovery. Public-sector as well as private-sector data leaders had to quickly create capabilities and facilitate access to new data while addressing ethical concerns, and operate in an agile, innovative, synchronized, and cooperative fashion to meet the data needs of key policy decision-makers and the public (Jaiani and Audet, 2020).

Capacity to Trace, Test, and Treat

Early detection of disease can play a key role in isolating and treating the patients and preventing further disease spread. Detection must be a smooth and efficient process. Medical establishments need to keep a lookout for uncommon patterns and report them upward to the management, and management should rapidly assess them, and if necessary, alert international authorities. This is because, depending on its pathology, a small outbreak could well be on its way to becoming a pandemic by infecting thousands or millions of people across the country and the world (Mearns and Parkinson, 2020).

It is also necessary to understand the scope and extent of disease spread. This requires the ability to contact trace the people who have come in contact with the infected people as well as a capacity to test a large number of individuals. The ability to contact trace and test also needs increase in human resources (for example, health care staff, emergency management, and armed forces) and other resources (for example, infrastructure and effective diagnostic kits). Relationships with workforce agencies, regulatory bodies, and academic institutions can assist in creation of surge workforce capacity (Ahern and Loh, 2020).

Education and Training

Education and training bring about an enhancement in knowledge and skills and a transformation in behavior and outlook of the personnel (Mahanti, 2019).

A new disease requires educating and training people (general public, healthcare workers, and organization employees) on different levels. For example, healthcare workers need to be trained with testing, detecting, and treating the disease.

Organizations need to educate employees, in advance, about the disease, the modes of transmission, the risks, and the symptoms, and to instruct them to isolate and to inform management if they have been exposed to the pathogen. Although disability discrimination laws protect employees with covered health conditions, limitations can usually be levied, in case it is a direct danger to the health or safety of others (Susser, 2006).

In the pandemic world where key decisions in different industry sectors (for example, health, retail, and pharmaceutical) are being increasingly driven by data, there is a pressing need for educating people about data in general as well in relation to crisis situation such as a pandemic, both from a perspective of usage and comprehension.

Different groups need to be training differently. For example, training employees responsible for inputting data to do so accurately and in accordance with predefined standards will be different from training business leaders and management throughout the organization to collaborate with the data team to extract insights. It is best to offer training right before employees can put these skills into practice. This accomplishes two things:

1. Employees are given an opportunity to understand and to absorb the concepts.
2. Employees have the knowledge and skills acquired in the training still fresh in their minds, hence can put them to practice more effectively.

With respect to managing the COVID-19 pandemic, Josh Martin, Chief Data Officer, State of Indiana, emphasized the need for citizens—both public trying to understand data and the visualizations created from the data and employees engaged in data related work to be educated in data literacy (Jaiani and Audet, 2020).

Educating the general public about the pandemic, technology, and data is very important. People need to be able to understand the implications of the pandemic, the significance of technology (for example, contact tracing apps) and comprehend the data, results, and visualizations related to the pandemic and make informed decisions. Reliable data are not of any use, if people do not have a data mindset or they are not able comprehend it. Hence, it is very important to work toward building a data literate population and educating people about data, needs to be a part of the strategy to manage a pandemic crisis.

Pandemic Preparedness and Strategies

"It's better to be prepared for something that doesn't happen than unprepared for something that does," says Michael Osterholm, Director of the University of Minnesota's Center for Infectious Disease Research and Policy (CIDRAP) (Zeidner, 2009).

One does not need to wait for catastrophe to strike before putting a plan into action. For diseases that can spread through droplets (such as influenza), simple preventive measures can restrict the spread of illness. Organizations and governments should promote better hygeine by providing hand sanitizers in work places and public places.

It is essential to track and plan for a disease that can have pandemic potential. Preparing for a pandemic and building suitable and quick response plans is important to manage the risk. Pandemic is a period of great uncertainty. A pandemic not only adversely affects the health sector, but also has a social, business, and economic impact. Hence, different strategies need to be devised at different levels to not only to prepare for the pandemic, combat disease, and save lives, but also deal with the social and economic impact, and plan for business continuity. Response strategies would involve a combination of preventive strategies and mitigation strategies to stop or at least slow down the spread of the disease. Appropriate risk communication strategies are required to communicate accurate and timely information to the public, so that they know what is expected of them. Since pandemics have a great degree uncertainty associated with them, strategies should be adaptive to be able to deal with the changes. It is also important to have strategies for recovery once the pandemic is over.

Data and technology can play a significant role in devising response strategies. Mathematical models can be used to appraise parameters of pathogen spread, investigate probable future scenarios, assess retrospectively the effectiveness of specific interventions, and identify potential strategies. However, good modeling requires facts, that is, accurate data.

As initial pandemic responses are put in place and data accrues, the focus shifts to retrospective evaluation of the effectiveness of particular strategies. Statistical inference algorithms can be used to fit core epidemiological models to case data and data on the timing and nature of control interventions. Retrospective evaluations of specific interventions and comprehensive modeling efforts lead to the identification of more targeted prospective strategies. For example, different countries, states, cities, and localities differ in their ability to act in response to the pandemic and hence require distinct strategies for tightening or relaxing interventions (Metcalf et al., 2020).

The COVID-19 pandemic has been unparalleled in terms of real-time collection and distribution of diverse datasets, ranging from disease outcomes, to mobility, behaviors, and socio-economic factors. The data sets have been crucial from the standpoint of disease modeling and analytics to support policymakers and devising response strategies (Adiga et al., 2020).

Strategies for dealing with a digital age pandemic are not to limited to response strategies in combating the disease, but also strategies around educating different groups of people about the pandemic, the related terms (example, super spreaders and various epidemiological parameters), about data and how to interpret data and visualizations related to the pandemic, as well as strategies to combat misinformation and designing effective communication strategies. Pandemic are characterized by sudden changes, and agility is very important to minimize adverse impacts.

Chapter 9 discusses pandemic planning and strategies to manage a pandemic in greater detail.

Communication

Effective communication of risks is vital to be able to control a pandemic. Pandemic destroys social cohesion and when the disease is severe or deadly, people become fearful of one another. Confusing or irrelevant messages can create greater uncertainty in an already uncertain situation. It is important to assess gaps in information as well as remove misinformation.

Accurate, concise information and status updates need to be communicated through multiple channels to provide the right information, at the right time, to the right audience, so that it provides reliable guidance and triggers the right behaviors and actions, and enables people to take adequate measures to effectively prevent disease transmission.

Pandemics evolve, sometimes rapidly, and accurate and reliable information needs to be adapted to the changing circumstance and communicated.

How a message is delivered during a crisis is also important. Communication during crisis situation needs to be transparent, that is providing honest and accurate descriptions of reality—being as clear as humanly possible about what is known, what is anticipated, and what it means for people. It is also important to be empathetic. For example, New Zealand Prime Minister Jacinda Ardern demonstrated empathy when she stated in her early national address (Kerrissey and Edmondson, 2020):

> *I understand that all of this rapid change creates anxiety and uncertainty. Especially when it means changing how we live. That's why today I am going to set out for you as clearly as possible, what you can expect as we continue to fight the virus together.*

Communication also needs to be clear, honest, and compassionate. For example, New Zealand Prime Minister Jacinda Ardern's communication recognized the daily sacrifices to come and stimulated people to forge ahead in bearing them together. She concluded her early national address on March 21, 2021, by thanking New Zealanders for all they were about to do. Her parting words were (Kerrissey and Edmondson, 2020):

> Please be strong, be kind, and unite against Covid-19.

At the same time, communication during a crisis situation such as a pandemic should have a hopeful vision that prevents people from despairing (Kerrissey and Edmondson, 2020).

Technology and Data

Data and technology have a critical role to play in managing a pandemic. It is important to be able to understand the nature of contagion, and the measures that help manage, contain, and prevent spread of the disease. Data sit at the heart of this exercise.

As stated by Dr. Tedros Adhanom Ghebreyesus, director-general of the World Health Organization (WHO), said: "You cannot fight a fire blindfolded." The right information in the hands of the right people can save lives in a time of crisis.

Insights into the nature of the contagion and spread of a disease can help countries respond more effectively to a pandemic. Data leveraged by technology can not only help in understanding the impact of a pandemic across different geographies and forecast the spread of a disease, but can also help plan suitable response to controlling the spread as well as allocation of resources. The role of data in managing a pandemic and the application of data analytics during pandemic have been discussed in detail in Chapters 5 and 6, respectively.

Basic data hygiene and data quality are very important, as critical data need accurate reporting. Bad data quality can lead to wrong conclusions as well as wrong decisions. Data governance is also equally important, as it ties together different aspects of data management, and helps establishing policies, processes, controls, roles, responsibilities, accountabilities, and decision rights around data. For example, it is very important to develop well-defined data analytics-related roles and responsibilities. It is also important to establish policies and practices for individual data steward-ship responsibilities, and provide guidance on how and when data analytics should be used, and formalize the decision-making process (RS&F, 2020). In addition, ethical and privacy concerns need to be taken into consideration to create an organization-wide code of conduct for ethical data use and to socialize and enforce the same across the organization.

In addition to data quality and effective data governance mechanisms, interoperability of systems of records and data, and analytics capabilities are critical elements for leveraging data to help manage a pandemic. In order for analytics to yield effective results, data scientists must have close contact with business leaders and also have a comprehensive understanding of the business challenges. A number of organizational structures may be suitable, but it is crucial to ensure that those with data expertise and deep business knowledge, have the prospect to work together to solve complex business challenges (RS&F, 2020).

Collaboration, Coordination, and Global Solidarity

Pandemic generally effects multiple countries across the world. It is usually a global problem which has several unknowns. It is also an interdisciplinary problem, as it not only has a health impact but also a social, demographic, and economic impact, and requires diverse skill sets. Such a global, interdisciplinary problem requires coordination, collaborative effort, and global solidarity to finding viable global solutions which would lead collective success.

In the globally connected world that we are currently living in, isolated action, will not be sufficient to combat a full blown pandemic (for example, COVID-19). The COVID-19 pandemic has been the world's combined learning exercise.

In order to be successful in fighting a pandemic it is necessary to pool, build, and pass innovation from strength to strength. This will require proactive and well-coordinated actions rather than passive monitoring and reporting of activities. One example of collaboration in the private sector to handle the COVID-19 pandemic is the alliance between Apple and Google to improve contact-tracing apps.

In order to work together on COVID-19-related big data sources and applications (policies, best practices, and research) which are distributed globally, global collaboration is a must. However, the open flow of information hardly exists in the healthcare domain. Shared access to reliable global medical data and insights are still lacking (Qiong et al., 2020). Due to sensitive and confidential nature of certain personal health information, there is a deceleration of globalization and an increase in protectionism (Khoday, 2020). These are barriers in adopting a collaborative approach in big data analytics for disease prevention (Qiong et al., 2020).

Cooperation, unparalleled on a global scale, is a critical element in managing a pandemic. A new disease requires research for finding cure as well as vaccine for preventing it. Scientific cooperation with governments, organizations, and universities opening up and sharing their research can facilitate faster and more robust discoveries.

Data and technology sharing arrangements can facilitate expedited discovery and early development efforts in relation to pathogen and treatment, while also creating a foundation for long-term research and development beyond the current outbreak. However, this requires ongoing coordination and collaboration across stakeholders, and mechanisms should be in place to facilitate and ensure the same (WHO, 2020).

Since pathogens and diseases respect no borders, countries need to work in global solidarity to fight a pandemic—share treatment options, cure, and vaccines if available, as well as their experiences and lessons learnt.

Concluding Thoughts

Pandemic is not an isolated crisis, but a crisis that impacts multiple geographies. It can create stress situations for long periods of time, and place extraordinary demands on health systems and community services. It is important to plan and prepare for pandemics. There are number of elements that play a crucial role in controlling a disease outbreak and pandemic. Each of these factors has been discussed in detail in this chapter. The current age is the digital age, which is driven by data and technology. Data and technology play critical roles in managing a pandemic as these feed into all the rest of factors—leadership, education, and training, communication, collaboration, coordination and global solidarity, capacity to trace, test, and treat, and pandemic preparedness and strategies as shown in Figure 8.3.

Figure 8.3   Pandemic critical success factors model.

References

Adiga, A., Chen, J., Marathe, M., et al. (2020) Data-driven Modeling for Different Stages of Pandemic Response. *Journal of the Indian Institute of Science*, 100, 901–915. https://doi.org/10.1007/s41745-020-00206-0

Ahern, S., and Loh, E. (September 30, 2020) Leadership During the COVID-19 Pandemic: Building and Sustaining Trust in Times of Uncertainty. *BMJ Leader*. https://doi.org/10.1136/leader-2020-000271

Al Saidi, A. M. O., Nur, F. A., Al-Mandhari, A. S., El Rabbat, M., Hafeez, A., and Abubakar, A. (2020) Decisive Leadership is a Necessity in the COVID-19 Response. *The Lancet*, 396(10247), 295–298. https://doi.org/10.1016/S0140-6736(20)31493-8

Boin, A., and 't Hart, P. (2003) Public Leadership in Times of Crisis: Mission Impossible? *Public Administration Review*, 63(5), 544–553. https://doi.org/10.1111/1540-6210.00318

Boin, A., 't Hart, P., Stern, E., and Sundelius, B. (2005) *The Politics of Crisis Management: Public Leadership under Pressure*. Cambridge University Press.

Brilliant, L. (May 2006) Policy: What to Expect from Government. *Harvard Business Review*. Last accessed on July 3, 2020, from https://hbr.org/2006/05/preparing-for-a-pandemic

Brummer, K. (2016) 'Fiasco Prime Ministers': Leaders' Beliefs and Personality Traits as Possible Causes for Policy Fiascos. *Journal of European Public Policy*, 23(5), 702–717. https://doi.org/10.1080/13501763.2015.1127277

Daniel, D. R. (September–October 1961) Management Information Crisis. *Harvard Business Review*, p. 111.

D'Auria, G., and De Smet, A. (March 16, 2020) Leadership in a Crisis: Responding to the Coronavirus Outbreak and Future Challenges. *McKinsey and Company*. Last accessed on December 3, 2020 www.mckinsey.com/business-functions/organization/our-insights/leadership-in-a-crisis-responding-to-the-coronavirus-outbreak-and-future-challenges

Dirani, K. M., Abadi, M., Alizadeh, A., Barhate, B., Garza, R. C., Gunasekara, N., Ibrahim, G., and Majzun, Z. (2020) Leadership Competencies and the Essential Role of Human Resource Development in Times of Crisis: A Response to Covid-19 pandemic. *Human Resource Development International*, 23(4), 380–394. https://doi.org/10.1080/13678868.2020.1780078

The Economist (January 7, 2021) What is the Economic Cost of Covid-19?, https://www.economist.com/finance-and-economics/2021/01/09/what-is-the-economic-cost-of-covid-19

Forster, T. and Heinzel M. (2021) Reacting, Fast and Slow: How World Leaders Shaped Government Responses to the COVID-19 Pandemic, *Journal of European Public Policy*, 28:8, 1299–1320, DOI: 10.1080/13501763.2021.1942157

Glenn, J., Chaumont, C., and Dintrans, P. V. (2021) Public Health Leadership in the Times of COVID-19: A Comparative Case Study of Three Countries. *International Journal of Public Leadership*, 17(1), 81–94. https://doi.org/10.1108/IJPL-08-2020-0082

Howitt, A., and Leonard, H. B. (eds) (2009) *Managing Crises: Responses to Large-scale Emergencies*, 1st ed. Washington, DC: CQ Press.

Jaiani, V., and Audet, R. (September 17, 2020) 8 Data Leaders on Leveraging Data During and after COVID-19. *GCN, Data Leaders Roundtable*. https://gcn.com/articles/2020/09/17/data-leaders-roundtable.aspx

Johnson, J. A., and Friesen, M. (1995) *The Success Paradigm: Creating Organizational Effectiveness through Quality and Strategy*. New York: Quorum Books.

Jong, W. (2017) Meaning Making by Public Leaders in Times of Crisis: An Assessment. *Public Relations Review*, 43(5), 1025–1035. https://doi.org/10.1016/j.pubrev.2017.09.003

Karesh, W. B., and Machalaba, C. M. (August 27, 2013) 7 Common Myths about Pandemics and New Diseases. *HuffPost Blog*. Last accessed on December 3, 2020, from www.huffpost.com/entry/pandemics-common-myths_b_3498381

Kerrissey, M. J., and Edmondson, A. C. (April 13, 2020) What Good Leadership Looks Like During This Pandemic. *Harvard Business Review*, https://hbr.org/2020/04/what-good-leadership-looks-like-during-this-pandemic

Khoday, T. (May 24, 2020) Impact of Deglobalization on Global Trade Post COVID-19, Amid Rising Protectionism. *Money Control News*. Last accessed on 15 August 2020, from www.moneycontrol.com/news/business/markets/impact-of-deglobalization-on-global-tradepost-covid-19-amid-rising-protectionism-5306101.html.

King, A. (August 17, 2020) Characteristics That Give Viruses Pandemic Potential. *The Scientist*. Last accessed on December 3, 2020. www.the-scientist.com/feature/characteristics-that-give-viruses-pandemic-potential-67822

Lipscy, P. Y. (2020) COVID-19 and the Politics of Crisis. *International Organization*, 74(S1), E98–E127.

Mahanti, R. (2019) *Data Quality: Dimensions, Measurement, Strategy, Management, and Governance*. Quality Press, ASQ. ISBN: 9780873899772

Mearns, E., and Parkinson, G. (2020) The Pandemic Playbook: Successful Strategies That Save Lives. *CTGN News*. Last accessed on July 3, 2020, from https://newseu.cgtn.com/news/2020-04-29/The-Pandemic-Playbook-Successful-strategies-that-save-lives-PIKqCFMHEk/index.html

Metcalf, J. C. E., Morris, D. H., and Park, S.W. (July 24, 2020) Mathematical Models to Guide Pandemic Response. *Science*, 369(6502), 368–369. https://doi.org/10.1126/science.abd1668

Plümper, T., and Neumayer, E. (2020) Lockdown Policies and the Dynamics of the First Wave of the Sars-CoV-2 Pandemic in Europe. *Journal of European Public Policy*, 1–21. http://dx.doi.org/10.1080/1350 1763.2020.1847170

Qiong, J., Guo, Y., Wang, G., and Barne, S. J. (August 2020) Big Data Analytics in the Fight against Major Public Health Incidents (Including COVID-19): A Conceptual Framework. *International Journal of Environmental Research and Public Health*, 17(17), 6161. https://doi.org/10.3390/ijerph17176161

Reicher, S., and Stott, C. (2020) On Order and Disorder During the COVID-19 Pandemic. *British Journal of Social Psychology*, 59(3), 694–702. https://doi.org/10.1111/bjso.12398

Rockart, J. F. (March 1979) Chief Executives Define Their Own Data Needs. *Sussex Business Review*.

Rockart, J. F. (1986) A Primer on Critical Success Factors. In *The Rise of Managerial Computing: The Best of the Center for Information Systems Research*, edited by Christine V. Bullen. Homewood, IL: Dow Jones-Irwin, 1981, OR, McGraw-Hill School Education Group.

RS&F (2020) The Data Analytics War Room: Lessons Learned from the Covid-19 Pandemic. Last accessed on July 3, 2021, from www.rsandf.com/news/2020/06/the-data-analytics-war-room-lessons-learned-from-the-covid-19-pandemic/

Susser, P. (2006) The Law: Limiting Exposure—of the Legal Kind. *Harvard Business Review*. Last accessed on July 3, 2020, from https://hbr.org/2006/05/preparing-for-a-pandemic

Swinkels, M. (2020) Beliefs of Political Leaders: Conditions for Change in the Eurozone Crisis. *West European Politics*, 43(5), 1163–1186. https://doi.org/10.1080/01402382.2019.1635802

van Esch, F., and Swinkels, M. (2015) How Europe's Political Leaders Made Sense of the Euro Crisis: The Influence of Pressure and Personality. *West European Politics*, 38(6), 1203–1225. https://doi.org/10.10 80/01402382.2015.1010783

WHO (2020) COVID-19 Strategy Update. Last accessed on December 3, 2020, from www.who.int/docs/default-source/coronaviruse/covid-strategy-update-14april2020.pdf?sfvrsn=29da3ba0_6

Zeidner, R. (September 23, 2009) H1N1 Flu Presents Management Challenges. *SHRM Online*. www.shrm.org/ResourcesAndTools/hr-topics/risk-management/Pages/SwineFluPresentsManagementChallenges.aspx

Chapter 9

Pandemic Preparedness and Strategies

"By failing to prepare, you are preparing to fail."

—Benjamin Franklin

"Preparedness is the ultimate confidence builder."

—Vince Lombardi

"Life isn't about waiting for the storm to pass. It's about learning how to dance in the rain."

—Vivian Greene

Any pandemic creates social disruption as well as economic turmoil. In severe outbreaks, human life is endangered. Pandemic is much more than a health emergency. Managing such a crisis requires different response strategies at individual, community, regional, national, organizational, and global level depending on the scale and intensity of the impact.

The COVID-19 pandemic has created unprecedented challenges, shown exponential growth and has had adverse impacts of a scale that have not been faced earlier by mankind. The key to devising a strategy to combat COVID-19 or any other disease pandemic lies in not only understanding the disease itself but also the challenges and the impacts. Data and technology can play a crucial role in building successful strategies around beating and recovering from a disease outbreak.

The executive summary of Joe Biden national COVID-19 strategy reads as follows (Jercich, 2021):

> "We can and will beat COVID-19. America deserves a response to the COVID-19 pandemic that is driven by science, data, and public health—not politics,"

Countries set aside funds to prepare for and respond to risks and threats such as chemical, biological, and nuclear threats that can cause continued, universal disruption. Generally, these are isolated crises with global impact. In contrast to these isolated crises, pandemic is a risk and threat that is global, and can have a massive adverse multi sector impact including health, social, political, business, and economic impact. Hence, it is necessary to invest funds to plan and prepare for a pandemic.

DOI: 10.4324/9781003270911-9

In the previous chapter, we discussed the success factors or the elements critical in managing a pandemic. Pandemic preparedness and strategies to manage a pandemic is one of the critical success factors. In a world that is inundated with data, digital strategies powered by different varieties of data (for example, mobility data, infection data, and epidemiological parameters) can provide insights into the pandemic and drive decisions to deal with the pandemic.

In this chapter, we discuss the strategies for preparing for and combating a pandemic.

COVID-19 pandemic has a put a full-stop on business as usual and has acted as a launching pad for organizations to become virtual, digital-centric, and agile—and to do it all at lightning-fast speed (McKinsey, 2020). Data can play a key role in managing a crisis situation such as pandemic and organizations need to have a data strategy that can be adaptive to changes brought about by the pandemic. The role of data strategies in managing a pandemic, and the key data strategy lessons learnt during the COVID-19 pandemic have also been discussed in this chapter.

Preparing for a Pandemic

"Can we create a pandemic-free world? There is no such thing as a guarantee, but with meticulous preparation and rapid response, we can prevent most outbreaks from getting out of control, and limit the impact of those that spread internationally."

—Dr. Tedros Adhanom Ghebreyesus, Director-General of the World Health Organization

"A pandemic is a lot like a forest fire. If caught early it might be extinguished with limited damage. If allowed to smolder, undetected, it can grow to an inferno that can spread quickly beyond our ability to control it."

—George W. Bush, 2005*

It is essential to track and plan for a potential pandemic. Real-time data and analytics can be used to track a pandemic, and the results can be used to chalk out an action plan. As the pandemic is characterized by high degree of uncertainty and sudden changes, real-time data and analytics followed by quick decision-making is needed.

Pandemic planning helps countries to be prepared to manage a pandemic. Planning may help to reduce transmission of the pathogen, resulting in lesser number of infected individuals, and subsequently lesser number of hospitalizations, and decreased mortality, help continuation or minimized interruption of essential services, consequently reducing the health, economic, and social impact of a pandemic.

WHO has a six-phase pandemic-tracking model that provides a global framework to aid countries in pandemic preparedness and response planning. The six phases have been discussed in detail in Chapter 2 which shows the WHO's assessment of the threat (see Table 9.1).

It is important for countries, states, and organizations to develop risk mitigations plans in phase 3 when scattered or isolated incidence of cases or small clusters of the disease are seen to be occurring in humans and there are possible cases of human-to-human transmission, but not at a level to cause community-level outbreaks. At this stage, it does not indicate that the disease has gained the level of transmission among human beings that will certainly cause a pandemic. However, it is imperative for all countries to start preparing for the possible crisis situation, should the disease spread and

---

*   Matthew, M. April 20, 2020. George W. Bush in 2005: 'If We Wait for a Pandemic to Appear, It Will Be Too Late to Prepare', abc NEWS, Last accessed on May 2, 2021, from https://abcnews.go.com/Politics/george-bush-2005-wait-pandemic-late-prepare/story?id=69979013

Table 9.1 Six-Phase Pandemic-Tracking Model

Interpandemic phase New virus in animals No human cases	Low risk of human cases	1
	Higher risk of human cases	2
Pandemic alert New virus causes human cases	No or very limited human-to-human transmission	③→ Organization should develop risk mitigation plans at Phase 3
	Evidence of increased human-to-human transmission	4
	Evidence of significant human-to-human transmission	5
Pandemic	Efficient and sustained human-to-human transmission	6

reach pandemic levels. Mobility data and digital contact tracing can be very useful at this stage to break the chain of spread. This can prevent cases from spreading and developing into clusters, and clusters from further growing fast to becoming explosive outbreaks.

However, in regions or countries, where the disease spread reaches a phase, characterized by widespread transmission (that is community transmission has led to outbreaks with near exponential growth), physical distancing measures and movement restrictions across population need to be enforced in order to slow the disease spread and set in place other control measures. Physical distancing measures and movement restrictions, often referred to as "shut downs" and "lock downs," can slow disease spread for certain diseases like COVID-19 by limiting contact between people.

However, these measures can have a profound negative impact on individuals, communities, and businesses by bringing social and economic life to almost a halt and curtail their freedom significantly resulting in psychological and physical health issues. Such measures have a disproportionate adverse impact on underprivileged groups, such as people in poverty, immigrants, internally displaced people and refugees, who most often live in congested and under resourced surroundings, and are usually dependent on daily labor for subsistence (WHO, 2020).

Hence, strategies need to focus on a phased transition from extensive transmission down to a stable state of low-level or no transmission, while enabling the resumption of some parts of economic and social life, prioritized by carefully balancing socio-economic benefit and epidemiological risk. Without careful planning for prevention and control of the disease, and in the absence of scaled up public health and clinical care capacities, the premature lifting of physical distancing measures is likely to lead to an uncontrolled resurgence in disease transmission and a more intense second wave of cases (WHO-EMRO, 2020). Real-time data related to number of infections in an area, and use of analytics to locate clusters and high-risk, medium-risk, and low-risk areas can help implement plans to tighten or relax these measures.

The WHO has developed a checklist for influenza pandemic preparedness planning. This checklist can also be used for wider contingency plans involving other disasters caused by the emergence of new, highly transmissible, and/or severe communicable diseases. The checklist reflects international expert opinion and includes the following essential elements in the checklist (WHO, 2005a):

■ Preparing for an emergency;
■ Surveillance;

- Case investigation and treatment;
- Preventing disease spread in the community;
- Maintaining essential services;
- Research and evaluation; and
- Implementation, testing, and revision of the national plan.

Pandemic and Strategies

Liddell and Scott (1999) define strategy as a high-level plan to achieve one or more goals under conditions of uncertainty. The term strategy does not have a universally accepted definition. Therefore, in different contexts and to different individuals, strategy means different things. Pandemic is a period of great uncertainty with a multisector impact, and different strategies need to be devised to handle it.

Pandemics do not only adversely affect the health sector, but also have a social, business, and economic impact. Pandemics can be extremely disruptive, and can cause slowdown and/or interruption of supply chains, interruption of essential services, overflooding of hospitals, weakened economies, public place closures, closure of schools and/or businesses, border and travel restrictions, transportation problems, misinformation, confusion, and public panic.

Hence, different strategies and measures need to be devised at different levels (that is, individual, community, regional, organizational, country, and global levels) to not only combat disease, and save lives, but also deal with the social and economic impact, and plan for business continuity. It is also important to have strategies for recovery once the pandemic is over.

Governments and organizations need to do the following (see Figure 9.1) (Brilliant, 2006):

1. **Create pandemic preparedness and response plan.**

    It is important for governments and organizations to devise strategies around pandemic preparedness and response based on general principles that guide preparedness planning for any acute threat to public health. The aim should be to strengthen existing systems than to build new systems, and adequate resources should be allocated for pandemic preparedness and response.

2. **Act to prevent the disease in the country.**

    This step involves understanding the disease characteristics, and devising and implementing preventive strategies to stop the disease from entering the country. This could range from conducting health screening of people entering the country/region and quarantining them, restricting travel from infected countries or closing borders. Collection and analysis of disease data, such as, but not limited to the number of infections sourced from other countries can help taking the appropriate decisions.

3. **Minimize the outbreak and stamp it out if it gets into the country.**

    If preventive strategies are not successful in keeping the disease out of the country, mitigation strategies would be needed to minimize the outbreak and to make the country disease free. It is very important to have good quality data related to number of infections, rate of transmission of infection, and number of causalities, to plan appropriate response strategies.

    Response strategies include communicating adequate disease and risk information to the public, imposing travel restrictions including closing borders, shutting down of effective areas, quarantine of high-risk areas, imposing restrictions on social gatherings, contact tracing, and organizing non-pharmaceutical and pharmaceutical interventions, including

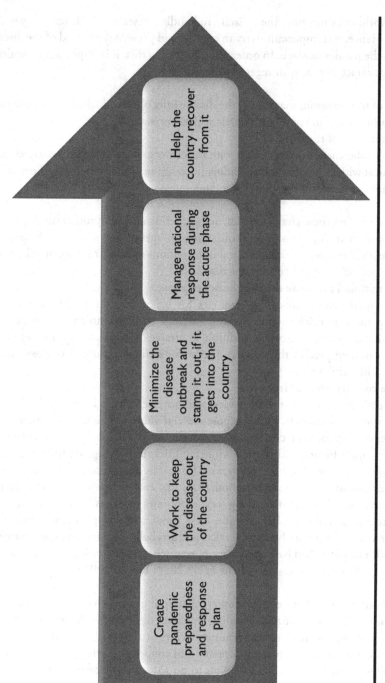

Figure 9.1 Pandemic preparedness and response steps.

organizing testing and treating patients, researching prevention (for example, development of vaccine) and cure, and implementing strategies to protect frontline staff, health workers, and public.

The world does not have the capacity to handle a disease once it reaches pandemic proportions. Hence, it is important to try to contain and prevent the spread of the disease, before it reaches the pandemic stage. In order to be able to do this, it is important to understand the following characteristics, with regard to the disease:

- mode of transmission, that is how the disease infects individuals, for example through the respiratory tract (air) or digestive system (food or water),
- the symptoms of the disease,
- the time difference between contact with the carrier and the symptoms to develop, and
- the rate at which the disease is spreading in communities (for example, the number of new infections in a specific geography per day).

Understanding these characteristics, and gathering and analyzing related data would help devise appropriate risk communication strategies, quarantine strategies, help planning for pharmaceutical and non-pharmaceutical interventions required to stop, or at least slow down the spread of a disease and combat the disease.

4. **Manage national response during the acute phase.**

   This would involve allocating resources for ballooning the health system to treat the increasing number of sick patients, closing interstate borders, implement surge capacity plans for all other impacted sectors in addition to strategies implemented in step 3. Data and analytics can help predict the resource needs (for example, number of hospital beds, ICU facilities, and ventilators).

5. **Help the country recover from it.**

   Pandemic is a crisis that has a widespread adverse impact including health, economic, business and social impacts, and it exposes several vulnerabilities. Governments along with businesses need to focus on creating policies and strategies that help creation of a more robust economic future by addressing these vulnerabilities, improving productivity, and building and strengthening innovation ecosystems—from state, business, and academia-led research and development to commercialization, start-up, entrepreneurship, and venture capital. Governments should focus on making local economies more resilient through diversification of their economic activities. For example, New York City's divergence away from finance and in the direction of tourism, business service, and arts helps the city to endure market volatility better. With its diversified base in education, research, and technology, Austin was able to add jobs during the Great Recession (Cheng et al., 2020; Hartley, 2015).

Individuals must protect themselves and others by adopting right behaviors. In case of COVID-19, washing hands, using hand sanitizers, avoiding touching of face, practicing good respiratory etiquette, social distancing, isolating in a community facility or at home if sick, identifying themselves as a contact of a confirmed case when appropriate, and cooperating with physical distancing measures and movement restrictions when called on to do so, are some of measures at the individual level (WHO, 2020).

Communities must be enabled to ensure that services and aid are designed and improved based on their feedback and local contexts. Critical functions, such as community education, protecting vulnerable groups, supporting health workers, case finding, contact tracing, and cooperation with physical distancing measures can only happen with the support of every part of affected communities (WHO, 2020).

Organizations generally have a business continuity plan to deal with crisis situations. However, these business continuity plans might not be sufficient to deal with a pandemic. This is because a pandemic is dynamic. Hence, while it necessary to plan for crisis, it necessary that both governments (at different levels) and business communities are quick to respond and adaptive to the changing circumstances.

In the words of Charles de Gaulle:

You have to be fast on your feet and adaptive or else a strategy is useless.

Businesses need to plan along the following lines:

- Risk mitigation.
- Supply chain management.
- Education continuity.
- Business continuity.
- Security.
- Transportation.
- Minimization of interruption to essential services.
- Staffing and resource planning, and
- How to prevent transmission?

However. it is important to note that pandemic does not impact all businesses adversely. For example, with the COVID-19 pandemic, tourism, airlines, and travel-related businesses have been hit badly. However, e-commerce and food have benefited from the restrictions (Ugarte, 2021).

Organizations should start by looking at their mission statement. While mission for most organizations will not change, there would be still certain organizations that would need to revise their mission to deal with the pandemic. For example, with the COVID-19 pandemic, if an organization's mission is to have a large number people in a certain area (for example, in cruise ships and for catering functions), then with social distancing required to stop spread of disease, these missions need to revisited (Conerly, 2020).

Pandemic highlights need for a more data-driven business strategy (Olano, 2020).

As per Joel Friedman, Co-Founder, Chief Technology Officer and Head of Software Development at Aclaimant (Olano, 2020):

Even before the pandemic, sophisticated use of data was transforming business to an unprecedented degree. And now, with so many past ways of doing work no longer viable for the time being, businesses must adapt to a dramatically changed set of expectations, norms and possibilities. Because these changes tend to involve an even greater technology component than before, the insightful use of data has become a fundamental determinant of the success or failure of business strategy.

Sales methods, channels, and consumer needs need to be re-evaluated during a pandemic. Sales transaction data and consumer buying trends can give an insight on which products are more in demand as well as the channels of purchase.

For example, with the COVID-19 pandemic which has been characterized by lock downs and social distancing restrictions, on-line shopping, phone deliveries, and work from home, (specifically for technology job streams) have become the new normal. Planning needs to be done to handle increase in home deliveries because of on-line shopping. Data can be used to increase efficiency in shipping and delivery functions. For example, e-commerce giant Amazon uses its data to model their warehouses so as to achieve the best possible shipping efficiency (Ugarte, 2021). In case of work from home, the technologies that enhance the work from home experience needs to be explored, security measures need to enhanced, and remote connectivity needs to be tested to ensure that it is able handle the large number of connections owing to the entire workforce working remotely.

Also, whether these trends will continue to thrive after the pandemic is over, are few things that organizations need to think about. Collecting data through surveys and analyzing the same can give some insight as to what might or might not work in the future. For example, collection and analysis of data in relation to customer satisfaction on various aspects of on-line/phone shopping, such as product quality, delivery, preferences, frequency of ordering, and more, can help understand how many customers are likely to continue with online shopping or organizing through phone calls, post the period when social distancing and lockdown restrictions are lifted as well as post the pandemic period.

Organizations also need to do revisit strategic planning around staffing, products, finances, operations, and other services at different stages of a pandemic.

Data Strategy and the Pandemic

Data, data-driven insights, and data strategies have never been a part of global crisis situation before COVID-19. Hence, many public-sector chief data officers (CDOs) and data leaders did not have the far-sightedness to account for the data requirements needed during the COVID-19 pandemic (Audet and Jaiani, 2020).

These organizations will have to revisit their data strategies and data infrastructure roadmaps with a goal of improving the ways they acquire, store, manage, share, and use data.

Data quality, data architecture, data governance, data security, and data privacy, and more recently analytics have been important elements of a data strategy, but have become more so during the COVID-19 pandemic, and data strategies need to revisited to address specific requirements in each of these areas.

For example, data architecture needed to be revisited as COVID-19 pandemic resulted in a sudden transition to a virtual environment, with a lot of data being stored virtually on the cloud. A shift to cloud-based tools has accelerated innovation and information-sharing as well as increased connectivity across the ecosystem.

Data quality, data governance, data security, and privacy in relation to pandemics have been discussed in detail in Chapter 5 of this book.

Governments and organizations that have used data to combat the effects of COVID-19 have realized several key data strategy lessons that can shape governments' data strategy even beyond the pandemic. These lessons are as follows (Corporate Member News, 2020):

1. Real-time data is central to resilience.
2. Data presentation is most productive when it's focussed on users.

3. Cloud transforms data from a luxury to a utility.
4. Data governance is critical.
5. A data strategy is not complete without quality, governance, privacy, and security.
6. Data-sharing facilitates research, problem solving, and innovation.
7. Identifying and fixing data issues can strengthen decision-making.

The COVID-19 pandemic has forced businesses to change the way they operate, and has resulted in digital acceleration, in fast tracking the digitalization of the world economy and transition toward a digital marketplace (Westley, 2021). More than 70% of attendees at the Metis Strategy Digital Symposium noted that their digital transformation efforts accelerated as a result of the pandemic, with 42% noting a significant acceleration (Metis Strategy, 2020). At the heart of digital transformation is data and technology, and a robust data strategy is an essential component of an organization's digital transformation journey.

As per the forecast by Gartner, IT spending in India is projected to total $81.9 billion in 2021, an increase of 6% from 2020. This is attributed to the fact that the pandemic situation has fast-tracked digital transformation, which has sparked an innovation of a new kind (Rohatgi, 2021).

With the COVID-19 pandemic, consumer behaviors, company operations, and supply chain behaviors have changed. As a result of these changes, the underlying data have also changed and will continue to change through the duration of the pandemic as well as beyond the pandemic. Organizations need to adapt their data strategies to align with the changes and at the same time need to be in tandem with the organizations' wider business strategies.

Organizations also need to reassess priorities for in-flight or planned data initiatives, assess their current-state data maturity to identify data capability gaps, and reprioritize data needs and capabilities that will enable leadership and the public to confidently make data-driven decisions to manage the pandemic and support economic recovery (Audet and Jaiani, 2020).

Concluding Thoughts

Pandemic not only creates a multiple geography wide health crisis, but a social and economic crisis too. There is no single silver bullet which can combat a pandemic crisis; a combination of approaches needs to be applied to reduce the communication and spread of the new disease and subsequently save many lives. It is necessary to develop, test, and adapt strategies for mitigating the severity of a new pandemic.

Data and analytics can be help understanding the disease spread patterns, areas of high concentration, and provide inputs needed to create appropriate response and mitigation strategies. With the COVID-19 pandemic, consumer behaviors, company operations, and supply chain behaviors have changed. As a result of these changes, the underlying data have also changed, and will continue to change as the pandemic evolves and finally disappears. Organizations need to be agile enough to adapt their data strategies to align with changes.

A key to managing a disease spread of the scale of a pandemic is flattening the curve, that is to reduce and slow down the number of infections over a time scale by applying and enforcing prevention and containment strategies so as to not overwhelm the healthcare systems. Prevention and containment strategies can be considered under the broad categories of vaccine and non-pharmaceutical (case isolation, household quarantine, school or workplace closure, and restrictions on travel) measures (WHO, 2005b). Mathematical models powered by good quality and sufficient data are powerful tools for exploring this complex landscape of intervention strategies and quantifying the potential costs and benefits of different options (Ferguson et al., 2001; Keeling et al., 2001; Riley et al., 2003; Lipsitch et al., 2003).

Like COVID-19, in the face of a serious pandemic, much of the world's public health infrastructure will be pathetically overworked. One sure way to ease the suffering that will be encountered in any future pandemic is to invest in construction of a robust public health infrastructure in places where one is lacking and reassess the existing health infrastructures at regular intervals. The effects of pandemic and epidemic diseases have been and are going to be far worse in locations that are inadequately equipped and hence least able to respond (McMillen, 2016).

The economic toll of the COVID-19 pandemic is incalculable. As per the semi-annual Global Economic Prospects report released by the World Bank in early 2021, the world economy probably shrank by 4.3% in 2020, a setback matched only by the Great Depression and the two world wars (The Economist, 2021).

In a conversation with TIME, Bill Gates called for research into drugs and vaccines that can target multiple diseases; shots that are thermostable and longer-lasting than current COVID-19 vaccines; and shots that could deliver the equivalent of multiple doses one time (Ducharme, 2021).

He also stated the following on the cost of COVID 19 and stressed on the need for future pandemic preparedness (Ducharme, 2021):

"The COVID-19 pandemic has cost the global economy trillions of dollars."

"We lost trillions of dollars because we weren't prepared [for this pandemic]. For tens of billions of dollars . . . you can invest [in things like surveillance, vaccines and therapeutics] and make the chance of this happening again extremely low."

References

Audet, R., and Jaiani, V. (July 2020) 5 Tactics for Data Leaders During the Pandemic, *GCN*, *Data Leaders Roundtable*, https://gcn.com/articles/2020/09/17/data-leaders-roundtable.aspx

Brilliant, L. (May 2006) Policy: What to Expect from Government, *Harvard Business Review*, Last accessed on July 3, 2020, from https://hbr.org/2006/05/preparing-for-a-pandemic

Cheng, W.-L., Dua, A., Jacobs, Z., Kerlin, M., Law, J., Safran, B., Schubert, J., Ying Wang, C., Xu, Q., and Zegeye, A. (August 14, 2020) *Reimagining the Postpandemic Economic Future*, McKinsey & Company, Last accessed on December 3, 2020, from www.mckinsey.com/industries/public-and-social-sector/our-insights/reimagining-the-postpandemic-economic-future

Conerly, B. (June 23, 2020) Business Strategic Planning During the Pandemic: What's Changed, What Hasn't? *Forbes*, Last accessed on May 2, 2021, from www.forbes.com/sites/billconerly/2020/06/23/business-strategic-planning-during-the-pandemic-whats-changed-what-hasnt/?sh=786e78f82ca2

Corporate Member News (September 30, 2020) Seven Lessons COVID-19 has Taught Us About Data Strategy, *NDTA*, www.ndtahq.com/seven-lessons-covid-19-has-taught-us-about-data-strategy/

Ducharme, J. (November 9, 2021) The World Wasn't Prepared for This Pandemic. Bill Gates Says We Can Do Better, *Time*, https://time.com/6115046/bill-gates-pandemic-preparedness/

The Economist (January 7, 2021) What Is the Economic Cost of Covid-19?, https://www.economist.com/finance-and-economics/2021/01/09/what-is-the-economic-cost-of-covid-19

Ferguson, N. M., Donnelly, C. A., and Anderson, R. M. (2001) Transmission Intensity and Impact of Control Policies on the Foot and Mouth Epidemic in Great Britain. *Nature*, 413, 542–548.

Hartley, K. (June 2, 2015) Flexible Economic Opportunism: Beyond Diversification in Urban Revival. *New Geography*, Last accessed on December 3, 2020, from www.newgeography.com/content/004934-flexible-economic-opportunism-beyond-diversification-urban-revival

Jercich, K. (January 21, 2021) Biden's COVID-19 Plan Depends on a Data-Driven Approach for Efficacy, Equity, *Healthcare IT News*, Last accessed on May 1, 2021, from www.healthcareitnews.com/news/bidens-covid-19-plan-depends-data-driven-approach-efficacy-equity

Keeling, M. J., et al. (2001) Dynamics of the 2001 UK Foot and Mouth Epidemic: Stochastic Dispersal in a Heterogeneous Landscape. *Science* 294, 813–817.

Liddell, H. G. and Scott, R. (1999) *A Greek-English Lexicon*, Perseus.

Lipsitch, M., Cohen T., Cooper B., Robins J.M., Ma S., James L., Gopalakrishna G., Chew S. K., Tan C. C., Samore M. H., Fisman D., Murray M. (2003) Transmission Dynamics and Control of Severe Acute Respiratory Syndrome. *Science* 300(5627), 1966–1970.

McKinsey (August 12, 2020) How Six Companies are Using Technology and Data to Transform Themselves, Last accessed on May 1, 2021, from www.mckinsey.com/business-functions/mckinsey-digital/our-insights/how-six-companies-are-using-technology-and-data-to-transform-themselves#

McMillen, C. W. (2016) *Pandemics: A Very Short Introduction*, Oxford University Press.

Metis Strategy (December 24, 2020) Preparing for a Post-Pandemic World of Work, www.metisstrategy.com/preparing-for-a-post-pandemic-future-of-work-covid-technology-preview/

Olano, G. (November 4, 2020) Pandemic Highlights Need for a More Data-Driven Business Strategy, *Corporate Risk and Insurance*. Last accessed on May 2, 2021, from www.insurancebusinessmag.com/us/risk-management/operational/pandemic-highlights-need-for-a-more-datadriven-business-strategy-238142.aspx

Riley, S., et al. (2003) Transmission Dynamics of the Etiological Agent of SARS in Hong Kong: Impact of Public Health Interventions. *Science,* 300, 1961–1966.

Rohatgi, S. (February 17, 2021) Unlocking Flexibility in Your Post-Pandemic Data Strategy, *LinkedIn*. www.linkedin.com/pulse/unlocking-flexibility-your-post-pandemic-data-strategy-sanjay-rohatgi/

Ugarte, R., (April 16, 2021) Data Science: 3 Strategies of Successful Companies, *The Enterprisers Project*, Last accessed on May 2, 2021, from https://enterprisersproject.com/article/2021/4/data-science-strategy-3-best-practices

Westley, J. (January 2021) The Importance of Formulating a Decisive Data Strategy in 2021, *Information Age*, www.information-age.com/importance-formulating-decisive-data-strategy-2021-123493422/

WHO (2005a) WHO Checklist for Influenza Pandemic Preparedness Planning, www.who.int/influenza/resources/documents/FluCheck6web.pdf?ua=1, WHO/CDS/CSR/GIP/2005.4

WHO (2005b) WHO Global Influenza Preparedness Plan, Last accessed on July 3, 2020, from www.who.int/csr/resources/publications/influenza/GIP_2005_5Eweb.pdf

WHO (April 14, 2020) COVID-19 Strategy Update, Last accessed on Dec 1 2020, from www.who.int/docs/default-source/coronaviruse/covid-strategy-update-14april2020.pdf

WHO-EMRO (April 28, 2020) Statement by WHO's Regional Director Dr Ahmed Al-Mandhari on our Collective Fight Against COVID-19, Last accessed on May 2, 2021, from www.emro.who.int/media/news/statement-by-whos-regional-director-dr-ahmed-al-mandhari-on-our-collective-fight-against-covid-19.html

Chapter 10

Pandemic—Lessons Learned and Future Ahead

"They say, never waste a crisis."

—Anirban Ghosh

"Life is a lesson, we learn and continue to learn every day."

—Andrijana Kamcheva

Introduction

A pandemic does not last for eternity; however, while it lasts, it changes lives beyond recognition on several fronts, ranging from healthcare to social customs, and has an adverse impact on economy that can take several years to revive. A pandemic forces humankind to acknowledge the uncertainty of human existence, vulnerability of human life, and the interdependence of nations across the globe, as disease respects no boundaries. It shows that human beings need to be prepared to handle a pandemic and that despite advancements in research and technology, most of the nations in the world are acutely unprepared to handle a pandemic. The COVID-19 pandemic which has touched the lives of everyone across the globe, and continues do so, either significantly or trivially, will continue to be a stark reminder of these facts.

A pandemic presents challenges at several levels, namely:

- *global level* for international bodies such as WHO,
- *national level*, where countries need to implement policy decisions to manage a pandemic, and
- *local level*, where people decide on whether to comply with government guidelines.

There have been several pandemics in the history of mankind and WHO has declared a few disease outbreaks (such as SARS, Swine flu, HIV/AIDS, and COVID-19) as pandemic. However, COVID-19 pandemic has affected a large number of people in a large number of countries and as

DOI: 10.4324/9781003270911-10

of date (December 02, 2021) continues to do so. No other pandemic except COVID-19 has had such a drastic impact.

The effects and after effects of COVID-19—from how people conduct their daily lives to the way people travel across the globe, to the way researchers study infectious diseases to the social and economic upheaval—are so far-reaching that the world will never be the same. There is an increase in reliance on services that decrease social contact—grocery delivery services replace store visits; contactless courier deliveries; virtual meetings supersede their real-life counterparts; virtual education blends with traditional schooling; working from home is increasingly common; and live streaming services replace in-person gathering. By the time a vaccine is in place or the disease vanishes, people may have acclimatized to these changes, which is functionally an acceleration of where present technology is leading us already (Rohrich et al., 2020).

While some countries around the world have managed the COVID-19 pandemic better than others, in a proactive as well as reactive manner, through rigorous surveillance and on-going monitoring to track and counteract disease spread, there are a number of lessons to be learnt from disease outbreaks, and to be applied in the event of future disease outbreaks, epidemic, and pandemics.

Each novel disease presents a new contest and creates a new tragedy, but it also provides an opportunity for change. When COVID-19 is finally behind us, while returning to normal life, we must hold on to the lessons learnt from the fight against pandemics. This chapter discusses the mistakes made in handling the COVID-19 pandemic and lessons learnt from past pandemics as well as the COVID-19 pandemic.

Lessons from Past Pandemics—With Special Reference to 1918 Spanish Flu

"It is not so much about what life hands you, but what you do with what you get."

—**Idowu Koyenikan**

There have been several lessons that have been learnt from the history of pandemics but quite a lot have been forgotten after the event. Some of these are:

- ■ **Quarantine**

    The concept quarantining high-risk areas in case of an infectious disease outbreak has been there since ancient ages. In 1918, when the severity of the second wave of Spanish flu became evident, many countries levied strict quarantine measures on all incoming ships to try and prevent the spread of Spanish flu (Johnson, 2006). However, in case of COVID-19, not all countries imposed quarantine early on.

- ■ **Facemask and good hygiene**

    Facemasks were a common preventative measure employed during the 1918 pandemic. While the public was uncertain of the etiological agent of the pandemic, the agreement was that it was an airborne disease and wearing a facemask would prevent infections (Crosby, 1976). Accordingly, many cities and regions, including Guatemala City, San Francisco, and certain prefectures of Japan, made wearing a facemask in public places compulsory, and special task forces and education campaigns were established to impose this regulation (Crosby, 1976; Rice and Palmer, 1993; Rice, 2011). However, in order for a facemask to be at least moderately effective against influenza virus, it must be (Short et al., 2018):

(i) worn at all times,
(ii) properly made and fitted, and
(iii) made of appropriate material.

Practicing good hygiene such as effective hand washing helps limiting the spread of infection, as influenza viruses are transmissible via hand to face contact. We have all been taught to wash our hands with soap from time to time. While, this is not actively practiced by all, the COVID-19 pandemic did see a marked increase in sale of soaps and hand sanitizers. However, in poorer populations, these simple measures may not be feasible.

In the context of COVID-19 pandemics, facemasks and handwashing/hand sanitizers have been used as preventative, non-pharmaceutical interventions.

■ **Imposing restrictions on social gatherings**

As a part of non-pharmaceutical interventions to restrict the viral spread during 1918 Spanish flu, most cities imposed restrictions on social gatherings where person-to-person spread could occur (Short et al., 2018). As a result, institutes, theatres, churches, and dance halls were shut down, while mass gatherings such as weddings and funerals were banned in order to prevent overcrowding (Frost, 1919; Johnson, 2006; Bootsma and Ferguson, 2007; Hatchett et al., 2007, Short et al., 2018). These restrictions have also imposed by many countries during COVID-19 pandemic, and this preventive measure has helped slowing down the spread of infection where people have abided by these restrictions.

The peak death rate during 1918 Spanish flu was lesser in cities that rapidly implemented these non-pharmaceutical interventions within a few days after the first local cases were recorded, compared to those cities which delayed responding until a few weeks had passed (Bootsma and Ferguson, 2007; Hatchett et al., 2007). The timing when these interventions were revoked also had an impact on the overall mortality (Bootsma and Ferguson, 2007; Hatchett et al., 2007). Thus, while restrictions on congregations of people helped decrease the spread of the influenza virus, as soon as these restrictions were relaxed (typically within 2–8 weeks of their implementation) efficient spread of the virus commenced again (Hatchett et al., 2007).

■ **Shutting down affected areas**

Shutting down affected areas can prevent infection spread. Ebola did not kill millions of people when it occurred, because the shutdown of the affected area was prompt and complete which prevented spread of the pathogen. However, with the COVID-19 pandemic, not all countries or regions implemented shutdown early on; this allowed the spread of the virus across the world (Ghosh, 2020).

COVID-19 Pandemic—Specific Lessons

"The mistakes of the past are valuable lessons for the future."

—Lailah Gifty Akita

The COVID-19 pandemic highlights the necessity to learn from the mistakes of the past, battle on, and be prepared for the next pandemic. There are several lessons to be learnt from the COVID-19 pandemic as follows (see Figure 10.1):

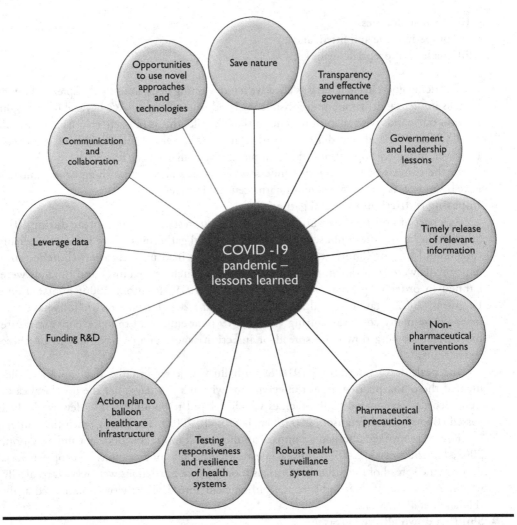

Figure 10.1 COVID-19 pandemic—lessons learned.

1. Save Nature

Rapid urbanization and human beings' incursion into forest lands and deforestation have resulted in many species losing their habitat. This has created a new interface between humans and wildlife, and exposed humans to unfamiliar organisms often involving the consumption of exotic wildlife and subsequently creating a prolific ground for the propagation of zoonotic viruses.

Each year, 5 million hectares of forest are lost across the globe. As per satellite data assessment, researchers at Global Forest Watch reckon that global deforestation in 2019 was around 5.4 million hectares [Ritchie].

As stated by the UN Environment Chief, Inger Anderson "*Our continued erosion of wild space has brought us uncomfortably close to animal and plants that harbor diseases that can jump to humans.*" She said, "*If we don't take care of nature, we can't take care of ourselves.*" (Khanna et al., 2020)

With COVID-19, nature is sending out a message that we need to acknowledge the interrelationship between animals, including pets, livestock, and wildlife (Khanna et al., 2020, Carrington, 2020) and look out for solutions that ensure the well-being of ecology.

2. Government and Leadership Lessons

Different government leaders reacted differently to the COVID-19 crisis and chose different strategies to deal with the pandemic with varying results. There were countries that applied fairly strict measures early on, but did not have sufficient finances or adequate infrastructure to continue to deal with it (Howell, 2021). There were some countries that adopted a herd immunity approach resulting in rapid spread of infection and high mortalities. The UK, along with many other countries in Europe and North America made a serious early error in adopting herd immunity by infection approach, and not considering a more emphatic and rigorous approach to stopping the spread of the virus as adopted by many East and South East Asian countries (HSCC, 2021).

It has been noted that the inadequate implementation of lockdowns (for example, in United States and India) or delayed implementation of lockdowns (for example, in Russia, United Kingdom, and France) could have reduced their effectiveness in slowing down the spread of COVID-19 infections in many countries (Verma et al., 2020; Stenseth et al., 2021). A resurgence in case numbers could be attributed to premature lifting of restrictions (for example, in India) (Bhuyan, 2021a, 2021b; Stenseth et al., 2021).

Countries that recognized the problem, embraced strategic thinking, were agile, responded earlier and aggressively, tended to have better responses. Two examples of where leaders (Adam Silver, the Commissioner of the National Basketball Association (NBA), and New Zealand Prime Minister Jacinda Ardern) acted with urgency early on during the COVID-19 pandemic (Kerrissey and Edmondson, 2020) has been discussed under the "Government and Leadership" section in Chapter 8.

Taiwan has been a testimony to how early action and aggressive monitoring can help combating a pandemic. Taiwan quickly closed its borders and banned exports of surgical masks, and used contact tracing and mobile Sim-tracking to identify and ensure those in quarantine were actually abiding by the rules. Medical officials held briefings for the public daily, and businesses were kept open by using aggressive precautionary measures (Bremmer, 2021).

Realizing its preliminary response mistakes, China combated the COVID-19 epidemic within its borders by implementing a mix of stringent measures which included extensive testing and contact-tracing, legally imposed physical (social) distancing measures, and use of modern technologies such as automated robot cleaners and facial recognition for contact-mapping. China effectively slowed the spread to a halt on March 19, 2020—for the first time since the outbreak began in 2019 (Togoh, 2020).

The early and aggressive approach by the Singapore government to contact-tracing and widespread testing by using technology and the powers of the state to enforce strict monitoring to ensure transmission remained at a minimum have helped the country combat the COVID-19 pandemic. In retrospect, Singapore was well positioned to outperform others in its pandemic response given its previous lessons learned from the SARS epidemic, its small size (5.7 million people total), and centralized "nanny state" approach not just to healthcare crises, but other facets of policy as well. The government built temporary bed spaces at breakneck speeds to house COVID-19 patients, keeping the casualty rate low (<0.1% of confirmed cases) (Bremmer, 2021).

South Korea has been able to keep COVID-19 cases and fatalities to a minimum, by aggressively dealing with outbreaks before they become a risk to the bigger population. This has been possible because the government has taken the essential measures such as testing, tracing and quarantining, as well as the public abiding by those policies for the greater good (Bremmer, 2021).

New Zealand's quick and aggressive lockdown measures alongside consistent messaging, strong political leadership, and emphasis on testing helped combat the pandemic effectively. Australia opted for early measures to limit travel from outside the country and within it, which helped keep transmission at a minimum. Also, authorities moved quickly to shut things down, when new cases surfaced (Bremmer, 2021).

Anecdotal evidence suggests that leaders' reliance on scientific advice (or absence thereof) was pivotal in the early stage of the outbreak. Some leaders were more reluctant to incorporate scientific expertise in their daily decision-making than others. For instance, the U.S. response was heavily criticized because President Donald J. Trump largely ignored scientific advice (Evanega et al., 2020). By contrast, German Chancellor Angela Merkel, and her government's early response, was hailed by the media because of her science background (Miller, 2020). During periods of substantial uncertainty such as a pandemic crisis, leaders should continuously seek relevant information and intelligence regarding the course and impact of the crisis from reliable sources. These sources comprise of health professionals, researchers, managers, industries, and related sectors. Shared stories and experiences from international colleagues, networks, and collaborative partners also need to be taken into consideration. Leaders need to act in accord with trustworthy expertise and advice (Ahern and Loh, 2020).

There are various lessons to be learnt from COVID-19 pandemic. From the varied COVID-19 responses and outcomes, it is clear that fast, aggressive strategies and informed decision-making based on scientific evidence are more effective to combat pandemics.

Governments such as Taiwan which planned well after lessons learnt from SARS pandemic were able to tackle the COVID-19 pandemic more efficiently. There will be more pandemics in the future. Hence, it is important for governments and leaders all over the world to learn from the COVID-19 pandemics and have actions plans in place to tackle future pandemics. There is a vital need for improved preparedness to quickly recognize and limit the spread of emerging pathogens (Stenseth et al., 2021). However, this needs funding and governments and leaders across the world need to set aside and assign funding to make sure this happens.

There are also certain behavior lessons to learn when comparing the leadership responses to the COVID-19 pandemic crisis, that can be applied in future crisis situations. While in crisis situations, the natural human instinct is to wait for additional information, downplaying the threat and suppressing bad news, the tendency to resort to defensiveness or blame when mistakes are made, what is required of leadership is to acknowledge the seriousness of the situation and act quickly, communicate with transparency but be empathetic, take responsibility and solve problems, be adaptive and correct course when a mistake is made, and engage in constant updates (Kerrissey and Edmondson, 2020).

3. Transparency, Effective Governance, and Timely Release of Relevant Information

In case of a disease outbreak, prompt and early release of information pertaining to disease cases can help implement preventive measures to minimize spread of infection. In olden days when the world was not so globally connected, spread of pathogens was slow. In his seminal book, *The Columbian Exchange*, AB Alfred W Crosby Jr writes:

> When the isolation of the New World was broken, when Columbus brought the two halves of the planet together, the American Indian met for the first time his most hideous enemy; not the white man nor his black servant, but the invisible killers which these men brought in their blood and breath.

Within a period of around 70 years, approximately 80 to 100 million inhabitants succumbed to the diseases brought by Europeans from across the seas. These diseases included smallpox, influenza, and diphtheria (Srivastava, 2020). However, with COVID-19, owing to extensive travel and globalization, the disease spread quickly to different parts of the world.

While COVID-19 was first reported to WHO Office in China on December 31, 2019, as "Pneumonia of an unknown cause" (WHO, 2020), healthcare professionals had warned Chinese authorities that a SARS-like illness was spreading among patients, weeks earlier than the reported date. However, instead of notifying the novel illness to those higher in the system, Wuhan authorities detained and silenced physician Dr. Li Wenliang on a charge of spreading false rumors after he reported a novel illness in his patients in early December, 2019 (Davidson, 2020; Forman et al., 2020).

Hence, there was a delay in release of information regarding COVID-19, a time lapse that could have otherwise been utilized by countries all round world to devise strategies to prevent and prepare for managing the new disease. Modelling data indicates that the spread of the virus could have been controlled significantly, if action had been taken even a few days earlier. (Forman et al., 2020). This highlights the critical importance of transparency and speed in a crisis. The lesson for governments was highlighted by Michael Ryan, a surgeon and the Executive Director of the World Health Organization's health emergency programs, in a press conference in March, 2020. His statement was as follows (Safi, 2020):

> Be fast. Have no regrets. You must be the first mover. The virus will always get you if you don't move quickly. If you need to be right before you move, you will never win. . . . Speed trumps perfection.

People have an innate wish for certainty in the face of crisis situations as frightening as a pandemic. However, the science advising the pandemic response, by its nature, functions through probabilities. This does not belittle the impact of epidemiology, but, instead, emphasizes the significance of sustaining a constant and transparent dialog between researchers, policymakers, and the public (*Nature* Editorial, 2021).

Also, it is important to establish clear whistleblowing policies and early warning systems for possible global health emergencies (Sohrabi et al., 2020). This is because in a globally connected world, contagious diseases can spread rapidly. This is reinforced by Dr. Swadeep Srivastava when he says (Srivastava, 2020):

> Unlike in the past, viruses in the 21st century not only are "hyperactive", but also leave their tales of devastation with "viral speed".

Another problem that surfaced with the COVID-19 pandemic was repeated cases of corruption due to lack of transparency. As stated by Jonathan Cushing, who leads on global health at the anti-corruption non-profit Transparency International (Buguzi et al., 2021):

> This is a tale of two pandemics. . . . We've seen repeated cases of corruption, and that is the second pandemic in many ways.

Data manipulation has been identified as a key marker of COVID-19 corruption, with some statistics, having been massaged to reveal a rosier version of reality. Researchers in India found that COVID-19 infections had been grossly underestimated and could be up to 95 times higher than the official numbers. Transparent and effective governance systems are needed to prevent corruption, improve trust and promote healthy societies (Buguzi et al., 2021).

Lack of transparency allows rumors, assumptions, and misinformation to be spread among the public. Transparency, governance, and open access to all information are essential to avoid misinformation (Sohrabi et al., 2020).

4. Non-Pharmaceutical Interventions and Pharmaceutical Precautions

A number of non-pharmaceutical interventions, such as travel restrictions, restrictions on social gatherings, use of facemasks, practice of good hygiene, quarantine of high-risk areas, shutting down affected areas, and social distancing, can limit spread of an infectious disease and slow down the pandemic (see Figure 10.2). These interventions are effective in delaying the onset of wide community transmission and reducing peak incidence.

While the first report of COVID-19 was released on December 31, 2019, Wuhan (the city where the outbreak took place), began to quarantine on January 23, 2020, nearly a month later. This resulted in individuals potentially infected with COVID-19 to travel outside Wuhan and spread the infection both nationally and internationally. It is important to quarantine high-risk areas as soon as a possible health threat is identified (Sohrabi et al., 2020). Mobility data and digital contact tracing powered by analytics and visualization can help identify case clusters.

Aviation services operated across the globe for over a month following the initial outbreak of COVID-19 with minimal health screening at international borders. Citizens travelling from

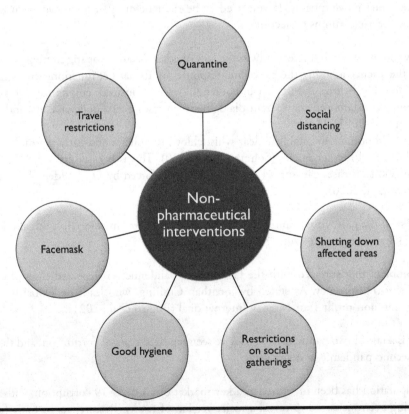

Figure 10.2   Non-pharmaceutical interventions that can slow down a pandemic.

high-risk areas as well impacted areas were able to freely pass through large airports without prior tests or health screening. Precautions such as screening citizens returning from high-risk countries should have been implemented earlier (Sohrabi et al., 2020).

Also, social distancing should become a practice and a part of the cultural fabric and life, even in the absence of a new virus or any other pathogen. Intimacy may reflect part of some cultures, but social distancing, without hurting somebody's feelings, is the best. This is because, there are quite a few infectious diseases, and social distancing can reduce or stop spread of infection. Prevention is better that cure.

When a new pathogen surfaces, self-imposed social distancing can break the chain of spread of the disease. This is because highly contagious diseases can have a butterfly effect, with COVID-19 being a live example of the "butterfly effect" as shown in Figure 10.3 and discussed in detail in Chapter 3. The "butterfly effect," implies that small things can have non-linear impacts on a complex system and a big phenomenon comprises a long chain of successive small events (Mahanti, 2019). The butterfly effect is certainly a reflection of the "domino effect" or "chain reaction"—the cumulative effect produced when one event sets off a faraway change. However, the chain can totally be broken-down or guided differently by moving just one domino a little bit. In case of a highly contagious disease, social distancing can be thought of as one of the dominos that break the chain or slow it down.

5. Robust Health Surveillance System

Public Health Emergency of International Concern was declared by WHO on December 30, 2019, approximately a month following the initial outbreak of COVID-19. The severity of the disease outbreak was not broadly aired or accepted. This may have delayed containment measures. Framework should be developed for fast-spreading diseases in order to escalate a threat status earlier (Sohrabi et al., 2020). Also, what is important is, the development of a robust health surveillance system at the state level and a constantly updated registry of population on a national scale. The vulnerable sections of the society need to be pre-identified through strong data collection (Srivastava, 2020). COVID-19 is caused by zoonotic virus. There are many viruses, including coronaviruses, that are currently circulating among wildlife and most of these have the potential to infect humans (Bhatia, 2020). There is necessity for undertaking joint surveillance for human health and animal health (Bhatia, 2019), for early detection of zoonotic infections.

6. Testing Responsiveness and Resilience of Health Systems and Action Plan to Balloon Healthcare Infrastructure

The healthcare systems, especially the critical care segment, have been overburdened in a large number of countries in their battle against COVID-19. Although high-income countries have strong health systems, they often lacked sufficient capacity to treat huge numbers of patients with COVID-19 and personal protective equipment (PPE) to protect health workers from infection. There has been a shortage of ventilators and respiratory equipment with the large number people hospitalized due to COVID-19. In the US, hospitals and states had to compete for access to ventilators and personal protective equipment. Resilient health systems require surge capacity to deal with health emergencies in the event hospitals become overrun (Gostin, 2020).

With a pandemic, it essential to have an action plan that can be executed in the shortest time frame. Usually such an action plan involves the ability to balloon the healthcare infrastructure by eliminating bottlenecks and designing more critical care units and isolation centers without affecting

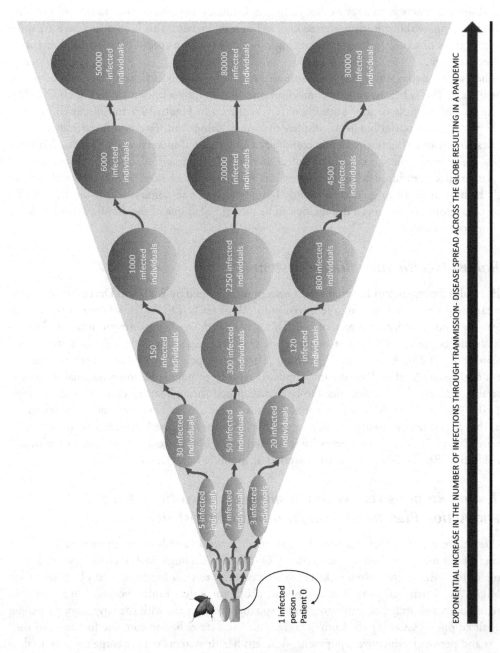

EXPONENTIAL INCREASE IN THE NUMBER OF INFECTIONS THROUGH TRANMISSION- DISEASE SPREAD ACROSS THE GLOBE RESULTING IN A PANDEMIC

Figure 10.3 COVID-19 pandemic—illustration of the butterfly effect.

non-pandemic critical care patients. This can be done by involving the private sector—both in the healthcare segment and hospitality sector which can become isolation units (Srivastava, 2020).

Many nations did not have enough testing kits and personal protective equipment (PPE) to deal with the COVID-19 crisis. When a disease outbreak occurs, the only way to curb community spread is testing. It is important to be able to ramp up production of testing kits, PPE, and other healthcare equipment in a short timeframe when a pandemic strike.

While health systems are essential to human well-being, the responsiveness and resilience of health systems to epidemics and pandemics are rarely tested. Even when an issue is found post testing, issues have been ignored. For example, after a major exercise in the UK in 2016 revealed a shortage of ventilators, the problem was disregarded (Lambert, 2020). Health systems should be tested at regular intervals to ensure that they are robust, and that any issues are addressed (Forman et al., 2020).

It is important to strengthen health systems built on the foundation of people-centered primary health care that focuses on health promotion and disease prevention, with a strong focus on surveillance systems. As stated by Dr. Tedros Adhanom Ghebreyesus, Director-General of the World Health Organization, "Delivering on these priorities will cost money of course, but only a fraction of what remaining unprepared will cost. In the end, prevention is not only better than cure; it's cheaper (WHO, 2018)."

7. Funding Research and Development (R&D)

There was a lack of funding in initial stages of research and development (R&D) of vaccine and treatment of COVID-19. A lot of patients worldwide have died due to COVID-19, and the death toll continues to rise weekly (at the time of writing this book). With COVID-19, vaccine development has taken place at record breaking speed, with the first vaccine ready for emergency use, in the less than one year since the disease was officially declared by WHO.

However, in general, further investment is required to produce successful treatments and to establish robust procedures to contain future outbreaks of infectious disease (Sohrabi et al., 2020). There is a need for nations to further strengthen their drug and vaccine development programs by speed-tracking vaccine and drug development when a new disease outbreak happens and also invest biomedical research in the absence of pandemics.

In addition, an improved understanding of the host-adaptation of influenza viruses and the existence of pre-existing immunity are likely to contribute to a more precise prediction of viral severity and possible impacts on human beings even before the influenza virus in question becomes established as a pandemic (Kreijtz et al., 2008; Lee et al., 2008; Herfst et al., 2012; Imai et al., 2012; Richard et al., 2013; Quiñones-Parra et al., 2014; van de Sandt et al., 2014; Wang et al., 2015). An improved understanding of the human immune response against (pandemic) influenza viruses will in due course of time assist the development of broad-protective influenza vaccines (Clemens et al., 2018).

Research into social sciences is also needed, to help comprehend the social facets of the pandemic, to help foster engagement, trust in societies, improve education to be more adaptive, and target misinformation (Saqr and Wasson, 2020).

8. Opportunities to Use Novel Approaches and Technologies

Technology has played and continues to play a significant role in tackling the COVID-19 pandemic. For example, in some countries, drones have and are being used to monitor people in lockdown and to deliver supplies and equipment; in other countries, robots are screening patients and thus helping in lessening the duties of healthcare workers. Additionally, robots, which deliver provisions and medicines, and even ones that dance, are offering emotional support and communication for those in isolation. Robots with UV units are being used to disinfect hospitals and other large buildings (Yang et al., 2020; Forman et al., 2020). Artificial intelligence, IoT, and big data technologies have been used to track the spread of the COVID-19 virus, identify the high-risk patients, predict the mortality risk by adequately analyzing the previous data of the patients (Vaishya et al., 2020), make employment decisions, and in areas of cash management.

Companies have had to be shifted to remote-working models and have had to alter their practices in a very short time as a result of the COVID-19 pandemic. With social distancing, travel restrictions, restrictions on public gatherings, and closing of borders, there has been accelerated migration to digital technologies at a stunning scale and speed, across every industry sector to ensure business continuity. For business continuity, companies need to adjust to new working paradigms (such as work from home and virtual meeting), new ways of servicing clients (via phone and mobile apps), new ways communicating with their employees and new technology to support these changes. The development of digital solutions has been the key to keep afloat during the unpredictable times brought about by the COVID-19 pandemic (Kirubi, 2020). Work from home models and virtual meetings have proved effective and could become the new normal eliminating the need for business travel and reduction of office infrastructure.

The battle against novel diseases presents opportunities to use novel approaches and technologies and will necessitate looking at all options, while ensuring that they are subject to evaluation (Forman et al., 2020).

9. Leverage Data

Data have a crucial role to play in managing a pandemic. At the heart of technologies, such as artificial intelligence and big data technologies is data. Data can not only help in understanding the impact of a pandemic across different geographies and forecast the spread of a disease, but can also help plan suitable response to controlling the spread as well as allocation of resources. While a lot of data have been collected and continues to be collected from different sources to fight the COVID-19 pandemic, the major issues are data manipulation, the lack of clarity, data quality issues, and inconsistency of data definitions, which can result in reporting and formatting discrepancies. It is very important to have an international agency that defines data definition standards. There should be effective governance processes for collection of different data elements in relation to a new disease and pandemic and ensuring the data collected has adequate quality levels.

Also, with all information and misinformation, available, it's crucial to separate signal from noise, or good data from bad data. In turn, the opportunities that having all of this data creates for technology to provide meaningful insights are massive, and should be kept in mind when dealing similar crisis situations.

10. Communication and Collaboration

Pandemic is not only a health event but also a political, social, and economic event. It is very important that communication happens along all these lines. Disease respects no boundaries, be it interstate, national, or international. It does not discriminate between the rich and poor. We are all connected and interdependent, and there is a need for collaborative solutions.

The Internet provides a valuable channel for communication. However, prevailing risk and health communication guidelines do not provide guidance or principles on the best way to use the Internet—specifically use of social networking tools such as Facebook and Twitter during disease outbreaks as well as for more intense health crises such as epidemics and pandemics. This is undoubtedly a zone where guidance based on evidence needs to be developed (Abraham, 2011).

Some of the mistakes in dealing with COVID-19 occurred because there was little information known about the virus as well as the disease it causes. Faced by the massive threat of the new pandemic, the policy makers and scientists were largely inconsistent and perhaps contradictory in communication. For example, the face masks issue — at first, the general advice was against, even warning people against. It did not take long before the advice was reversed. A complicated dynamic problem needs a different communication strategy so that the message does not erode the public trust. The communication strategy should prioritize credibility, communicate the future consequences, and outline the factors involved in the pandemic, the uncertainties, the unknowns, and limitations of our knowledge. The public can understand uncertainty and risks better than contrary messages (Saqr and Wasson 2020). Also, closer collaboration between nations and a more extensive exchange of information could have assisted governments to introduce the appropriate measures more effectively (Lockton, 2020).

Concluding Thoughts

"Lessons learned" is a rather over used term. However, a pandemic is a crisis and there are lessons to be learnt from a crisis. This is essential to be able to respond more effectively to future events. In words of Anirban Ghosh, Chief Sustainability Officer, Mahindra Group—"never waste a crisis."

However, what is equally important is to implement the lessons during and after the crisis. This is reinforced by Anirban Ghosh when he states (Ghosh, 2020):

> If we adopt half of what we have learnt, we will be better off.

For example, post lessons learnt from SARS pandemic in 2003, Taiwan established the Central Epidemic Command Center (CECC), which it activated during COVID-19 to ensure resilience against the spread. Taiwan responded quickly to COVID-19 by leveraging real-time data and technology. They adopted diversified strategies to combat the crisis that included (Eggers et al., 2020; Apple Podcasts, 2020):

- testing flight passengers from Wuhan, China as early as in December 2019;
- mapping real-time availability of face masks to avoid shortage;
- addressing tales and collusion schemes on social media very quickly, within two hours—to prevent the spread of misinformation.

These approaches enabled Taiwan to keep infection rates as low as 45 infections per million people (Dark Daily, 2020).

As stated by Dr. Tedros Adhanom Ghebreyesus, Director-General of the World Health Organization (WHO, 2018):

> Global health security is only as strong as its weakest link. No-one is safe until everyone is safe.

Hence, it is important to build and sustain resilient capacities at national, regional, and global levels to prevent, detect, and respond to disease outbreaks, in agreement with the International Health Regulations. Also, it is important to ensure that populations affected by emergencies have rapid access to essential lifesaving health services, including medicines and vaccines (WHO, 2018).

COVID-19 has touched everyone's lives across the globe. Biocon Executive Chairperson Kiran Mazumdar-Shaw states (The Economic Times, 2020):

> Ultimately, the greatest lesson that COVID-19 can teach humanity is that we are all in this together, that what affects a single person anywhere affects everyone everywhere, that as homo sapiens we need to think and act unitedly rather than worrying about race, ethnicity, nationality, religion, economic status, and such artificial groupings.

COVID-19 has occurred during the digital age, that is, characterized by availability of massive amounts of different varieties of data as well as sophisticated technologies available to leverage data to derive insights. Data and analytics have played a crucial role in managing the pandemic and they should be kept in mind and applied when dealing with similar crisis situations.

The pandemic has reinforced the need for countries to make serious investment in research and development to prepare for the possible future pandemics. Also, investments in innovation are important to be able to adapt to the dynamic environment.

With reference to the COVID-19, Madanmohan Rao stated [Rao, 2021]:

> The pandemic has been a great teacher.

While the lessons learnt certainly help in dealing with future pandemics or to tackle diseases before they acquire pandemic status, there might be several new challenges that we face in the context of later influenza pandemics that would need new practices and require human beings to adapt to changes. We have to be more open to learn, unlearn, and relearn.

References

Abraham, T. (2011) Lessons from the Pandemic: The Need for New Tools for Risk and Outbreak Communication. *Emerging Health Threats Journal*, 4(1). DOI: 10.3402/ehtj.v4i0.7160.

Ahern, S., and Loh, E. (September 30, 2020) Leadership during the COVID-19 Pandemic: Building and Sustaining Trust in Times of Uncertainty. *BMJ Leader.* DOI: 10.1136/leader-2020-000271

Apple Podcasts (June 1, 2020) How Taiwan used Digital Tools to Solve the Pandemic with Audrey Tang. *The TED Interview.*

Bhatia, R. (2019) Implementation Framework for One Health Approach. *Indian Journal of Medical Research* 149: 329–331, https://doi.org/10.4103/ijmr.IJMR_1517_18

Bhatia, R. (2020) Need for Integrated Surveillance at Human-Animal Interface for Rapid Detection and Response to Emerging Corona Viral Infections Using One Health Approach. *Indian Journal of Medical Research* 151: 132–135.

Bhuyan, A. (2021a) Experts Criticise India's Complacency over COVID-19. *Lancet.* 397: 1611–1612. Doi: 10.1016/S0140-6736(21)00993-4

Bhuyan, A. (2021b) Covid-19: India Sees New Spike in Cases Despite Vaccine Rollout. *BMJ.* 372:n854. 10.1136/bmj.n854

Bootsma, M. C., and Ferguson, N. M. (2007) The Effect of Public Health Measures on the 1918 Influenza Pandemic in U.S. Cities. *Proceedings of the National Academy of Sciences of the United States of America* 104: 7588–7593. DOI: 10.1073/pnas.0611071104

Bremmer, I. (February 2021) The Best Global Responses to the COVID-19 Pandemic, 1 Year Later. *Time Ideas*. https://time.com/5851633/best-global-responses-covid-19/

Buguzi, S., Broom, F., Adriano, J., and Rueda, A. (April 2021) COVID-19 Lies and Statistics: Corruption and the Pandemic. Phys.org provided by *SciDev.Net*, Last accessed on September 30, 2021, from https://phys.org/news/2021-04-covid-lies-statistics-corruption-pandemic.html

Carrington, D. (March 25, 2020) Coronavirus: "Nature is Sending us a Message", Says UN Environment Chief, *The Guardian*. https://www.theguardian.com/world/2020/mar/25/coronavirus-nature-is-sending-us-a-message-says-un-environment-chief

Clemens, E. B., van de Sandt, C., Wong, S. S., Wakim, L. M., and Valkenburg, S. A. (2018) Harnessing the Power of T Cells: The Promising Hope for a Universal Influenza Vaccine. *Vaccines* 6(2): 18. DOI: 10.3390/vaccines6020018

Crosby, A. W. (1976) *Epidemic and Peace 1918*. Santa Barbara, CA: Abc-Clio.

Dark Daily (March 23, 2020) Taiwan's Containment of COVID-19 Outbreak Demonstrates Importance of Rapid Response, Including Fast Access to Clinical Laboratory Tests. Last accessed on October 17, 2021, from https://www.darkdaily.com/2020/03/23/taiwans-containment-of-covid-19-outbreak-demonstrates-importance-of-rapid-response-including-fast-access-to-clinical-laboratory-tests/

Davidson, H. (2020) *Chinese Inquiry Exonerates Coronavirus Whistleblower Doctor*. Guard.

The Economic Times (April 18, 2020) COVID-19 Will Reboot World into Virtual Reality: Kiran Mazumdar-Shaw. Last accessed on October 17, 2021, from https://economictimes.indiatimes.com/news/company/corporate-trends/covid-19-will-reboot-world-into-virtual-reality-kiran-mazumdar-shaw/articleshow/75223254.cms?from=mdr

Eggers, W. D., Chew, B., Nunes, N. M., Davis, A., and Rodrigues, G. (2020) Seven Lessons COVID-19 Has Taught Us about Data Strategy. *Deloitte*, Last accessed on May 17, 2021, from https://www2.deloitte.com/us/en/insights/economy/covid-19/government-data-management-lessons.html.

Evanega, S., Lynas, M., Adams, J., and Smolenyak, K. (2020) Coronavirus Misinformation: Quantifying Sources and Themes in the COVID-19 'Infodemic'. https:// allianceforscience.cornell.edu/wp-content/uploads/2020/10/Evanega-et-al-Corona virus-misinformation-submitted_07_23_20-1.pdf.

Forman, R., Atun, R., McKee, M., and Mossialos, E. (2020) 12 Lessons Learned from the Management of the Coronavirus Pandemic. *Health Policy* 124(6): 577–580. ISSN 0168–8510. https://doi.org/10.1016/j.healthpol.2020.05.008.

Frost, W. H. (1919) Public health weekly reports for August 15, 1919. *Public Health Reports* 34: 1823–1926. DOI: 10.2307/4575271

Ghosh, A. (April 29, 2020) 11 Lessons from the Coronavirus Pandemic. *The Indian Express*, Last accessed on November 14, 2020, from https://indianexpress.com/article/opinion/11-lessons-from-the-corona virus-pandemic-6384591/

Gostin L.O. (August 13, 2020) The Great Coronavirus Pandemic of 2020–7 Critical Lessons. *JAMA Health Forum, JAMA Network*, Last accessed on November 14, 2020, from https://jamanetwork.com/channels/health-forum/fullarticle/2769600

Hatchett, R. J., Mecher, C. E., and Lipsitch, M. (2007) Public Health Interventions and Epidemic Intensity During the 1918 Influenza Pandemic. *Proceedings of the National Academy of Sciences of the United States of America* 104: 7582–7587. DOI: 10.1073/pnas.0610941104

Herfst, S., Schrauwen, E. J., Linster, M., Chutinimitkul, S., de Wit, E., Munster, V. J., Sorrell, E. M., Bestebroer, T. M., Burke, D. F., Smith, D. J., Rimmelzwaan, G. F., Osterhaus, A. D., Fouchier, R. A. (June 22, 2012) Airborne Transmission of Influenza A/H5N1 Virus between Ferrets. *Science*. 336(6088): 1534–41. DOI: 10.1126/science.1213362. PMID: 22723413; PMCID: PMC4810786.

Howell, B. (October 4, 2021) The Countries Who've Handled Coronavirus the Best—and Worst. *MoveHub Blog*. www.movehub.com/blog/best-and-worst-covid-responses/

HSCC (2021) Health and Social Care Committee, October 2021, Coronavirus: Lessons Learned to Date. Sixth Report of the Health and Social Care Committee and Third Report of the Science and Technology Committee of Session 2021–22, Report, Ordered by the House of Commons. https://committees.parliament.uk/publications/7497/documents/78688/default/

Imai, M., Watanabe, T., Hatta, M., Das, S. C., Ozawa, M., Shinya, K., et al. (2012) Experimental Adaptation of an Influenza H5 HA Confers Respiratory Droplet Transmission to a Reassortant H5 HA/H1N1 Virus in Ferrets. *Nature* 486: 420–428. DOI: 10.1038/nature10831

Johnson, N. (2006) *Britain and the 1918–19 Influenza Pandemic: A Dark Epilogue*. Abingdon: Taylor & Francis Ltd.

Kerrissey, M. J., and Edmondson, A. C. (April 13, 2020) What Good Leadership Looks Like During this Pandemic. *Harvard Business Review*. https://hbr.org/2020/04/what-good-leadership-looks-like-during-this-pandemic

Khanna, R. C., Cicinelli, M. V., Gilbert, S. S., Honavar, S. G., and Murthy, G. V. S. (2020) COVID-19 Pandemic: Lessons Learned and Future Directions. *Indian Journal of Ophthalmology* 68(5): 703–710. DOI: 10.4103/ijo.IJO_843_20

Kirubi, C. (May 26, 2020) COVID-19: Lessons Learned and Future Direction for Entrepreneurs, *Capital Business*, Last accessed on November 14, 2020, from www.capitalfm.co.ke/business/2020/05/covid-19-lessons-learned-and-future-direction-for-entrepreneurs/?doing_wp_cron=1607081867.640392 0650482177734375

Kreijtz, J. H., de Mutsert, G., van Baalen, C. A., Fouchier, R. A., Osterhaus, A. D., and Rimmelzwaan, G. F. (2008) Cross-recognition of Avian H5N1 Influenza Virus by Human Cytotoxic T-lymphocyte Populations Directed to Human Influenza A Virus. *Journal of Virology* 82: 5161–5166. DOI: 10.1128/JVI.02694-07

Lambert, H. (2020) Government Documents Show No Planning for Ventilators in the Event of a Pandemic. *The New Statesman* UK Edition, Last accessed on September 30, 2021, from. https://www.newstatesman.com/politics/2020/03/government-documents-show-no-planning-ventilators-event-pandemic

Lee, L. Y., Ha do, L. A., Simmons, C., de Jong, M. D., Chau, N. V., Schumacher, R., et al. (2008) Memory T Cells Established by Seasonal Human Influenza A Infection Cross-react with Avian Influenza A (H5N1) in Healthy Individuals. *Journal of Clinical Investigation* 118: 3478–3490. DOI: 10.1172/JCI32460

Lockton (July 29, 2020) Lessons Learned from the COVID-19 Pandemic. Available at: www.locktoninternational.com/apac/articles/lessons-learned-covid-19-pandemic

Mahanti, R. (2019) *Data Quality: Dimensions, Measurement, Strategy, Management and Governance*. Quality Press, ASQ. ISBN: 9780873899772

Miller, S. (19 April, 2020) The Secret to Germany's COVID-19 Success: Angela Merkel is a Scientist. *The Atlantic*.

Nature Editorial (January 27, 2021) How Epidemiology Has Shaped the COVID Pandemic. *Nature*, Last accessed on September 30, 2021, from www.nature.com/articles/d41586-021-00183-z

Quiñones-Parra, S., Grant, E., Loh, L., Nguyen, T. H., Campbell, K. A., Tong, S. Y, et al. (2014) Preexisting CD8+ T-cell Immunity to the H7N9 Influenza A Virus Varies Across Ethnicities. *Proceedings of the National Academy of Sciences of the United States of America* 111: 1049–1054. Doi: 10.1073/pnas.1322229111.

Rao, M. (April 1, 2021) The Pandemic Has Been a Great Teacher' – 25 Quotes from India's COVID-19 Struggle. *Yourstory*, Last accessed on September 10, 2021, from https://yourstory.com/2021/04/quotes-storybites-covid19-pandemic-teacher/amp

Rice, G. W. (2011) Japan and New Zealand in the 1918 Influenza Pandemic: Comparative Perspectives on Official Responses and Crisis Management. In *Spanish Influenza Pandemic of 1918–1919: New Perspectives*, ed. D. Killingray. Melbourne, VIC: Routledge.

Rice, G. W., and Palmer, E. (1993) Pandemic Influenza in Japan, 1918–19, Mortality Patterns and Official Responses. *Journal of Japanese Studies* 19: 389–420. DOI: 10.2307/132645.

Richard, M., Schrauwen, E. J., de Graaf, M., Bestebroer, T. M., Spronken, M. I., van Boheemen, S., et al. (2013) Limited Airborne Transmission of H7N9 Influenza A Virus between Ferrets. *Nature* 501: 560–563. DOI: 10.1038/nature12476

[Ritchie] Ritchie, H. Drivers of Deforestation, *Our World in Data*. https://ourworldindata.org/drivers-of-deforestation

Rohrich, R. J., Hamilton, K. L., Avashia, Y., and Savetsky, I. (April 2020) The COVID-19 Pandemic: Changing Lives and Lessons Learned. *Plastic and Reconstructive Surgery—Global Open* 8(4): e2854. DOI: 10.1097/GOX.0000000000002854

Safi, M. (Friday May 1, 2020) 10 Key Lessons for the Future to Be Learned from Fighting Covid-19. *Guardian*. www.theguardian.com/world/2020/may/01/10-key-lessons-for-future-learned-fighting-covid-19-coronavirus-society

Saqr, M., and Wasson, B. (2020) COVID-19: Lost Opportunities and Lessons for the Future. *International Journal of Health Sciences*, 14(3), 4–6.

Short, K. R., Katherine, K., and van de Sandt, C. E. (2018) Back to the Future: Lessons Learned from the 1918 Influenza Pandemic. *Frontiers in Cellular and Infection Microbiology* 8. DOI: 10.3389/fcimb.2018.00343, Last accessed on November 14, 2020, from www.frontiersin.org/article/10.3389/fcimb.2018.00343

Sohrabi, C., Alsafi, Z., O'Neill, N., et al. (April 2020) World Health Organization Declares Global Emergency: A Review of the 2019 Novel Coronavirus (COVID-19). *International Journal of Surgery (London, England)* 76: 71–76. DOI: 10.1016/j.ijsu.2020.02.034.

Srivastava, S. (April 2020) Eight Key Lessons to Learn from COVID-19 Pandemic. *EH News Bureau, Express Healthcare*, Last accessed on November 14, 2020, from www.expresshealthcare.in/blogs/eight-key-lessons-to-learn-from-covid-19-pandemic/419184/

Stenseth, N. C., Dharmarajan, G., Li, R., Shi, Z.-L., Yang, R., and Gao, G. F. (2021) Lessons Learnt from the COVID-19 Pandemic. *Frontier in Public Health* 9: 694705. DOI: 10.3389/fpubh.2021.694705

Togoh, I. (2020) China, Where COVID-19 Was First Detected, Reports No New Local Cases of Coronavirus. *Forbes*.

Vaishya, R., Javaid, M., Haleem Khan, I., and Haleem, A. (2020) Artificial Intelligence (AI) Applications for COVID-19 Pandemic. *Diabetes & Metabolic Syndrome: Clinical Research & Reviews* 14(4): 337–339. ISSN 1871–4021. DOI: 10.1016/j.dsx.2020.04.012. www.sciencedirect.com/science/article/pii/S1871402120300771

van de Sandt, C. E., Kreijtz, J. H., de Mutsert, G., Geelhoed-Mieras, M. M., Hillaire, M. L., Vogelzang-van Trierum, S. E., et al. (2014) Human Cytotoxic T Lymphocytes Directed to Seasonal Influenza a Viruses Cross-react with the Newly Emerging H7N9 Virus. *Journal of Virology* 88: 1684–1693. DOI: 10.1128/JVI.02843-13

Verma, B. K., Verma, M., Verma, V. K., Abdullah, R. B., Nath, D. C., Khan, H. T. A., et al. (2020) Global Lockdown: An Effective Safeguard in Responding to the Threat of COVID-19. *Journal of Evaluation in Clinical Practice* 26: 1592–1598. DOI: 10.1111/jep.13483

Wang, Z., Wan, Y., Qiu, C., Quinones-Parra, S., Zhu, Z., Loh, L., et al. (2015) Recovery from Severe H7N9 Disease is Associated with Diverse Response Mechanisms Dominated by CD8+ T Cells. *Nature Communications* 6: 6833. DOI: 10.1038/ncomms7833.

WHO (2018) Managing Epidemics: Key Facts about Major Deadly Diseases. ISBN 978-92-4-156553-0, Last accessed on November 14, 2020, from www.who.int/emergencies/diseases/managing-epidemics-interactive.pdf

World Health Organization (WHO) (2020) *Pneumonia of Unknown Cause—China*. World Health Organization. www.who.int/csr/don/05-january-2020-pneumonia-of-unkown-cause-china/en/

Yang, G.-Z., Nelson, B. J., Murphy, R. R., Choset, H., Christensen, H., Collins, S. H., et al. (2020) Combating COVID-19—The Role of Robotics in Managing Public Health and Infectious Diseases. *Science Robotics*, 5. DOI: 10.1126/scirobotics.abb5589eabb5589

Appendix A: Abbreviations and Acronymns

AI	Artificial intelligence
CDCP	Centers for Disease Control and Prevention
COVID-19	Coronavirus Disease 2019
CSFs	Critical Success Factors
CT	Computed Tomography
DPA	Data Protection Authorities
EID	Emerging Infectious Disease
EUA	Emergency Use Authorizations
FAO	Food and Agriculture Organization
FDA	U.S. Food and Drug Administration
GPS	Global Positioning System
HIPAA	Health Insurance Portability and Accountability Act
HR	Human Resources
IDEA	Institute for Data Exploration and Applications
IFAD	International Fund for Agricultural Development
ILO	International Labour Organization
IMF	International Monetary Fund
IoT	Internet of Things
MERS	Middle East Respiratory Syndrome
ML	Machine Learning
POS	Point of Sale
PPE	Personal Protective Equipment
RFID	Radio Frequency Identification
RNA	Ribonucleic Acid
RPI	Rensselaer Polytechnic Institute
SARS	Severe Acute Respiratory Syndrome
SARS-CoV-2	Severe Acute Respiratory Syndrome, Coronavirus 2
WGS	Whole Genome Sequencing
WHO	World Health Organization
WWW	World Wide Web

Appendix B: Glossary of Terms

Analytics: Analytics or data analytics is the analysis and consolidation of data from a number of heterogeneous sources, with the aid of specialized applications, systems, tools, technology, and software to derive insights.

Asymptomatic: Asymptomatic means presenting no symptoms of disease (Merriam-Webster Dictionary) or having very mild symptoms that the symptoms are missed entirely. An asymptomatic individual has the potential to infect other individuals.

Big data: Big data is high-volume, high-velocity, and/or high-variety information assets that demand cost-effective, innovative forms of information processing that enable enhanced insight, decision-making, and process automation [Gartner Information Technology Glossary].

Butterfly effect: Butterfly effect is the sensitive dependence on initial conditions in which a small change in one state of a deterministic nonlinear system can result in large differences in a later state (Boeing, 2016; [Wikipedia]).

Contact tracing: Contact tracing is the process of identifying individuals with close contact with infected patients and can be considered as one of the main weapons to tackle the spread of a contagious disease.

COVID-19: COVID-19 is contagious respiratory and vascular disease caused by a coronavirus named severe acute respiratory syndrome coronavirus 2 (SARS-CoV-2).

Coronavirus: Coronaviruses are a large family of viruses that are known to infect both humans and animals. Coronaviruses cause respiratory illness in humans which can range from the common cold to more serious infections.

Critical success factors (CSFs): Critical success factors (CSFs) are the specific elements that are vital for an initiative or program to be successful.

Data: Data are information, especially facts or numbers, collected to be examined and considered, and used to help decision-making. From an IT perspective, data can be defined as information in an electronic form that can be stored and used by a computer (Cambridge Dictionary).

Data set: A data set is a set of records (both rows and columns) extracted from data files or database tables, for a specific purpose.

Data quality: Data quality is the capability of data to satisfy the stated business, system, and technical requirements of an enterprise. Data quality is an insight or an evaluation of data's fitness to serve their purpose in a given context (Mahanti, 2019).

Data governance: Data governance is the exercise and enforcement of policies, processes, guidelines, rules, standards, metrics, controls, decision rights, roles, responsibilities, and accountabilities to manage data as a strategic enterprise asset (Mahanti, 2021a, 2021b).

Data management: Data management is the process of capturing, processing, storing, organizing, and maintaining the data that is created and/or collected by an organization. It encompasses all disciplines associated with managing data as an asset resource.

Digital contact tracing: Digital contact tracing is a method of contact tracing relying on tracking systems, most often based on mobile devices, to determine contact between an infected patient and a user.

Endemic: An endemic is something that belongs to a particular group of people or a particular country. Endemics are a perpetual presence in a specific location but at low frequency.

Epidemic: An epidemic is a disease that affects a large number of people within a community, population, or region.

Epidemiological parameters: Epidemiological parameters are measurable factors that can help in for planning of strategies to mitigate and control diseases, as well as provision of care to those infected and sick (Guerra et al., 2020).

Internet of Things (IoT): The Internet of Things refers to a large number of devices and people connected to the internet all collecting and sharing information.

Outbreak: An outbreak is "a sudden rise in the incidence of a disease" and typically is confined to a localized area or a specific group of people.

Pandemic: A pandemic is an occurrence of a disease that affects many people over a very wide area [Collins Dictionary]. It is a global outbreak of a disease or an epidemic that travels.

Patient zero: Patient zero refers to the first person infected in an epidemic (Dictionary.com).

Super spreader: A super spreader is an extraordinarily infectious organism who has been infested with a disease. In relation to a human-borne disease, a super spreader is an individual who is more liable to infect others than a normal infected person.

Zoonosis: Zoonosis or zoonotic disease is a disease that can be transmitted from animals, birds, or insects to humans or, more specifically, a disease that normally exists in animals but that can infect humans.

References

Boeing, G. (2016) Visual Analysis of Nonlinear Dynamical Systems: Chaos, Fractals, Self-similarity and the Limits of Prediction. *Systems*, 4 (4): 37. DOI: 10.3390/systems4040037

Gallo, L. G., Oliveira, A. F. M., Abrahão, A. A., Sandoval, L. A. M., Martins, Y. R. A., Almirón, M., dos Santos, F. S. G., Araújo, W. N., de Oliveira, M. R. F., Peixoto, H. M. (2020) Ten Epidemiological Parameters of COVID-19: Use of Rapid Literature Review to Inform Predictive Models During the Pandemic. *Frontiers in Public Health*, 8. DOI: 10.3389/fpubh.2020.598547, ISSN=2296–2565, www.frontiersin.org/article/10.3389/fpubh.2020.598547 (last accessed 25 April 2021)

[Gartner Information Technology Glossary], Big Data, Last accessed on June 20, 2021, from www.gartner.com/en/information-technology/glossary/big-data.

Mahanti, R. (2019) *Data quality: Dimensions, Measurement, Strategy, Management, and Governance.* ASQ Quality Press, Milwaukee, WI, p. 526, ISBN: 9780873899772

Mahanti, R. (2021a) *Data Governance and Compliance: Evolving to our Current High Stakes Environment.* Springer Book, number 978-981-33-6877-4

Mahanti, R. (2021b) *Data Governance and Data Management: Contextualizing Data Governance Drivers, Technologies, and Tools.* Springer Book. DOI: 10.1007/978-981-16-3583-0; Print ISBN—978-981-16-3582-3

[Wikipedia], Butterfly Effect, https://en.wikipedia.org/wiki/Butterfly_effect (last accessed January 2021)

Index

Note: Page numbers in *italics* indicate a figure and page numbers in **bold** indicate a table on the corresponding page.

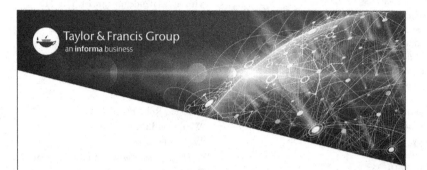

Printed in the United States
by Baker & Taylor Publisher Services